Thomas C Lynch

The masons', bricklayers' and plasterers' guide

a book on the art and science of the masons' trade

Thomas C Lynch

The masons', bricklayers' and plasterers' guide
a book on the art and science of the masons' trade

ISBN/EAN: 9783742858856

Manufactured in Europe, USA, Canada, Australia, Japa

Cover: Foto ©ninafisch / pixelio.de

Manufactured and distributed by brebook publishing software (www.brebook.com)

Thomas C Lynch

The masons', bricklayers' and plasterers' guide

THE
Masons', Bricklayers' and Plasterers' Guide.

A BOOK ON THE ART AND SCIENCE OF THE

MASONS' TRADE.

Dedicated to the Bricklayers' and Masons' International Union of America and all Subordinate Unions.

COMPILED, WRITTEN AND ARRANGED

By THOMAS C. LYNCH,

OF ALBANY, N. Y.

RIGGS PRINTING HOUSE, ALBANY, N. Y.
1892.

PREFACE.

In presenting the *Mason's Guide* to his fellow workman the writer has been actuated to the task from his own experience as a mechanic of a great want that existed among a large body of our workmen of an industrial Guide in the execution of the art and science of the mason's trade, and properly adapted for the practical wants of the mechanic, many of whom have been forced in their earlier days to enter the hard road of the bread-winner just as their minds began to taste the benefits of culture. And efficient, however, as many have became in the handiwork portion of their craft in after life, it is a fact that many are found uninformed and wholly deficient in the scientific principles and knowledge on which the whole superstructure of their handiwork rest for stability. It cannot but be evident that this condition has been a drawback and an encumbrance to the prosperity of many a competent workman. We believe in the present work that we have succeeded in placing before him such useful and practical information that if properly utilized will add greatly to his prosperity, and which he should possess to be considered a proficient and reliable mechanic.

We have found as a rule from our own experience as a mechanic, that when the workman has ventured to pass his judgment in regard to the construction and stability of certain kinds of work, pertaining to his art, in the presence of those who consider that they have been particularly educated to possess such knowledge, that his opinion, rather than being received with respect by them as being of any reliable authority, was looked upon with rather a contemptuous good humor, and placing the mechanic in rather a ridiculous and humiliating position before those contemplating or erecting an edifice.

PREFACE.

As a rule works upon construction are generally written in an abstruse and perplexing manner to the practical mind of the mechanic and designed more for those who work with the pencil than for him who labors with the trowel, and too expensive for him to procure; but we have endeavored in the present work to overcome that difficulty by presenting each subject treated in a plain and intelligent manner.

That the mechanic may be bold and confident in expressing his opinion on any subject treated in this book, we have given subjoined a list of works and authorities that have been consulted, quoted and used in the compilation of this work. They are the best. I have perused them for many years in the State Library in Albany, N. Y., and otherwise; that which I have considered most essential for him to possess I have embodied in this work:

American Architect, Gwilt's Encyclopædia of Architecture, Weale's Civil and Naval Architecture, American Architect and Building News, Ferguson's Hand Book of Architecture, Downing's Rural Homes, Chambers' Encyclopedia, American Cyclopedia, Encyclopedia of Practical Receipts and Processes, Trautwine's Engineers' Manual, Imperial Journal of the Arts and Sciences, American Mechanical Dictionary, Rudiments of the Art of Building, American Journal of Science and Art, Ure's Dictionary of Arts, Manufactures and Mines, Scientific American, Industrial World, Cassell's Popular Education, Architecture and Building, Native and Foreign Art Journals, Baldwin Steam Heating, Various Papers read before Scientific Societies, Brown's Book of Secrets. Carpentry and Building: From Wren, Gen. Totton, Mr. Hope, Mr. McAlpine, Mr. Hodgson, Gen. Gilmore, Mr. Roudelet, Mr. Decournean, Mr. Blackburne, Dr. Alexis A. Julian, Prof. J. C. Draper, Mr. Rawlinson, M. Coignet, Mr. Wilkinson, Mr. Hooke, Mr. Black, Reports of Engineers to Congress, etc. etc.

INDEX.

	PAGE
Abaciscus, Abutment, Alabaster	1
Angle-float, Assize, Artificial Stone	2
Architrave, Architecture	3
Arch	11
Groined Arches	15
Dome	16
Niche, Skew Arches	17
Equilibrium of Arches	18
Drawing, Cutting, Setting Arches	22
Bond	41
Brick	46
Bond Stones, Bastard Stucco	52
Caisson, Counter-forte	53
Cements and Lime	60
Center, Coffer-dam, Cornice	55
Chimney-piece and Mantle-piece	58
Cisterns	57
Coloring Cements	68
Concrete	70
Coursed-rubble, Copings	54
Coying, Creasing, Cross-springer	54
Crushing height of Bricks and Stone	56
Crypt, Conical Arch	54
Mortars, proportions Sand, Lime, Cement	69
Mortar for setting Boilers, etc	74
Dampness	79
Damp Courses	80
Dentils, Dwarf-walls	81
Darby, Diamond Work	81
Discharging Arch, Dots	81
Drove, Dry Arch	81

INDEX.

	PAGE
Dead-man, Derrick	81
Deafening, Dowel-pin	82
Draft, Drip-stone	82
Discoloration of Brick Walls	82
Drains, etc	84
Encaustic Tile, Entabliture	86
Excavating	86
Float Stone, Floors for Cellars and Walks	90
Grout, Hawk	90
Hair, Grounds	90
Impost, Incrustation	91
Jack Arch, Jointer	91
Level, Lintel, Ledger	91
Masonry*	91
Cost of Masonry	108
Stone	112
Durability of Building Stone	116
The Preservation of Building Stone	119
Mensuration	121
Plain and Ornamental Brick-work, Foundations, etc	126
Tuck-pointing	169
Fire-proof Building	173
Boiler-setting	174
Baker's Ovens	177
Brick Stack	178
Retorts, Brick Measurement	181
Plain and Ornamental Plastering	184
Interior Decoration	191
Whitewash, Kalsomine and Coloring	203
Washes, Interior and Exterior	206
Terra Cotta	215
Walls	217
Beton	221
Tests for Bricks	222
Thin Joints	223
Union of New and Old Work	223
To Stay-lath Walls	223

Masons and Builders' Guide.

Abaciscus.—A small square stone, or tessera for a tesselated pavement. It is more correctly applied as a square compartment, enclosing a part or entire pattern or design of mosaic pavements.

Abutment.—A structure that receives the lateral thrust of an arch. The abutment may be a pier or wing wall forming a horizontal arch; or the arch may be continued to a piled or hewn foundation, which is then the abutment. In the construction of abutments great care is required in laying the foundations, the joining of the stones and the filling up or backing, for every portion of the structure has to bear its proportionate strain.

Walls and abutments are usually exposed to two forces—their own weight acting in a vertical direction through their centre of gravity, and the pressure occasioned by the extraneous load which they have to sustain; and upon the magnitude and direction of the resultant of their pressures the stability of the structure depends. They may yield or give way in three different ways: namely, the wall or abutment may separate into two portions, one sliding or slipping upon the other, or it may similarly separate and the upper portion turn over about one or other of its edges; or the material of the wall may be crushed by the pressure exceeding its cohesion. Or, in case the wall or abutment is too strong to be broken or crushed, it may still yield in any one of the above ways by either sliding upon the surface of the ground, or turning over upon one of its lower edges, or from the ground yielding under the pressure. (See Walls.)

Alabaster.—A species of marble white or colored. Sometimes call Oriental alabaster. A granular, compact, semi-pellucid gypsum which is found in masses, white or colored, and is readily turned into vases and ornaments. When calcined or roasted and powdered, it forms the substance known by the name of *Plaster of Paris*, of which the inferior kinds only are manufactured into.

Angle-float.—A float made to fit any internal angle of the walls of a room.

Assize.—A layer of stone, or one of the cylindrical blocks in a column.

Artificial stone.—Many attempts have been made, from time to time, to introduce an artificial stone, but however successful these may have been in so far as the making was concerned, none have been commercially successful, or have withstood the hard tests of our winters throughout the Northern States. But some claim from a process which consists in uniting the particles of sand into a solid mass by means of a solution of flints in caustic soda; the mixture of solution and sand is thoroughly incorporated by means of a mill, and is then moulded into any desired form by hand, or specially prepared moulds if the object is much ornamental. But although the mass—in large objects the core may be of broken brick, etc.—is thoroughly solid, hard and dense, the solution (a silicate of soda) is soluble, so that if the mass was exposed to the weather it would be washed out; to render it insoluble the object is dipped into or saturated with a solution of chloride of calcium, by which means the top whole is hardened and rendered impervious to the action of the rain.

An improved process in this work consists in making a mortar of sand and cement and casting it in wooden and iron molds. The next and new step in the work is to submit the window-sills, caps and other articles thus made to the action of carbonic acid gas in an air-tight chamber. The gas is easily obtained by burning charcoal and passing the products of combustion through water to reduce the temperature, the gas being turned into the chamber for two or three days without intermission. The gas is absolved by the damp mortar, and in time it becomes very hard, and some claim that it will withstand as well as some natural stone. The articles are plunged in water for a short time, and are then ready for use.

Architrave.—A molding around a door or window.

Architecture.—Or the art of erecting edifices, is as old as civilized man himself; from a dweller in the mound, the cave, the grotto, hut and tent, he has evolved to the possession of the luxuries of a palace.

The Egyptian style of building had its origin in the cavern and mound; the Chinese structure, with its pavilion roofs and pointed minaret, is moulded from the Tartar tent; the Grecian is derived from the wooden cabin; and the Gothic from the bower of trees.

After mankind learned to build houses, they commenced the erection of temples to their gods, and these they made more splendid than private dwellings. Thus architecture became a fine art, and at last became a universal want to society. All the architecture of ancient times sinks into insignificance when compared with that of Egypt. The obelisks, pyramids, temples, palaces, and other structures of this country, are on the grandest scale, and such as could only have been perfected by a people considerably advanced in refinement. From Egypt, the architectural art spread to Greece, where it passed from the gigantic to the chaste and elegant. Aided, doubtless, by the examples of Egyptian art, the Greeks gradually improved the style of architecture, and originated those distinctions which are now called the *Orders of Architecture*. By this phrase is understood certain modes of proportioning and decorating the column and its entablature. The Greeks had three Orders, called the Doric, Ionic, and Corinthian; these were adopted and modified by the Romans, who also added two others, called the Tuscan and Composite.

Explanation of terms used in Architecture.—The *front* or facade of a building, made after the ancient models, or any portion of it, may represent three parts, occupying different heights; the *pedestal* is the lower part, usually supporting a column; and its place supplied by a *stylobate;* the stylobate is either a platform with steps, or a continuous pedestal, supporting a row of columns. The lower part of a finished pedestal is called the *plinth;* the middle part is the *die*, and the upper part the *cornice* of the pedestal, or *surbase*. The *column* is the middle part, situated upon the pedestal or stylobate. It is commonly detached from the wall, but is sometimes buried in it for half its diameters and is then said to be engaged. *Pilasters* are square or flat columns attached to walls. The lower part of a column, when distinct, is called the *base;* the middle, or longest part, is the *shaft;* and the upper, or ornamental part, the *capital*. The swell of the column is called the *entasis*. The height of columns is measured in diameters of the column itself, taken always at the base. The *entablature* is the horizontal continuous portion which rests upon the top of a row of columns. The lower part of the entablature is called the *architrave*, or *epsitylium*. The middle part is the *frieze*, which, from its usually containing sculpture, was called *Zophorus* by the ancients. The upper or projecting part is the *cornice*. A *pediment* is the triangular face produced by the extremity of a roof. The middle or flat portion inclosed by the cornice of the pediment is called the *tympanium*. Pedestals for statues, erected on the summit and extremities of a pediment, are called *acrosteria*. An *attic* is an upper part of a building, terminated at top by a horizontal line instead of a pediment. The different mouldings in architecture are described from their sections, or from the profile which they present when cut across. Of these, the *torus* is a convex, but its outline is only the quarter of a circle; the *echinus* resembles the *ovals*, but its outline is spiral, not circular; the *scotia* is a deep concave moulding; the *cavetto* is also a concave, and occupying but a quarter of a circle; the *cymatium* is an undulated moulding, of which the upper part is concave and the lower *convex;* the *ogee*, or *talon*, is an inverted cymatium; the *fillet* is a small square or flat moulding.

In architectural measurement, a *diameter* means the width of a column at the base. A *module* is half a diameter. A *minute* is a sixtieth part of a diameter.

I have'nt space to give in this book an extensive explanation of the different styles of architecture which should be interesting to every man working at the art of construction; but will make use of some remarks of Mr. Henry

Van Brunt, in an able essay lately written on Architecture in the West, which I know will be instructive. "No people in the world understands cheap construction and economical methods of building so well, and is so inventive in providing for it. But, unwilling to let it appear what it is, and to let it grow into a legitimate expression of art by natural processes of development, it has been forced to assume forms which do not belong to it, which contradict its proper functions, and which are devised to satisfy false and unsettled ideas of beauty and fitness. The facility with which wood and galvanized iron may be moulded, painted, and sanded to imitate stone or other nobler materials, makes this baleful process possible, and tempts the builder to mask his honest work with crude travesties of conventional art. It must be admitted that this method of architectural masquerading had its origin in the eastern part of our country; but there, under the influence of better examples and higher education, it soon fell into disrepute, because, theoretically, it is an offense against fundamental principles of art, so gross that it cannot survive its first touch of intelligent criticism; and, practically, because this architecture of pretense cannot stand the test of time. These devices have been invented by practical men to meet practical wants in a practical way. When freed from the misleading adornments imposed upon them by ignorance and pretense; from shams of wood, galvanized iron, machine made mouldings, and all other delusive made rubbish of cheap deceit, which have no connection whatever with the structure, these practical devices will develop style. Until these quips and cranks of undisciplined imaginations shall have shabbily descended into their inevitable oblivion, and have been replaced by methods of decoration developed out of the construction according to the spirit of precedents furnished by the best eras of art which remains to us for our delight and instruction, deliberate and permanent architecture will not come into existence. The manner in which these opportunities have been used during the past eight or ten years gives encouragement to the hope so long cherished, that we may at last have an American architecture, the unforced and natural growth of our independent position in art. The hope that we are entering upon such an era rests mainly upon the fact that the characteristics of the best new work of the West are based, not on the elegant dilettanteism, which is appreciated only by the elect, but by the frank conversion of practical building into architectural building without affectations of mannerisms, thus appealing directly to the common sense of the people, and creating a standard which they may be capable of comprehending. It is based on a sleepless inventiveness in structure; on an honest and vigorous recognition of the part which structure should play in making a building fitting and beautiful. It is in making the wisest use of these that the leading architects of Chicago have achieved their characteristic successes. A ten story office and bank building, fire-proof throughout; with swift elevators for passengers and freight, a battery of boilers in the deep sub-basement, giving summer heat throughout, and supplying energy for pumps, ventilating fans, and electric dynamos; equipped like a palace with marbles, bronze, and glass; with no superfluous weight of steam beam, fire-clay arch, or terra-cotta partition; no unnecessary mass of masonry or column; the whole structure nicely adjusted to sustain the calculated strains and to bear with equal stress upon every pier of the deep foundations, so that no one shall yield more than another as it transfers its accumulated burden to the unstable soil beneath,—such a problem does not call for the same sort of architectural inspiration as the building of a vaulted cathedral in the Middle Ages; but, surely, for no less of courage and science, and, in providing for the safe, swift and harmonious adjustment of every part of its complicated organism, for a far wider range of knowledge. Whether one compares a modern building of this sort with a cathedral of the first class, with one of the imperial baths or villas of Rome, or with the Flavian amphitheatre itself, it must hold equal rank as a production of human genius and energy, not only in the skillful economy of its structure, and its defiance of fire and the other vicissitudes of time, but as a work of fine art developed among practical considerations which seem fundamentally opposed to expressions of architectural beauty. Indeed, the architect's most anxious study must be bestowed on the structural part of the problem. If the artistic is one part, the *structural* is *nine parts* of his endeavor. The question which must pre-occupy his mind is how he can meet the practical conditions with the greatest economy of material and labor; how he may adjust the dimensions, forms, and connections of every girder, beam, column, pier, and other parts of his structure, so that each shall be adapted to the service which it has to perform, with no superfluity of weight and strength, on the one hand, and so that, on the other, all considerations of stability shall be duly provided for within the limit of safety. His inventive zeal must be constantly on the alert to improve on the known methods, for there are none which are not subject to improvement more or less fundamental. Fire-proof structure, in especial, makes a never-ceasing demand upon his resources. An envelope of fire-clay, porous terra cotta, plastic, or some other material impervious to fiercest heat, must cover every piece of structural iron or wood. There must be no brute masses of material, such as formed the basis of Roman structure. None of these devices and methods were dreamed of when the old masters of architecture perfected their forms and proportions; so that the decoration or artistic expression of this complicated and, in each case, to a certain extent, unprecedented organism, and the conversion of it into an object of architecture, as contrasted with one of engineering, must demand of the architect such a freedom from academical restraint, such a command of the resources of design, as to make his task at once inspiring and perilous. Under these conditions, error is far easier than success; the grooves of custom, if indolently followed, will, sooner or later, lead him astray from the opportunities of original expression which are lying in wait for his use. The silent growth of the building on the drawing-boards must be attended by a constant strain of doubt and anxiety. The spirit of a recognized historical style must be followed, in any case, but these new, practical conditions of construction and service compel him to various and perplexing degrees of divergence from consecrated types. To meet these difficult emergencies with adequate spirit, he must possess the thorough knowledge of the scholar, the exact training of the engineer, the enthusiastic zeal and inventive courage of an artist, and the prompt decision of the man of business. The stimulus of enterprise and the incitements of emulation are in the air which he breathes. The qualities which I have named have certainly been exhibited in some of the best buildings in the West to a degree and in a manner which distinctly differentiate them from any contemporary work of the Old World, which challenge the best endeavors of the East to emulate them, and are already giving cheering evidence of the establishment of a vigorous architecture characteristic of the West. Architecture has not kept pace with the advance of science and invention during the present century. This has been one of its gravest reproaches. But an architecture which, like this one of the West, is frankly based upon science and invention, must keep fairly abreast with them, and thus redeem the waning influence of this noblest of the arts. If it can thus be made a living art instead of a studio art, it will not be long before it will be justifying its function as an expression of our civilization." The relations of an architect and the mechanic are so intimately connected with the successful construction of a building, and the foregoing remarks that so explicitly explain the qualification that should be had by the former, are such, that his association with an inferior workman in the management of an edifice would be of the most undesirable kind; therefore, every mechanic should take a pride in cultivating and enlightening his mind on the scientific principles of construction; and by so doing, he will not leave himself, as is often the case, in the mercy of some picture drawer, whose knowledge of sound and durable construction is of the flimsiest and most clerical nature.

Plans and Drawings.—The various kinds of drawings used in the **erection** of buildings are generally **classed** under the name of *plans*.

The drawings consist of plans, elevations, sections and

working drawings; they are classed as follows. 1. Block plans; showing the mere outlines of the buildings, and their position in relation to the surrounding objects. 2. Excavation plans; showing the shape of the trenches to be dug for the foundations, cellars, underground kitchens, etc. 3. Basement plans; showing the foundations and works up to the level of the ground, or as it is called, the ground line. 4. Floor plans; including (1) the ground floor plan; (2) the chamber plans, showing the disposition of the different rooms, which are not always arranged as on the ground floor; but, of course, the main walls necessarily cause the general apportionment to be the same; other divisions are accomplished by means of partitions; and (3) the attic plan, showing how the garrets or attics are arranged. 5. Roof plans; showing the manner in which the roofs are disposed, so as to secure the fall required, that rain may at once pass off by the gutters and spouts. Plans resemble the appearance of any object viewed from a height above it. They represent not only the piece of ground occupied, but the space it overhangs as well. Plans, therefore, do not convey any notion as to the *appearance* of a building, but as to its *reality*. They do not show how a building looks, but how its different apartments are arranged. Nor are plans associated in the mind with what may have been seen; for, of course, a true view of a roof, such as would be given in a roof plan, could only be obtained from a point above it, looking immediately downwards. In fact, the ground plan of any finished building is, properly speaking, a section through the various walls; the only difference between it and a common section consisting in this: that the *common section* is taken *vertically*, whereas the actual section of a building which is exhibited in any ground plan of it, is supposed to be taken *horizontally*. Thus, if the workman can imagine a house cut through horizontally, immediately on the line of the first floor; that is, on the level of the top of the first flight of stairs; and the whole part above this cut, including the floor, to be removed; a drawing made of the edges of the walls, of the floors, and stairs they include, would be the plan of the ground floor. An elevation plan is the picture of the *front* or flank or rear of a building; and if extensive, is accompanied with working drawing that the mechanic may fully carry it out.

Scales used in Drawings.—The scale to which drawings or plans are constructed are conventional arrangements by which the proportion is maintained between the measurement which the drawings gives, and the actual length of the same parts when constructed, should be. Thus, a part of any building fifteen feet in length could obviously not be drawn full size on paper; but if the length of each actual foot was supposed to be represented by a distance of an inch, a piece of paper a little over fifteen inches in length would allow the line to be drawn; with a margin over, the line on the drawing paper would be fifteen inches in length; but if the conventional measurement adopted was named in the drawing, it would be known that the line would be representing a line which in actual practice would be fifteen feet in length. The formation of scales, of which the above is the general principle, is a matter comparatively simple, and will easily be understood by the mechanic.

Detail or Enlarged drawings.—These are constructed on the above principle, but are designed to give facilities for measuring fractions of an inch, and are designed principally for the mechanic to work from, and are therefore got up in an enlarged or more simplified manner. Plans are always accompanied with written specifications, furnished by the architect or builder, and should specify in a plain and thorough manner the work to be done and the quality to be expected from the mechanic, that he may base his estimate upon the same.

It is a common practice with architects and engineers to name the proportion of the scale on which the drawing is made. The meaning of the fraction $\frac{1}{8}$ is that *unity* is divided into equal parts expressed by the denominator. Thus, a scale of feet $\frac{1}{48}$ signifies that our standard foot is divided into 48 equal parts, each part representing a foot on paper, the result is $\frac{1}{4}$ inch to the foot. It also means that the original object, whether a building or piece of machinery, is 48 times larger than the drawing which represents it. If the scale had been written, yards $\frac{1}{18}$, it would be the same as $\frac{2}{3}$ inch to represent a yard. The way to arrive at this is as follows : $\frac{1}{18}$ of $\frac{12}{1}$ equals $\frac{1}{4}$ inch to the foot. $\frac{1}{18}$ inches of $\frac{36}{1}$ equals $\frac{3}{4}$ inch to the yard. The above method of stating the scale ought to be understood by every mason having anything to do with plans.

The *Color* represented in plans is generally that of the material which they represent. Thus—red for brick; pale India ink, for granite; and red sandstone by light red. The lighter woods are represented by Raw Sienna; oak or teak by Vandyke Brown; concrete works are colored with Sepia, with darker markings; clay or earth with Burnt Umber; slate with Indigo and Lake; lead with pure Indigo mixed with India ink; cast iron with Grey or Neutral Tint; and wrought iron with Indigo. Plans that have many tints, the architect generally explains their meaning so that the workman may not go astray. Although *views* or *perspectives* are constantly made by the architect, they are intended to show how the building will look when finished; but they are not in any way concerned in construction.

Arch.—Notwithstanding the great importance of the arch in building, and the changes which its use has introduced, as well as the style and taste of decoration as in construction, the era of its invention, its original form, the name or country of its inventor, are involved in the deepest obscurity. The shadowing wings of the cherubim meeting over the ark of the covenant, and the meeting of the branches of the palm-trees, with carved and gilded representations of which the walls of the temple of Solomon were adorned, have been cited by some authors of warm imaginations, and familiar with the mediæval structures, as suggesting the idea of a Gothic arch. Yet it is remarkable that in the detailed description of this magnificent fane, no contrivance similar to the arch appears to have been employed in its construction. In the immense palaces built by the same prince in Jerusalem, and in the forest of Lebanon (which required thirteen years to complete them), the walls were formed of immensely large stones 12 to 15 feet long, the *covering above* being of *cedar beams*, upon rows of cedar pillars. In the account of these buildings we find staircases regularly formed, but no indications of arches. In the second temple, built by Esdras, the temple itself, as well as the stately cloisters surrounding it, the apertures were of the lintelled kind; and when it was re-edified by Herod, the greatest part of these ambulatories are again described to have been roofed with beams of wood laid across, and resting upon massive stone pillars. The antiquity of the arch, says Wilkinson, is traced to the time of Amunoph I., who reigned 1540 B. C. He also thinks it probable that the chambers of the brick Pyramids at Memphis, erected by the successor of the son of Cheops, would prove to be vaulted over with arches, which would carry back the antiquity of the arch to 2020 B. C. In one of the Egyptian pyramids is an arch turned over three stones which formed a stone arched ceiling to the Sarcophagus chamber. The two outer stones were set edgeways and inclined inward, having the outer placed upon them, forming an arch. Over these stones was turned a brick arch. This tomb is of the time of Amunoph I., 1540 B. C.

The stone arch at Saccura is of the time of Psammeticus II., 600 B. C. Arches are found in Chinese bridges of great antiquity and magnitude; and, as before shown, those of Egypt far antedate the periods of Greece or Rome. Arched vaults are found among the ruins of Nineveh. The Greeks did not allow arches to appear in their visible architecture, but used them for covering drains and the like, as in the temple of the Sun at Athens, and that of Apollo at Didymos. It was, however, contrary to their architectural principles to admit any but straight lines into any visible part of a building, except, perhaps, as mere ornamentation, thus sacrificing in many instances convenience to secure that severe simplicity of outline by which their public structures were characterized. The Romans made very free use of the arch. The Cloaca Maxima, or Great Sewer, of Rome, is the oldest known example of Roman workmanship; it is believed to have been constructed more than five hundred years before the Christian era, and is yet in a perfect state of preservation, still continuing to perform its original functions. That people used arches also as triumphal monuments; the arch of Titus was erected A. D. 80; that of Trajan, A. D. 114; and of Constantine, A. D. 312. The Gothic style, which originated about the ninth century, and soon spread over the whole of Europe, was emphatically the style of arches. Its special characteristics are the clustered pillar and the pointed arch. The mediæval masons treated them with a boldness and freedom unknown to the builders of ancient Rome. Long before the properties of the century had been developed by Hooke, it is more than probable that they were known in practice to the old Freemasons, who built Henry VIII.'s chapel and other structures of similar and previous date. And now, at the present time, the arch assumes an importance of the greatest concern to the practical mason, for nowhere is there a structure of any importance being erected but what the arch forms a prominent feature; either of brick, stone or plaster, the construction of which should be intelligently understood by the mechanic.

Arch. In building.—A mechanical arrangement of separate inelastic bodies in the line of a curve, which preserve a given form when resisting pressure. A part of a building suspended over, or from, a given plan, and supported or resisted at its extremities and concave towards the plan. A concave structure raised or turned upon a mould, called its centering, in the form of an arc of a curve, and serving as the inward support of some superstructure. A *building* open below and closed above, standing by the form of its own curve. A *ceiling*, composed of stones, which, by acting against each other, are supported by the same *force* by which they would otherwise fall.

An aperture formed of bricks or stones of a wedge or like tendency, by which it is adapted to resist perpendicular and lateral pressure, so as to support the edifice built over it. An opening in a bridge, through or under which the water and vessels pass. A *concave* ceiling, or floor, of any material, or on any principal of construction. A tunnel. An excavation. The term *arch*, in its widest signification, is commonly understood to mean almost anything of a curved shape employed for the purpose of bearing weight or resisting pressure, but in its more restricted mechanical sense may be defined as a collection of wedge-shaped bodies, termed voussoirs, or arch stones, of which the first and last at each extremity are sustained by a sup-

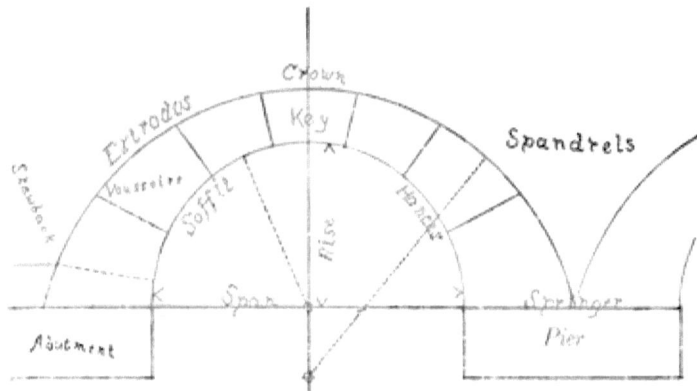

port or abutment, while the intermediate ones are held in position by their mutual *pressure* and the adhesion of the mortar or cement interposed between them.

The first, or lowest stones, or courses of stones, that form part of the arch, are called *springers;* and the line on which they are placed, or from which the arch begins to rise or spring, is the *springing line,* or reins of the arch.

The *impost,* or *platband,* is the upper end of the pier on which the arch rests. The stones ranged in the curved line are called *archstones,* or voussoirs; the lower end of the stones form the interior, or curve of the arch, the whole of which concave surface is called the *intrados* or soffit. The *extrados* is the upper or opposite *convex* surface of the archstones.

The *span,* or *chord of the arch,* is measured from the points or lines where the intrados rises from the impost. The *rise of the arch,* or its versed line, is the distance of the highest point of the intrados above the chord line.

This highest point being by some called the *vertex* of the arch, sometimes the *crown;* but among workmen, the highest point of the intrados, or vertex, is called the *under side of the crown*, the crown being the *upper end* of the stones highest in the arch.

The upper or centre stone of the series of archstones, or voussoirs, which connects the opposite portions of the arch, and binds them together, is the *keystone*, or *key*.

The *haunces*, or *hauces*, are the spaces included between a horizontal line drawn from the vertex of the arch, and a perpendicular touching the springing line of the intrados. *Flanks* are the spaces included between the extrados, and a horizontal line from the *crown* of the arch, and a vertical line from the springing of the extrados.

When this space is not built up with solid masonry throughout the breadth of the arch, the walls built upon the voussoirs to the same height are called *hauce* or *flank* walls; the outer wall forming the elevation of the arch is the *spandrel* wall. Sometimes a circle-arch is constructed through the spandrel and haunch walls, which workmen designate an *ox-eye*,—the extrados prolonged by an arch of a reversed curvature passing over the pier, and connected with a similar prolongation of the opposite arch, is called a *strutt arch*, or *strutt course*. In the decoration of arches, the archivolt is a collection of mouldings, on the face of the archstones, concentric with the intrados. The keystone, when ornamented, is sometimes named from its ornament, as a *console*,

Arches are also denominated from the similarity of their intrados to the periphery of the sections of various geometrical solids, as semi-circular, elliptical, parabolic, cycloidal, catenarian, etc., etc.

Groined arches.—A groin is the angular curve formed by the intersection of two semi-cylinders or arches. The centerings which are used in forming these arches will guide the mason in this work. The turning a simple arch on a centre only requires care to keep the courses as close as possible, and to use very little mortar on the inner part of the joints.

In executing a brick groin, the difficulty arises from the peculiar mode of making proper *bond*, at the intersection of the two circles as they gradually rise to the crown, where they form an exact point. In the intersection of these angles, the inner rib should be perfectly straight and perpendicular to a diagonal line drawn to the plane; after the centres are set, the application of the brick to the angle will show in what direction it is to be cut.

As for the sides, they are turned as for common cylindric vaults. It is usual for the mason, when laying out the courses for a groin arch, whether of stone or brick, to use a thin rod which will bend over the centre, and from it mark the number of courses, which should be odd in number. From these spaces he may snap chalk lines on the centering bounds, which will guide him in cutting his groin and keeping his courses uniform.

Arches intersecting a coved ceiling are similar to groins. Such arches are called *lunettes*, and are generally practiced for semi-circular-headed windows piercing the coves in the ceiling.

Dome.—The dome is a hemispherical arch, or any other curve, constructed to cover a circular, elliptical, or polygonal area. There is an important difference between the dome and the common arch, usullay called a cylindrical, or cylindroidal arch, to distinguish it from the former. The common arch cannot stand at all without its centering, unless the whole curve be complete; and when finished, the crown or upper segment tends to overset the haunches or lower segments. The dome, on the contrary, is perfectly strong, and is a complete arch without its upper segment, thus, as the pressure acts differently, there is less strain upon the haunches and abutments of a dome than on those of a common arch of the same curve. Hence, a sufficient dome may be constructed with much thinner material than would be proper for a common arch of same curvature. However, to construct a stone dome on a large scale, so that it shall resist the effects of time and climate, and last for several centuries without repair, may be considered one of the greatest triumphs of architectural and masonic art, which circumstance may account for the very few examples in the world that are really satisfactory, either in design, execution or durability. At first sight, it would appear that the dome is a much more difficult piece of work than a plain arch; this is, however, not actually the case in absolute practice; for when we examine potters' kilns, bakers ovens, and glass-house cones—some of the latter of which are of vast extent, erected by ordinary bricklayers, with materials, in many cases, of an inferior nature, as compared with good stone—our wonder ceases, and we naturally come to the conclusion that the fact of curvature in the horizontal direction, or the continuous abutment of a circular basement, gives considerable extra stability to the superstructure.

Some authorities have placed the niche relatively with the dome in construction, but the

Niche is now, for the most part, an ornamental figure in construction, and inconsidered in the light of its former application. As now used, there are three classes corresponding in character with the order or composition in which they are employed. The first agreeing with the Doric, expresses strength and simplicity, and should be without decoration; the second, following the character of the Ionic, exhibits a moderate enrichment and lighter proportion than the former, and is usually adorned with archivolt and impost; and the third extreme, delicacy and richness, according with the Corinthian, and showing usually entablature, pediment, and columns.

For the bricklayer, the construction of niches is, perhaps, one of his most difficult operations. It is usual for him to form all of his courses standing, and the bricks must thus be reduced very thin at the inner circle, as they cannot extend beyond the thickness of one brick at the crown.

Skew arches.—In ordinary cases, the plan of an arch is rectangular, the face of the abutments being at right angles to the fronts; but of late years the necessity which has arisen on railway works for carrying communications across each other without regard to the angle of their intersection, has led to the construction of *oblique* or *skew* arches. In an ordinary rectangular arch, each course is parallel to the abutments, and the inclination of any bed joint with the horizon will be the same at every part of it. In a skew arch it is not possible to lay the courses parallel to the abutments, for, were this done, the thrust being at right angles to the direction of the courses, a great portion of the arch on each side would have nothing to keep it from falling. In order to bring the thrust into the right direction, the courses must, therefore, be laid as nearly as possible at right angles to the fronts of the arch at an angle with the abutments; and it is this which produces the peculiarity of the *skew arch*. The two ends of any course will then be at different heights, and the inclination of each bed joint with the horizon will increase from the springing to the crown, causing the beds to be *winding* surfaces instead of a series of planes, as in a rectangular arch. The variation in the inclination of the bed joints is called the *twist* of the beds, and leads to many difficult problems in masonry and stonecutting, which requires considerable skill on the part of the mechanic to execute. The general principles employed in the erection of cylindrical arches and corridors should be followed in the work, but the most extreme care should be exercised in the proper development of the arch stones or brick, which, from their cross direction, require great nicety of adjustment and strict regard to radiation.

As a general thing, attending the construction of skew arches, bridges, domes, and vaulting, a skilled engineer superintends the work, and a mechanic, who understands the general principles of arching, will find but little trouble in getting along. For, practically speaking, we know that this work is now within the domain of civil engineering, and in stone construction, the various parts and geometrical curves are, or should be, so shown on the working drawings by the engineer that the practical mason, who does understand the sound principles of arching, should have but little difficulty in cutting or setting his stone.

Equilibrium of arches.—When an arch is in a state of perfect equilibrium, each stone or voussoir is acted upon by three forces, namely, the weight of itself and the load above it acting in a vertical direction; and the pressure of each of the two contiguous stones acting in directions perpendicular to their surfaces of mutual contact; then, since their forces must be all in equilibrium, their lines of direction must all intersect in some common point within the stone.

If we suppose its abutments incapable of yielding, it can only fail in consequence of the crushing of its material, the cohesive power of which is then the limit of the strength of an arch. When, however, an arch is not in a state of equilibrium, it may fail in two ways: in the first case, the stones may slide or slip past each other, and so become displaced; and, in the second case, they may yield by turning upon some of the joints, the arch separating into three or four large portions, and turning on the inner and outer edges of certain of the joints. Now, the voussoirs of the arch cannot slide upon each other unless the angle which the line of pressure makes with a perpendicular to the joint is equal to or greater than the limiting angle of resistance for the material of which the arch is composed, which is usually sixty degrees for stone; and as this is very much greater than the angle which the line of pressure ever makes with the perpendicular to the joint, an arch may be considered in no danger of giving way from the slipping of its voussoirs; to which we may add, that the cohesion of the cement interposed between the stones, is an additional security against the failure of an arch from this cause. The second mode of failure, which is also the most usual, takes place whenever the line of pressure deviates so far from the position of equilibrium as to pass entirely out of the substance of the arch, so as not to cut the joints at all. The more the line of pressure deviates from the center of the joints, the less will be the stability of the arch; but so long as it continues to cut the joints, no motion can take place; the moment, however, that it passes without the joint, the motion will take place, the two voussoirs will turn upon their edges nearest the line of pressure, and the arch will fall. If, however, there be a deficiency of weight at the crown, then the line of pressure will fall within the intrados and rise above the extrados, the arch separating as in the former case, but now turning about the outer edges, and the inner edges the crown rising and the haunches falling in. We see, then, that when we deviate so far from the arch of equilibrium as to cause the line of pressure to approach either the intrados or extrados of the arch, we begin to endanger its stability, actual contact with either being the ultimate limit; and the stability of the arch being greater, as we make the line of pressure approach nearer the center of the joints. When an arch has all its parts in equilibrium, the horizontal strain on every joint is the same, and therefore the perpendicular pressure, tending to crush the keystone of the arch, is equal to the horizontal thrust against its abutment. Therefore, the power of an arch to resist the horizontal strain at the crown is proportionate to the depth of the keystone and to the cohesive power of the material of which the arch is composed. The *stability of an arch is*, therefore, directly proportional to the depth of its keystone, multiplied by the cohesive power of the material, and is inversely proportional to its radius of curvature, multiplied by the weight on every foot of its surface.

So convinced were the Egyptians and Greeks of this principle in an arch, that they never used any other constructive expedient than a perpendicular wall or prop, supporting a horizontal beam, and half the satisfactory effect of their buildings arises from their adhering to this simple, though expensive, mode of construction. They were perfectly acquainted with the use of the arch and its properties; even to the present day the Hindoos refuse to use the arch, though it has long been employed in their country by the Mahometans. As they express it, "*An arch never sleeps,*" and it is true that by its thrust and pressure it is always tending to tear a building to pieces: and when the smallest damage is done, and surely if it be imperfectly *constructed*, it hastens the ruin of a building, whereas, if it was perfectly and mechanically built, might last for ages. One of **the great principles that** ought to be carefully studied **in constructing arches is,** that the **longer** the joints of the voussoirs the greater the strength of the arch will be.

It is quite evident that the old Gothic architects were well aware of this fact; for in the construction of their vaulted roofs they introduced what are technically called ribs, adopted in many cases both diagonally and at right angles, which materially augment the strength of support required for the spandrills that come between the ribs.

In designing an arch, two methods of proceeding present themselves; we may either confine the load to the weight of the arch itself, or nearly so, and suit the shape of an arch to a given curve of equilibrium, or we may design the arch as taste or circumstances may dictate, and load it until the line of resistance coincides with the curve thus determined upon. Those arches which differ most from their curves of equal horizontal thrust are semi-circles and semi-ellipses, which have a tendency to descend at their crowns and to rise at their haunches, unless they are well *backed up*. The *depth* of the voussoirs in an arch must be sufficient to contain the *curve* of equilibrium under the greatest load to which it can be exposed; and, as the pressure on the arch stones increases from the crown to the springing, their depth should be increased in the same proportion. Each joint of the voussoirs should be at right angles to a tangent to the curve of equilibrium at the point through which it passes.

To find the depth of keystones for cut stone arches, whether circular or elliptical.—Find the radius which will touch the arch at its soffit. Add together this radius and half the span of the arch. Take the square root of the sum. Divide this square by 4. To the quotient add $\frac{2}{10}$ of a foot.

For second class work, this depth may be increased about $\frac{1}{8}$th part; or for brick, or rubble, about $\frac{1}{4}$. Trautwine, C. E.

The above manner of ascertaining the depth of arch stones will agree with all the present arches that have proven successful in practice.

To find the radius of an arch, whether the arch be circular or elliptical, square half the span; square the whole rise;

add these squares together; divide the sum by twice the *rise*.

DRAWING, CUTTING AND SETTING ARCHES.

' Arches are generally divided into the triangular-headed arch, the round-headed, and the pointed arch.

Of round-headed arches there are four kinds: the semi-circular, the stilted, segmental, and the horse-shoe. The stilted arch is semi-circular, but the sides are carried downwards in a straight line below the spring of the curve till they rest upon the imposts. In the horse-shoe arch, the sides are also carried down below the center, but follow the same curve. The pointed arch may be divided into two classes, those described from two centers, and those described from four. Of the first class there are three kinds: the equilateral, the lancet, and the obtuse. The equilateral is formed of two segments of circle, of which the radii are equal to the breadth of the arch, and the obtuse shorter, while the lancet is longer.

Of the complex arches, there is the Ogee and the Tudor. The Tudor arch is described from four centers, two on a level with the spring and two below it. Of foiled arches, there are the round-headed trefoil, and the square-headed trefoil.

The elliptic arch is not always truly elliptical, but is sometimes formed by the combination of the arcs of several circles.

For the *true ellipsis* is derived from a *diagonal cut* through the cone or cylinder; no portion of its curve, strictly speaking, is any part of a circle; it cannot, therefore, be drawn *correctly* either by the compasses or from centres, and it must be remembered by the mason and the plasterer also, that for practical purposes, when describing or working this curve from the centres given, that a little modification in the curve by hand is frequently an artistic improvement, and as the purpose of this book is chiefly of a practical nature, we do not wish to burden its pages with geometrical definitions further than what is necessary for practical purposes.

The semi-circular arch is the Roman Byzantine and Norman arch; the Ogee and horse-shoe are the profile of many Turkish and Moorish domes.

The pointed and foliated arches are Gothic. Both domes and vaults are found in Roman works, but with the decline of Roman power the art of vaulting was lost, and the churches of all Roman Christendom remained with nothing but timber roofs.

But among the Greek Christians or Byzantines, it was retained, or else re-invented; but the Greek vaulting consisted wholly of spherical surfaces, whilst the Roman consisted of cylindrical ones.

The *beds* of all wedge-shaped forms, brick or stone, in arches, should converge towards a common *center*. The *joints* of all arches should be perpendicular to the surface of the *soffit*.

The arches that the mason has to deal with generally in the practical construction of buildings are termed *rough*, *plain* and *ornamental* arches.

Plain or *rough arches* are those in which none of the bricks are cut to fit the splay. Hence, the joints which are quite close to each other at the soffit, are wider towards the outer curve of the arch, and are generally used as *relieving, trimmer, tunnel, vaulting*, and all arches where *strength* is essential, and appearance no particular object. In constructing arches of this kind, that is, where the radius of curvature is small, not exceeding four or five feet, the best arrangement is to build two or more four-inch concentric brick arches over each other until the whole necessary thickness is obtained ; each of their successive rings should be built independent, having no connection with the others beyond the cohesion of the mortar in the *ring joint*. It is quite necessary that each course should be bonded alternately throughout the length of the arch, and the joint should be of a regular thickness. For, if one ring is built with a thin joint, and another with a thick one, the one having the most mortar will shrink, causing a fracture and depriving the arch of much of its power. The reason for building an arch composed of several rings, without attempting to bond them together, is plain enough.

The joints of such an arch diverge so rapidly from the soffit outward, that if it were built otherwise the brick work would not be sufficiently compact, for, at the upper part of the arch, the bricks would be separated to an extraordinary degree.

As the radius of the curvature of an arch increases, the joints diverge less rapidly; therefore, it is objectionable to build small span arches without *cutting the brick*, or forming them of several concentric rings. In arches, however, of greater radius, such as from six to eight feet, they may be built without cutting the brick, in the usual method of headers and stretchers, or *bonded*, from one side of the arch to the other.

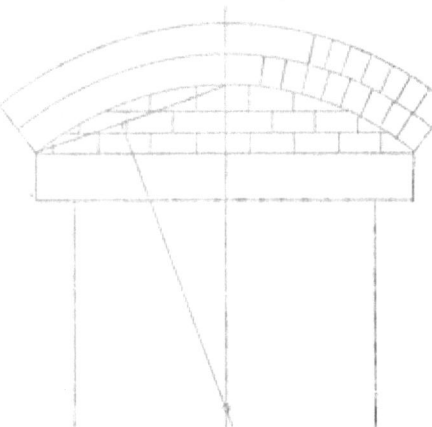

All plain **arches** should be built in the most substantial manner of hard burned **brick, t** h e joints tight, and formed of the best mortar. Subjoined figure **shows** the manner of forming a plain or rough archh over a lintel.

EXTERNAL OR ORNAMENTAL BRICK ARCHES.

These **consist of all** kinds **of** arches **that are** cut and brought **down to a given gauge,** and **are built of** pressed brick.

The **bricks used in** these arches always show their thickness or edge **in** the face of the wall, which thickness generally being **the** full width of the brick **at the** extrados of the arch, diminishes towards **the** soffit.

This splay is termed **the *sommering* of an** arch. The bricks used in external **arches** should **be** cut and rubbed with great **care to** the proper splay or wedge-like form necessary, and according to the gauges or regularly measured dimensions. This is not always done. Bricklayers are generally allowed sufficient time to rub the outside of each arch brick properly, so that their work may have a handsome appearance to the eye, but often slur over all the other parts of the work which are hidden from view. Hence, in order to save time, they are very apt to cut away the inside of the bricks of those arches to such a degree as may even deprive them of their proper wedge-like form everywhere, except at the external surface.

This neglect produces cracks, and causes the arch to bulge forward. It may even cause one of the bricks of a straight arch to drop down lower than the soffit or bottom of the arch, which defects may be frequently seen over the windows of many brick buildings.

It is well known that all ornamental arches, generally, are nothing more than mere shells, as far as strength is concerned, and support a portion of the wall towards the outside only. But if properly executed, well cut, rubbed and set, they answer the purpose for which they are designed. It is, therefore, necessary that the mason should understand this part of his trade thoroughly. Subjoined, we place before him the forms of the principal brick arches in use throughout the States; and when he is called upon to construct any of these in practice, all that is necessary for him to do is to apply the rules for designing them as laid down here.

The mason may use them also for cutting and setting his stone, and the plasterer for running his arches. All ornamental and cut brick arches, to be properly constructed, should be cut and rubbed first before they are placed upon the scaffold. It gives the mason a better opportunity to select his brick or stone; and when everything is ready, the sooner an arch is put in after it has been started the better, for the mortar will bond uniformly throughout the arch.

Every mason should have a pair of compasses, a T square, and a set square, a drawing board and his rule, and practice the drawing of these arches he is often called upon to construct, and thereby become familiar with every one of them, the higher problems connected with the cutting of stone, which in the past belonged to the mason trade, we know, at the present time in the United States, is executed by the stonecutters; and I trust there are sufficient number of examples given here to answer the requirements of the practical mason, who is often called upon to perform this work.

To draw and build a *semi-circular arch*.—Place the point of the compass at the center O, and with the radius O C describe the inner circle which will answer for the soffit;

Semi-circular Arch.

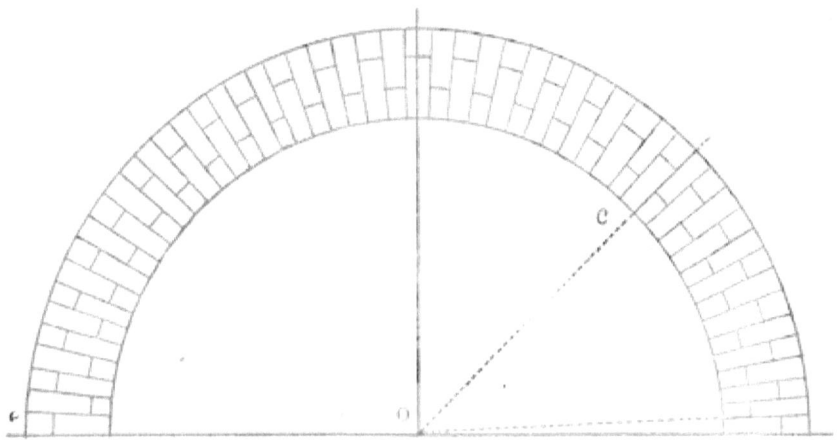

then with the same center describe the outer circle according to the depth of the arch required. The number of courses in a semi-circular arch is determined by finding how many thicknesses of a brick (the kind that is to be used) are required at the extrados or outside of the arch, as well as allowing for the thickness of the joint, which is generally one-tenth or one-eighth of an inch thick for pressed brick, and from these points of division, drawing to the centre of the arch, will determine the splay, and give the rule for rubbing the brick to their proper form. It must be remembered that all *bonded arches* must be spaced off into an odd number of courses, and the proper way to do this is to lay out the *key brick* or course first, divide it in the center of the perpendicular line, from which space downwards to the springing line of the arch, which number of spaces or courses should be alike on both sides of the key brick; if of an even number, the key brick, and the brick started at the springing line will be alike, that is, either stretcher or header, depending upon the disposition of the key brick at the soffit of the arch. The soffit line for the brick of the arch is got by placing a set bevel across the space occupied by one course of brick on the soffit lines this is reversed for the brick on the extrados line.

Segment Arch.

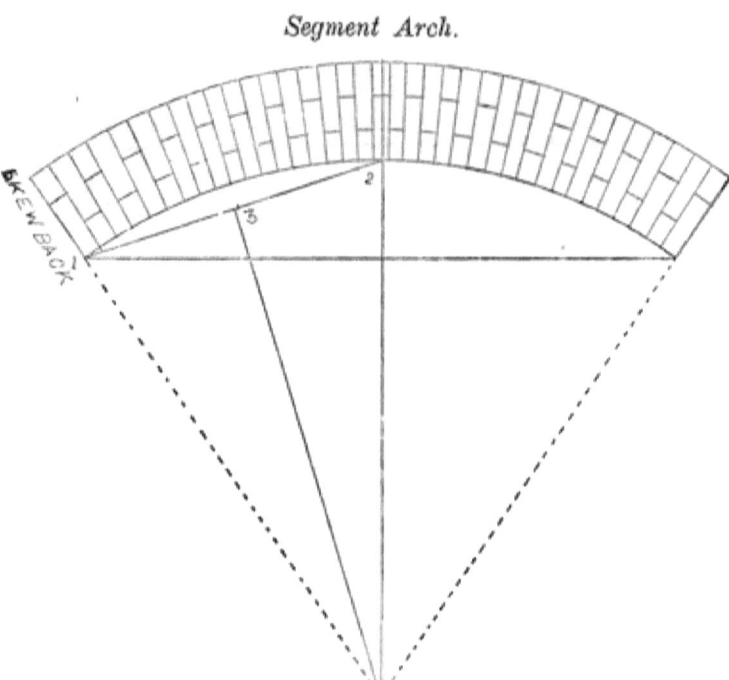

The Segment Arch may be worked in the same way as the semi-circular, the only difference being in taking the center line to strike it with. This is taken in the perpendicular line below the span, with radius according to the rise required, and this is the point to which all lines must be drawn, both to get the skew back and also size of the course.

Draw the tangent line 1, 2, bisect it at the point 3, place the set-square at the point 3 at right angles with the line

1, 2, which gives the line 3, 4, the intersection of which, with the perpendicular, gives the center from whence the segmental curve of the arch is drawn, and also the point from which all the joints of the arch must radiate.

SEMI-CIRCULAR ARCH WITH A GOTHIC HEAD.

To draw the outside portion of this arch, it is necessary to draw the line A. B., bisect it at C., draw a line with the set-square from C., at right angles with A. B. to any point D., and upon this line the center is taken to describe the outside curve of the arch, according to the haunch required; and the inner ring must be divided in the same manner as the outer ring of the semi-circular arch, but the bevels for the tops must be taken separately. If the depth of the arch be very deep, this inner circle must be so divided that the joint at the outer circle may not be too *large*.

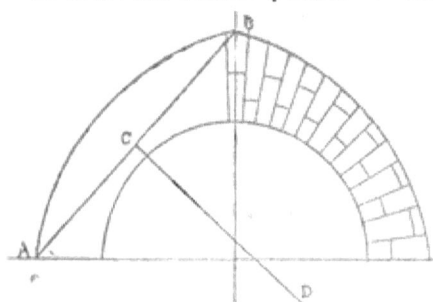

THE GOTHIC OR POINTED ARCH.

Set out the width of the arch a. b. on the horizontal line, then with a. for center, and the distance a. b. for radius, describe the arc c. b.; then with a. e. as radius and with the same center describe the inner arc d. e.; this forms one side of the arch; then with b. as center, and same radius used for the first half, describe

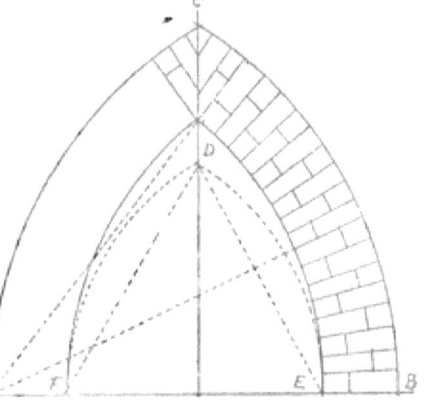

the second. It will be observed that this is not the equilateral Gothic arch, which arch is shown, however, by the dotted lines within the pointed arch, and is described by using the centre E. and F., and is built as follows according to the pointed Gothic:

Divide the extrados into courses according to the size of the bricks, and draw the lines to the point a., as shown, taking care in dividing out the courses that half a course shall be on each side of the perpendicular line at c., to answer for key brick. The bevel once set will answer for the whole of this arch, the same as semi-circular.

The bricklayer should observe with attention the manner in which this arch is *keyed*, for, in practice, pointed arches are often botched in a ridiculous manner in this respect, simply because the mechanic either did not know how to design it, or was not allowed sufficient time to execute it properly, which only way is, for ornamental pressed brick work, to draw the full size of the arch to be constructed first—form your moulds, and cut and rub your brick to them; then, when everything is all right, put the arch in as quick as possible.

Sometimes the Gothic arch is cut as represented in the following figure, but it is very seldom, on account of the extra work in soffiting the bricks; for, in this case, each course must be cut to a separate bevel, and the lines for each course must be drawn from the center O.

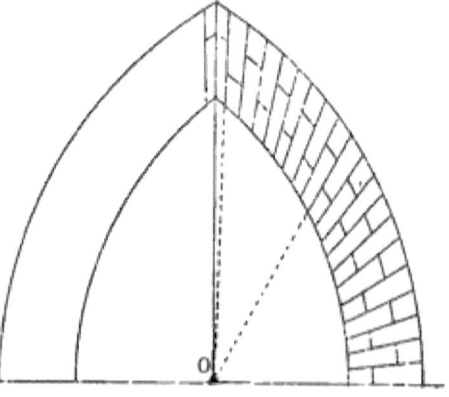

Modified Gothic.—To cut this arch, it is necessary to draw the lines a. b. and b. c. from the springing to the under side of the crown; bisect a. b. and b. c. at d. and e., and from these points of bisection draw the lines to the points F. F. with the set-square. And upon these lines the points are taken to describe the arch according to the depth required.

The extrados is then divided into courses and lines drawn to the points F. F. for the wedge-shape of the brick, if the arch is to be cut in the same way as the Gothic arch. But if it is to be *keyed in* with an upright key, the lines must be drawn to the center O. The manner of drawing and cutting the moulds of the Modified Gothic applies to any Gothic whether *greater* or *less* than the regular equilateral arch.

Modified Gothic.

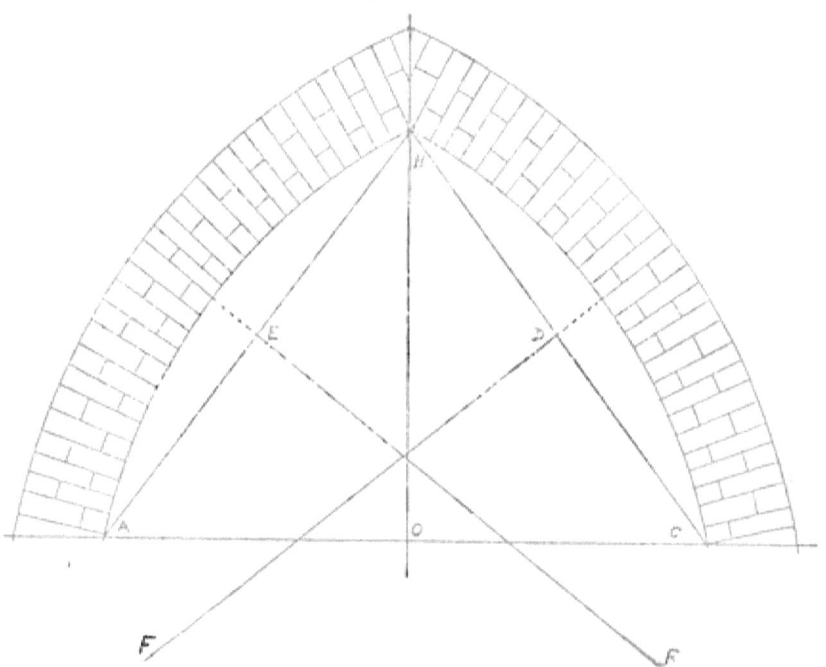

Segment Gothic.—To draw the segment Gothic, lay out the span a. b., and describe the soffit from the perpendicular line according to the rise required as at O.; the extrados of the arch is obtained as shown for the modified Gothic. Care should always be taken in laying out the courses of

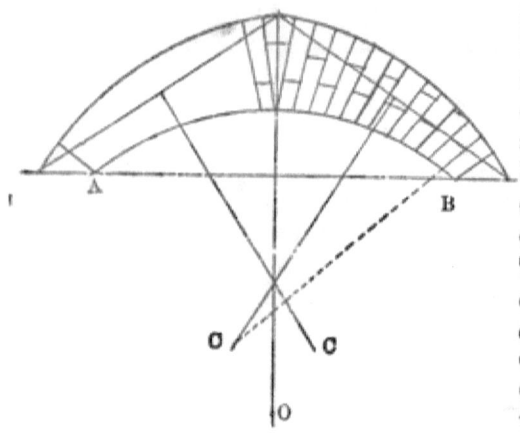

this arch that the key may appear as shown in the cut. The wedge-shape form of the brick are obtained from the centers C. C. The soffit and cross joints are obtained from the center O., but the extrados line of the arch must be cut from the centers C. C., as well the line of skew-back.

Camber arch.—When the curve of the segmental arch is very flat, the center from which it could be described is very distant from the intrados of the arch, the bricks have their joints converging to points near the arch, and are all, therefore, cut to different forms; the arch is called a *camber arch*. It will be seen that in a straight arch of this kind no two voussoirs, or bricks, are alike on the same side of the key, but those of the contrary side correspond with each other pair by pair. The ordinary way to describe this arch is to lay out the width of the opening, draw the soffit line with a *camber slip* (a piece of board $\frac{1}{2}$ inch thick and as long as the opening, and triangular in shape, having a rise of $\frac{1}{8}$ inch to the foot toward the center of the opening), bisect the perpendicular line with C. as center, and C. B. as radius; this is the point to which the lines are drawn to get the proper skew back. It is then necessary to measure the bricks to see how they will work. If $2\frac{1}{4}$ inches set off $1\frac{1}{4}$ inches on each side of the centre line A., and draw lines to the point C., as shown, this will give the shape of the moulds, of which there ought to be three, made of stiff cardboard, and about eighteen inches in length. If the arch is to be one foot in depth, and in proportion if more or less, then mark them all about three inches from the narrow end. Fix one of these upon the center line, as shown at A., so the line above mentioned shall be exactly at the soffit line of the arch, and then trace the other two alternately towards the skew back, keeping each line on the moulds to the soffit curve each time. The bevels must be taken for each course, and marked on the mould ready for working; one bevel will answer for soffit, cross-joint, and top of each course, if it is reversed for the two last named. But sometimes it would be best to leave the tops and cut them when setting the arch, for very often mistakes are made in taking the length of the courses with the template; be sure and have the cross joints in this arch level, and the courses uniform. Plain as this arch appears to be in appearance, it is, however difficult to execute properly in practice; the full size of the arch should be drawn first, and the moulds taken as described, of course, allowance being made for the joint when the cardboard or wood is being cut for the mould.

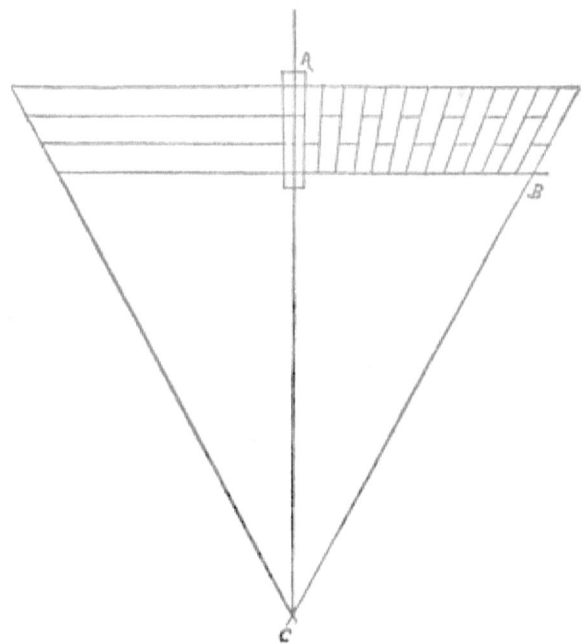

Camber Arch.

Segment Camber.—The Segment Camber is somewhat like the Camber arch, and is constructed with much less labor, and looks well in a building. Lay out the height of the arch as required on the perpendicular line, and draw a line parallel to the span of the arch and intersect it with the line of the skew-back drawn from the center. Lay the courses out the same as in the camber, and it is only necessary to cut for the beds and the upper line of the arch.

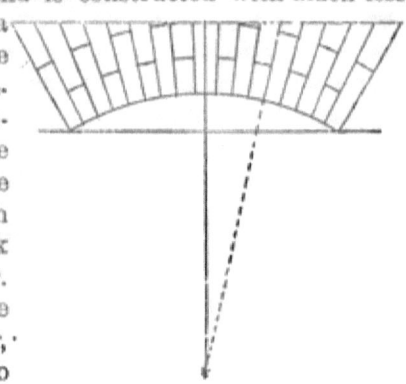

The Ellipse Gothic is rather more difficult in the working than the generality of Gothic arches, owing to the different striking points.

To draw this arch, let the distance a. b. be set off equally on each side of the perpendicular line; then divide it into four equal parts by marking the points c. d., and with d. as center, and the distance d. b. as radius, describe the arc from b. to E., mark the point b. e. equal with B. D., draw the chord F. E. and bisect it at G., from which point draw a line with the set-square to any point O., and upon this line the center is taken to draw the upper portion of that part of the arch as shown; the soffit curves are obtained in the same way. After the lines A. F. E. B. are drawn, they can be made to answer either for soffit or extrados by striking the other parts *greater* or *less* than those named; but the center will do for either. The moulds for this arch are taken in the same way as those in the *camber;* that is, it must be traced over with the moulds so that each course shall be *exactly of one size,* and the bevels must be taken separately. It is of the greatest importance that the mechanic should practice drawing this arch until he is thoroughly acquainted with every part; for **ellipse Gothic, or**

Tudor arch, or *four centered*, vary greatly, and by thoroughly understanding the principles of the one here described, he will be better able to reduce or elevate them to suit his requirements. The construction of this arch is slurred over more than any other we are apt to see, the mechanic forming two moulds to construct each side of the arch, which should *never be* done when the appearance of the arch is taken into consideration; and where great exactness in workmanship is required in ellipse Gothic, or any other form of arch, whether of stone or brick, the mason should set out the full size of the arch in elevation on a drawing, with the joints, soffit and extrados lines marked thereon. Lay the full size of drawing on a thin sheet of zinc, prick through the lines with a fine point into the zinc to the form of the required stones or bricks, and then cut them to their requisite shape, being numbered for their requisite situation in the arch; they can then be ap-

Ellipse Gothic.

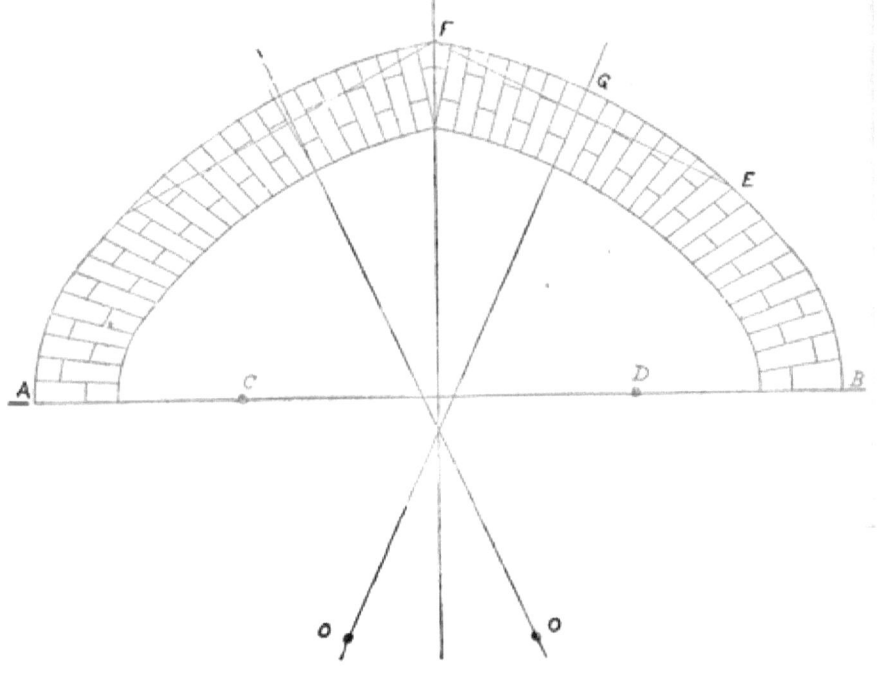

plied to either the stone or brick to be worked, and **when** they are formed they should be numbered or marked **also**, and when setting **the arch**, the above drawing should be at hand, and each **course** or voussoir placed as correspondingly marked on the **drawing**.

Semi-ellipse **Arch**, which is somewhat like the ellipse Gothic, the **difference being in** their crowns; but the drawing is quite different. In drawing this arch, divide the span into three equal parts, as shown at A., C., D., B.; then with D. as center and D. B. for radius, describe the arc from B. to E. equal to D. E., and the same on the opposite side to F.; then with D. for center and the distance D. C. for radius, describe an arc cutting the perpendicular line in G.; and from this point, with the distance G. F., describe the crown F. E.; the outer curves are taken from the same centers, only with a greater radius. To get the moulds correctly, that is, for ornamental brick work, where all the brick should be of the same size, this arch must be traced over in the same way as the camber and ellipse Gothic; that is, take the thickness of the brick and set it equally on each side of the center line at H.; then draw the lines to G.; this will give the size of the mould very nearly; then if they are worked alternately down to the springing line, it **will** easily be seen where they **want** easing. There is on

Semi ellipse Arch.

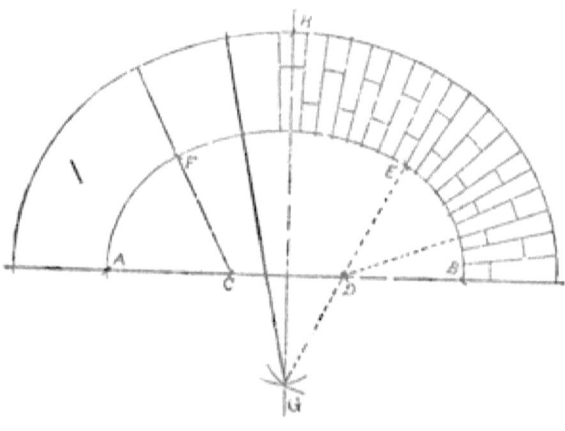

doubt but what these arches are stronger in every case when they are built from their centering lines, and is the easiest method; but the appearance is not so good as when the courses in the arch are all of the same size, and for face brick work their stability is sufficient for the amount of weight they have to bear.

The adjoining mode is probably the closest approximation that can be arrived at in showing the true ellipse by the compasses or from centers, which we know will be useful for the mason to understand. To draw it, erect the perpendicular line A. 1. at right angles to the conjugate axis A. B., and make it equal to O. C. Divide A. I. into two equal parts, and draw the dotted lines 2 C. and 1, 3, describe the arcs Q. R. from the centers 4 and C. Draw the line S. S. until it cuts the continued transverse axis at D., this being the center of the larger curve of the ellipse 4 C. T. Next draw the line 1 D., and where it cuts the conjugate axis at 5 is the center of the end curves of the figure. The foregoing is probably the most ingenious mode of drawing the ellipse by the compasses or by centers that has yet been discovered.

The necessity for taking the face moulds for brick or stone arches constructed from ellipse curve from the full-sized drawing of the arch, arises from the fact that these arches are generally *crippled* at the junction of the small and large curves T., and they should be nicely arranged in this respect by the mechanic; also, that all the face moulds of the arch should be exactly alike, especially for ornamental brick work or masonry. And for the plasterer, it lies

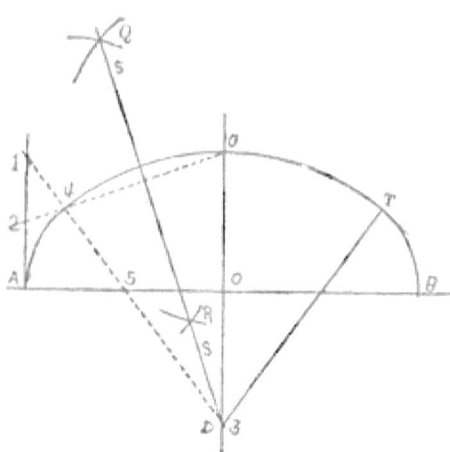

within his skill to nicely adjust whatever imperfection there is in the curve in this regard without the use of the instrument called the trammel, that we know has been used to run plaster arches of this description. The most pleasing proportion for the elliptical arch is to make the height equal to one-third of the width, which we have done in the cut.

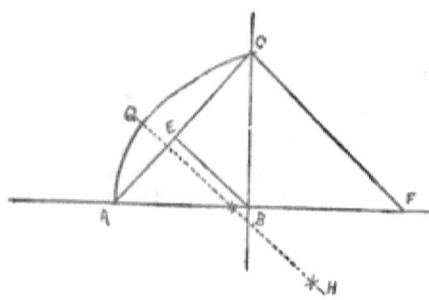

To draw arches whose height is greater than their *half width*. —For arches whose height is *greater* than their half width, draw C. F. and B. E. perpendicular to A. C.; then E. C. will be the smaller radius; and E. C. added to C. E. will be the longer radius H.

To draw an arch less in height than the half width.—
The following plan has been put forward for finding the curves of arches and *ribs*. The fundamental rule that the curves should spring from the line of the impost has been abandoned by many; one center was to be taken a litlte above this line, and so on. The following rule furnishes a principle which gives the centers of all these curves with perfect certainty and perfect harmony, at the same time furnishing what is further requisite, an independent projection for each *rib*. If the arch to be drawn be *less* in height than the half width, let A. B. be the half width; B. C. the

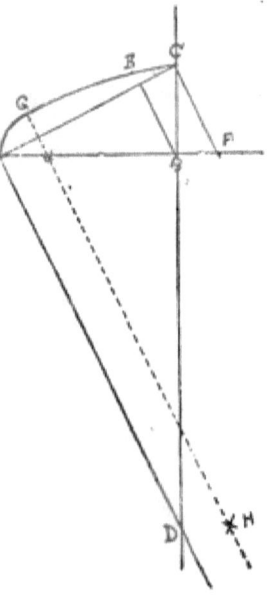

height; join A. C.; draw lines from B. and A. perpendicular to A. C., and the points E. D. are those required. Then E. C. will be the smaller radius, and E. C. added to A. D. will be the longer radius H.

SADDLES.

Saddles.—Where two or more arches are set close together, "saddles" ought to be cut, as shown and not a continual straight joint, for, although this is often done, there is no bond between the two arches. In the same cut is shown the manner in which ornamental Gothic arches are "keyed" when red, black, buff or white brick are used to build them, as well their disposition when tuck pointed for ornamental work, and the straight jointed key where strength is desired instead of ornament.

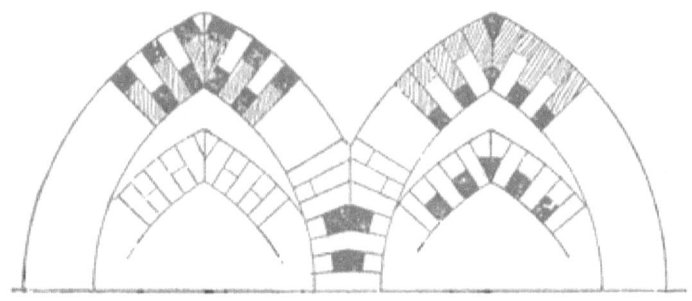

Saddles.

THE WHEEL ARCH, OR BULLS-EYE.

In this arch the outer circle is divided out in such a way that each line shall be in the center of the course; that each of these points shall show a key brick, in the same way as one key is shown in the semi circular arch.

To draw an Ogee arch of one point.—Bisect the span in D., draw the center line C. D., **describe the arc A. G.;** bisect A. G. in E., **and through** E. from A. draw a line cutting **the** centre **line in** H.; through **H.** draw **F. K.** parallel to the springing line, and through E. from D. draw a line cutting **F. K.** at M., **which will be the center for the upper part of** the ogee arch.

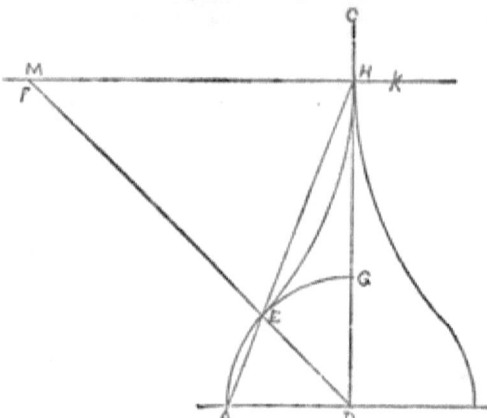

The various **forms and designs of** the arch **are** of an almost endless **description, and as** practiced in various countries form a **most interesting** study for **the** mechanic; but I **trust I** have described **enough to** answer the practical mason and to further his **knowledge** and examination of higher principles **of** arching, which are founded on **the** unerring laws of geometry and proportion.

In setting arches, the mason should be sure that **the** *centers* **are** set *level* **and** *plumb,* **that his arch brick or stone may rest upon them** *square;* **when his brick or stone are** properly **cut** beforehand, he may **gauge** his courses with them upon the center from the key **downwards** (never gauge from the *skew-back,* **as** this often leads to mistakes in setting arches), with **the** thickness **of the brick or stone, and** joint **at the** *soffit,* **as prepared. The** soffit of each course should **fit the center perfectly; and in order that it** should do so, **and the courses should come in** *right* **at the** *key,* it is necessary **to have a radius line, and draw it up** to each course as it is *set* from the gauged *points* on the center. This will prevent the **mason** from getting his work **too** high or too low as he builds towards the crown. If this is not done he is working at **random, and** often has to make his brick or stone smaller, or, otherwise, his bed joints thicker when he gets to the key; depriving the arch of its strength, and so causing a settlement when the centers are struck. It should ever be remembered by the mason that, when constructing an arch, its stability **does not depend on the cement or mortar** between **the stones or bricks of which it is built;** for the various parts **should be so arranged with such accurate skill** and **geometrical knowledge as to be** independent of **extraneous aid, and as much mortar should** be used only **to bed the stone or brick in an arch with a close joint, the size of which should be calculated beforehand when the stability or appearance of the work is taken into** consideration, **and performing this work at** random, **and** measuring, as **it were, your way up the center to execute it, is** *wrong*, **and contrary to the unerring** laws of proportion and geometry, **on which** the stability of all arch construction depends. **Every** arch should be put in by two masons, and as quick after began as possible, **so that the** mortar may all set, as near as possible, at the same time. All arches should *rise* evenly with the **face line of the building, and for the camber arch it is often necessary to have two or three lines across its face to be put in properly.** In setting cut stone arches (and all fine cut **stone** work), the delicate mouldings and projections should **have the joints left open at the outer edge, so that the pressure may be confined to the** solid parts of the stone until all is **set and sound; the stone** may then be stopped some time previous **to being** cleaned down. Plugs **of slate or** hard stone (not iron) may be **inserted** where required, and set with Portland **cement** and sand, **in** order to connect the voussoir stones more firmly together. **But in** brick arching **this** should **be avoided; all** the **joints** should be **properly flushed up,** and **the** arch receive sufficient time **for the** mortar to bond **before** the center is removed. **When there are a** long range of arches, *one* ought not to be set separately; but a line drawn the whole length, so that when all **are** set **they** shall be perfectly straight one with the other.

It is well known that the **mason** has little to do with **stone** arches more than the **setting of** them, as the preparation or cutting of these nowadays is generally done by the stonecutters; but there are many instances where he is called upon to cut them, and by making himself familiar with the rules here laid down, he can make them answer for almost any practical purpose. The plasterer also should understand the principles for *striking* arches; and then, when called upon to run plaster arches, he would not find any difficulty in fixing his *centers* to do so. There are many rules for describing some of the arches here given, but we know of none that are plainer than those given, and within the comprehension of the average workman.

A practical method of getting a voussoir of a stone arch.—No difficulty occurs in working a block of stone, of which the faces, beds and joints are to be either vertical or hori‑ 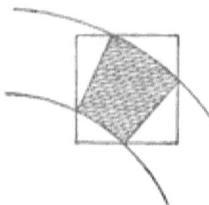 zontal planes, as the several dimensions required can be obtained directly from the plan and elevation. Nor is any dfficulty introduced if some of the sur‑ faces are cylindrical, as a cylindrical surface can be worked with almost as much facility as a plane; the only dif‑ ference being that a curved rule is used in one direction and a straight one in the opposite, whilst in the latter case the straight edge alone is used. Subjoined Fig. shows the man‑ ner of taking the vous soir shape of an arch stone from the plan, when it is spaced off into courses; the courses of all stone arches should be odd in number.

Bond.—In good brickwork the first thing to be consid‑ ered is *bond*. There are, properly speaking, in brickwork, but two sorts of bond; one is called *Old English* and the other *Flemish*.

English bond, so called, as it was the only style used in England up to the time of William III., consists of alter‑ nate courses of stretchers and headers; and the Flemish bond, introduced by Flemish workmen, who came over with the Flemish king, consists of alternate header and stretcher in the same course. Masons should pay great attention to *bond* in construction, and pride themselves upon its perfec‑

tion English bond is selected for heavy buildings on account of its superior strength. Mr. Furguson says: "I cannot, of course, deny that its strength might exceed that of Flemish bond if carried out in all its integrity, but this I do affirm, without fear of contradiction, that Flemish bond is equal to every possible and impossible emergency. I defy any architect to point out any one instance of its failure to sustain, without fracture, any superincumbent weight or pressure ever brought to bear upon it. The reason of *failure*, when any such has taken place, is not the weakness of the style of *bond*, but the want of *bond*, by the bricklayers snapping header after header, in order to *save* a few front bricks, and the contractor, to hurry the *rise* of the wall, has him to put in *bats* for headers, for five or six courses, and then *back* up the inside of the wall in a hurry, which should never be done in this style of bond; but, on the contrary, *each* and *every* exterior front course should be immediately *backed up* to admit a lap for the succeeding course. If the courses are laid regularly and fairly—the headers being properly and constantly placed their *whole length* in the wall—it cannot fail.

"Nevertheless, the old English bond should be used in rough work, inside and outside, or at least a header every three or four courses, as it is a little quicker in practice, and all the *bats* can thereby be used up. And in this there is no failure in regard to strength, as walls never split or separate in the center; these fractures are generally due to the foundation; for a heavy pier will settle more than a light one, and hence it frequently happens that the fracture takes place through the arches of windows or doors; but for appearance the English bond can never have the light appearance of the Flemish;" and it is a question with many mechanics whether the absence of headers altogether in the front of a building is any improve-

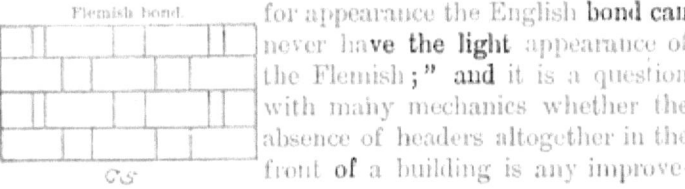

ment on the Flemish bond when accurately executed; especially front piers of a building, when they are nicely laid out in regard to bond. This bond, as before stated, consists of alternate header and stretcher in the same course. It should be started thus: First a stretcher, then a header and stretcher to the end of piece of wall or pier, always taking care that there be a stretcher at either corner (sometimes this cannot be done in very small piers; the bricklayer will then reverse one of the corners). This first course being *run out*, start the next course with a *header*, then a *closer* (a quarter brick), then a stretcher, etc., till the end of the second course, taking care that *both courses* are *started alike*, if it possibly can be done.

In a long pier or wall, if there be any *broken bond*, i. e., if in running out your bond you find it does not finish alike at both corners, then start from each corner and work to the centre, so that the broken bond, if there be any, may fall in the middle of the pier. (This should be avoided in first class work.) Sometimes it will require two headers instead of one; if so, let them follow each other all up the wall or pier until its finish; if you do not, it will detract from the entire piece. Sometimes it will require three headers; then you will find that it will require two stretchers in the next course, and so on all up the wall. (This is not considered broken bond.) In some instances it will require a three-quarter, but this should at all times be avoided, if possible. *Never*, under any circumstances, place a *closer* in the *middle*, or any other portion of the wall or pier, except at the *angles* next to the *header*. The beauty of brickwork will very much depend upon the *bond* being perfectly *kept*, that is, the perfect regularity of the perpendicular joints right up the wall. Stretcher over stretcher should be kept parallel; so also should the *broken bond*, if any occur. If this be neglected, as well the neatness required in *striking* or *trimming* the joints, the beauty of the whole work is entirely destroyed. The work should be also kept *plumb*, and *level* on the face, the bricks being laid square to the line for *flush* work; but where the joints are to be *cut* or *trimmed*, as in close pressed brickwork, it will be an advantage in regard to appearance to *roll* the brick (as it is called) a trifle, and the work will look all the better from a short distance. There are often piers **built in** Flemish bond as in No. 3 Fig., **which is** wrong, and **should** be as shown in No. 4 Fig., **as well in No.** 5 Fig., and should be as in No. 6 Fig.

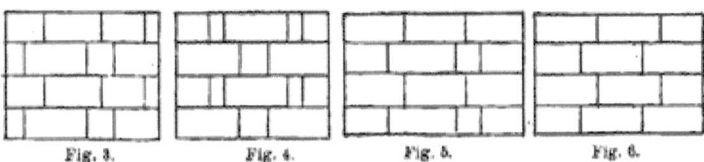

Fig. 3.   Fig. 4.   Fig. 5.   Fig. 6.

BLIND BOND is generally used now by the bricklayer to tie the front course to the wall in pressed brickwork, where it is not desirable that any headers should be seen in the face-work; and, when the *binders* are good hard burnt brick, and the *backing up* is properly executed, it appears to answer well enough for ornamental brickwork and fronts of structures; but to construct the exterior face of a wall, with costly hard pressed front brick, laid in a close putty joint, and then to back it up with soft brick, and the joints sometimes one-half inch thick or more, and a *binder* not put in for a dozen courses, is wrong and careless.

To form this bond, the face brick is trimmed off at both ends, so that it will admit a binder to set in transversely from the face of the wall, and every layer of these binders should be tied with a *header course* the whole length of the wall. Those binders should be put in every fifth course, and it is evident that the backing up of this work should be done in the most substantial manner of *hard* brick laid in a close joint; for the reason that the face work is laid in a fine putty mortar, and the joints consequently close and tight; and if the backing is not the same, the pressure upon the **wall will make** it settle and draw the wall inward.

Blind Bond.

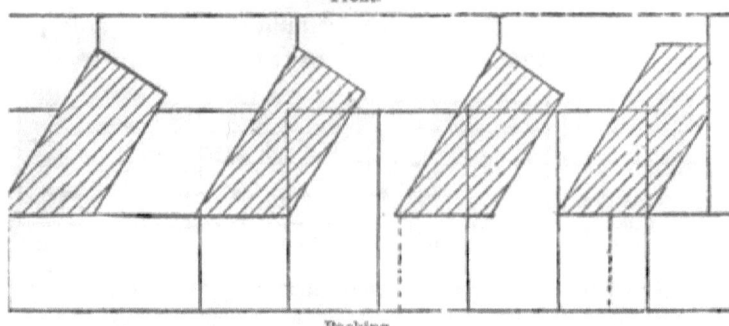

The bricklayer, in starting this manner of facework, should be careful in laying out his bond that no *bats* or closers appear in any part of it; and in a first class job the doors and windows are so arranged that such will be the case.

Bond, in masonry, consists in the placing of the stones in such relative positions that no joint in any course shall be in the same plane with any other joint in the course immediately above or below it. This is called *breaking* joint. Stones placed lengthwise in any work are called *stretchers,* and those placed in a contrary direction are called *headers.* When a header extends throughout the whole thickness of a wall it is called a *through.* It is always advisable, when a heavy load has to be supported on a few points, as in case of a large floor resting on girders, and where a heavy weight is thrown upon piers, to bring the weight as near as possible on the center of the wall, and to distribute it over a large bearing surface, by stone bonding through their whole thickness.

Perpend-bond signifies that a heading stone is placed through the whole thickness of the wall.

Binder, that it extends a part of the distance across the wall.

Heart-bond, in stone work. In this there are no perpend stones, but two *headers* meet in the middle of the wall, and the joint between them is covered by another header.

Chain-bond is the building into the masonry of an iron bar or heavy scantling.

Chain bond is also a preventive to the disruption of the foundation and other parts of large buildings, where continuous junction of parts is not always obtainable, when this bond is introduced, which is of a very old practice. This bond is sometimes of timber, but metal, properly protected from oxidation, is preferable on many accounts, if made of iron hooping, laid in long lengths, tarred, sanded and lapped or folded together at all joinings, and bedded in cement.

Cross-bond.—A block bond in which the joints of the second stretcher-course come in the middle of the first, a course of header and stretcher intervening.

Block and *cross-bond.*—The extrados of the wall is put up in cross-bond; the intrados in *block-bond*.

Breast wall.—A wall built against an embankment. The thickness and batter of a breast wall depend upon the character and inclination of the strata. It is held to be safe to make the base of the wall not less than one-fourth, and the batter not less than one-sixth of the vertical height of the wall.

Bricklayers' hammer.—A hammer for trimming bricks for caps, lintels, groins, etc., in ornamental brickwork, which is only in its infancy in the United States. Such edifices as exist in Turin, and in other cities in northern Italy, have no parallel on this side of the Atlantic.

Brick.—A kind of a factitious stone, composed of an argillaceous earth tempered and formed in moulds, dried in the sun, and finally burnt to a proper degree of hardness in a clamp or kiln. There are so many different kinds of bricks manufactured throughout the United States, which have a local value of their own, that it would be almost impossible here to enumerate them; but will treat of the matter in such a way that the mason, who is called upon very often to pass judgment upon brick, may do so in an intelligent manner.

The importance of selecting proper brick for constructing

buildings is so evident that it needs but the statement of the fact, without argument, to have it generally accepted. It is plain that in the construction of buildings care ought to be taken to have them of such architectural design as to present an agreeable impression to the eye; but as they are intended for the future, as well as for the present, they should be of such materials as to withstand, as far as may be, the destructive effects of time.

They should be, in fact, both in design and material, representatives of skill and judgment, that their valuation may not too readily fall before they have served the purpose of their construction.

Even a limited examination of edifices, public and private, discloses the fact that brick of the same general character vary greatly in serving the same purpose. While some preserve their soundness after years of exposure, others quickly show signs of decay and rapidly crumble, requiring continual repairs to keep them in proper condition. In some buildings cracks and fissures appear in them, the material not being in all cases of sufficient strength to resist the superincumbent pressure; in other buildings a similar variety of brick, though subject to equal or greater pressure, remain unimpaired.

The value of building-brick, therefore, may be briefly expressed as depending upon two causes:

1st, their physical constitution; and 2d, their chemical composition. The most important in its results of all experiments regarding brick, is the determination of the force required to crush them. The importance of determining the resistance of building material to pressure cannot well be overestimated. It gives accurate information obtainable in no other way. It enables us to make a classification of building materials according to one of their most vital qualities, so that those which are weak need not be placed where strength is required.

Without this knowledge errors are frequently made, resulting in some cases in bricks cracking and splitting, before the building in which they were placed was finished. In other cases the brick, though specially selected for strength, gives away in the course of a few years, causing sometimes the complete destruction of the edifice and even loss of life.

The effect, it is evident in both cases, is owing to the inherent weakness of the brick, it may not at once appear, but is gradually developed in accordance with the law that: "*When any material is strained beyond a certain extent, each time that the pressure is increased to that degree, or if it is continued at that degree, there is a permanent derangement of the structure of the material, which will eventually increase to such an extent, that the parts separate.*" The strain which produces this permanent derangement in the structure of materials, varies from one-fourth to three-fifths of that which would directly destroy their cohesion. On account of the many defects of bricks, and the different qualities of which they are composed it is not considered prudent ordinarily to subject a brick to more than one-eighth of its crushing weight.

Crushing strength of bricks of course varies greatly. A rather soft one will crush under from 450 to 600 pounds per square inch; or about 30 to 40 tons per square foot; while a first rate machine pressed brick will require about 6222 pounds per square inch, or 400 tons per foot. This last is about the crushing limit of the best sand stone; $\frac{2}{3}$ as much as the best marbles or limestones; and $\frac{1}{2}$ as much as the best granites or roofing slates. But masses of brickwork crush under much smaller loads than single bricks. It must, however, be remembered, that cracking and splitting usually commence under about one-half the crushing loads. To be safe, the load should not exceed $\frac{1}{8}$ or $\frac{1}{10}$ of the crushing load; and so with stone. Moreover, these experiments were made upon low masses; but the strength decreases with the proportion of the height to the thickness. The pressure at the base of a brick shot-tower, Baltimore, 246 feet high, is estimated at $6\frac{1}{2}$ tons per square foot; and a brick chimney at Glasgow, Scotland, 486 feet high, at 9 tons. Professor Rankin calculates that in heavy gales this is increased to 15 tons on the leeward side. The walls of both are much thicker at bottom than at top. With walls

100 feet high, of uniform thickness, the pressure at base would be 5.4 tons per square foot. With our present imperfect knowledge on this subject, it cannot be considered safe to expose even first class pressed brickwork *in cement*, to more than 12 or 15 tons per square foot, or good hand-moulded, to more than two-thirds as much.

Porosity of bricks; in no respect do bricks differ more than in the mode of the arrangement of their particles, the best hard burnt brick have their particles so closely compacted together, as to be free from sensible pores. Others, on the contrary, are imperfectly compacted; they have a porous or cellular structure, they readily absorb water, and this oftentimes proves a cause of disintegration. But all bricks absorb water, even the most homogenous and compact; the difference between them in this respect is only one of degree.

The effect of freezing and thawing in gradually disintegrating brick, is well known, and their comparative value depends largely upon the degree of their resistance to these influences. As ordinarily too much time would be taken by submitting them to frosts of numerous winters, experiments have been devised to imitate this operation of nature, hastening the effects by increasing the energy of the action. Subjoined we show the results obtained by Dr. Page with hard and soft brick treated by Brard's process:

Hard brick, specific gravity	2.294
Loss during treatment in grains	1.07
Soft brick, specific gravity	2.211
Loss in grains	16.46

It can be plainly seen that it is unsafe to trust any great amount of weight upon piers, and walls built of soft brick, and under no circumstance should a soft brick be exposed to the effects of *freezing* and *thawing*.

The presence of foreign ingredients in the clay used for bricks is frequently disastrous. Thus when vegetable fibres are present, they are consumed during the burning, leaving corresponding cavities, giving the bricks an open porous structure and rendering it of unequal strength in different parts.

The occurrence of fragments of limestone, or other calcareous matter occasion the destruction of bricks, owing to the caustic lime formation during the burning.

When the brick becomes moistened the lime slakes and tears it in pieces. The presence of foreign ingredients which are readily soluble, or which are rendered so by exposure is deleterious. They sometimes cause the brick to break down as if it was gradually slaked and always diminish its durability.

There is oftentimes found, as we can see every day in our cities, patches of a whitish color, that appear upon brickwork, which might at first sight be mistaken for vegetable mould. A close examination reveals the fact, that these patches are composed of a multitude of minute crystals, and that chemically they are composed of the alkalies or of lime and magnesia.

These salts are gradually dissolved by the moisture, and with it brought to the surface by capillary attraction. As the moisture is dissipated, the salts are left upon the surface. The presence of such substances is not only unfortunate as seriously disfiguring the appearance of the building, but further as indicating a porosity and a chemical character in the brick, that is certain to materially diminish the durability of the edifice. An interesting example of the efflorescence described, may be observed upon the walls of the Vassar Female College, Poughkeepsie, N. Y. Two kinds of brick were used in the construction of these buildings, viz.: the hard Hudson River brick, and the "Adams sand brick." No efflorescence ever appeared on the former, but there has always been more or less on the latter. It varies in quantity, and in the area of the spots, coming and going with variations of temperature and humidity, but finally disappearing entirely, sometimes in the second year after building. If, however, the wall becomes saturated with moisture, as by a leak in the gutter, the efflorescence reappears. It disappears latest from those parts of the walls which are protected from the rain, as under the cornices.

The efflorescence consists principally of compounds of potash and soda. It must be remarked that the reactions and changes mentioned in this section are generally increased by variations of temperature and alternate dryness and moisture (see Discoloration of Walls).

Bricks also have been experimented on which have withstood a compressive force of 13,000 pounds to the square inch, whilst others have failed under a pressure of less than 500 pounds. In construction, brick is seldom subjected to a pressure of over 100 pounds to the square inch.

Few structures have absolutely failed on account of the crushing of either brick or stone, but unequal settlements of foundations, or compression of the mortar in the joints may change the strain upon the material from a compressive to a transverse one and cause distractive cracks.

"In England the size of bricks is fixed by law, and the same should be the case in this country. For want of such a provision gross frauds are perpetrated. Few persons are aware of the loss they sustain in purchasing small bricks; not only in the bricks, but also in the laying by the thousand; and in the increased amount of mortar required. In our Eastern states a common sized brick is $8\frac{1}{4} \times 4 \times 2$ inches; making 66 cubic inches; but bricks as small as $8 \times 3\frac{3}{4} \times 1\frac{3}{4}$ are not unusual, containing only $52\frac{1}{2}$ cubic inches. One of $8\frac{1}{4} \times 4 \times 2$ inches is about $\frac{1}{4}$ part larger than this last. A good hand moulded brick of $8\frac{1}{4} \times 4 \times 2$ inches will weigh about $4\frac{1}{2}$ pounds, or 118 pounds per cubic foot; 1.4223 tons per cubic yard, or 498 bricks per ton. A machine pressed brick weighs about 5 pounds. If immersed in water, either of them will in a few minutes absorb from $\frac{1}{2}$ to $\frac{3}{4}$ pounds of water." (Trautwine.)

Fire bricks are made from a compound of silica and alumina, and the clay owes its refractory quality to the absence of lime, magnesia, potash, and metallic oxides, which act as fluxes.

Hollow-bricks are made for the purpose of warming, ventilating and removing moisture from the wall.

Water-proof brick; bricks are glazed or rendered waterproof by a composition which gives them a vitreous surface.

This is performed by treating the surface with a flux which melts the silex of the brick, or it may be applied to the surface in solution, the liquid being afterwards expelled by heat. Resinous compounds have also been used to render the surface non-absorbent.

They have also been treated with soluble silicate of soda, which has been decomposed, leaving the insoluble silex in the pores of the brick. Pigments added to the glazing compounds give an ornamental appearance.

Air-brick is a grating the size of a brick let into a wall to allow the passage of air.

Arch-brick usually means the hard burned partially vitrified brick from the arches of the brick clamp, in which the fire is made and maintained.

A brick made voussoir shape is known as a compass brick. Clinker, a brick from an arch of the clamp, so named from the sharp glassy sound when struck.

Feather-edge brick, of prismatic form for arches, vaults, niches, etc.

Pecking, place, sandal, samel brick are local names applied to imperfectly burned or refuse brick.

Baltimore and Philadelphia lead in regard to the quality of the finer of red pressed bricks in this country; but the ornamental bricks produced in Philadelphia are of the highest rank. In Ohio, Milwaukee, New York and New Jersey they are manufacturing a light colored pressed brick, which are being used extensively in many places.

Blocking course; a course of stones placed on the top of a cornice, crowning the walls.

Bond-stones.—Stones placed at intervals in brick piers, to give them additional strength; stones used in rubble work, having their length placed in the thickness of the wall. These stones are placed at regular intervals, both horisontally and vertically, so that every stone of one row falls on the vertical joint that is in the course below. Bondstones inserted the whole thickness of the masonry are called *perpends* or *perpend-stones*.

Bastard-stucco is a light putty finish with a little plaster of paris added, that the wall may receive paint or kalsomine.

Bosses, etc.—They are usually understood to be **projecting** ornaments placed at the intersection of the ribs of roofs and ceilings.

Corbels are a projection of stone, brick or other material supporting a superincumbent weight, and are decorative features, generally, in masonry, brickwork and plastering.

Consoles or *Ancones* are the brackets frequently attached as supports to the projecting cornices of classic doors and windows. In the proper signification of the term, namely, that of bracket from the French word *console*; it also applies, and perhaps more correctly, to the supports of a balcony or other projection. The modillions of the Corinthian cornice are strictly brackets or consoles.

Key-stone is of an arch the binding stone, and one of a number necessary to the substantiality and proper action of the others which compose it. It has a similar amount of duty to perform, and should not by any seeming operation of ornament be made to appear less able than its fellows to perform it.

Caisson is a large case or box floated over the area of a foundation, and sunk by building the foundation inside of it; as it sinks, the sides of the caisson are also carried up sufficiently high to keep the water out, and thus the great box containing the masonry gradually sinks to the bottom; the bottom must be levelled and prepared beforehand for it, with the help of a diving apparatus. Caissons are generally made of wood, but wrought iron has been used. Any soft stratum should be dredged away; and if the surface is irregular, a bed of hydraulic concrete should be laid over it, if the natural bed is too soft to carry the caisson piles must be driven over the area and a platform of planks and concrete formed on the top of them for the caisson to rest on. (See Foundation.)

Counter-forte.—A pier or buttress bonded as a revetment to the back of a retaining wall, to support and also tie the wall, such as the scarp of a forte to the bank in the rear. The buttress is sometimes on the face. When arches are turned between counter-fortes, it is called a counter-arched revetment.

Coving.—The overhang of the upper portions of a building beyond the limits of the ground plan. The splayed reveals or inclined jambs on the sides of a fireplace.

Creasing.—A layer of tiles forming a corona for a wall.

Cross-springer.—In a groined arch, the rib that springs from a pillar in a diagonal direction at the intersection of the arches forming the groin.

Crypt.—A vault beneath a church or mausoleum, and either entirely or partly under ground.

Conical-arch.—Is an arch built in the shape of a cone for kilns, glass works, or hop kilns. This arch has all the bricks or stones at right angles to the sides, and radiating towards the centre, and is remarkably strong, so much so that a kiln of the greatest usual height may be built of one brick thick only.

Coursed-rubble.—Is the employment of stones, not dressed or but roughly so as they come from the quarry, but chosen of sizes somewhat uniform and of the same thickness in each course so that a uniformity of line in the course is obtained; hence the name. The stones vary in depth dependent upon the condition in which they come or are sent from the quarry, but they are carefully fitted and well laid in mortar. Bond is obtained by the use of *headers* and *stretchers*, there serving the same office as the bricks, so termed in brickwork.

The angle quoins in coursed rubble are sometimes worked very neatly and with great care; they serve in fact as gauge courses for the others. A very nice appearance is produced by the quoins being tooled to a smooth surface corresponding to the dressings of the windows and doorways; this style is very much used in church building.

Copings.—These are either plain or ornamental. The plain are slightly projecting courses used to cover brick walls.

Ornamental are large moulded stone surmounting a cornice. Copings are worked with a plain, horizontal bed, two vertical faces, and an inclined or *weathered* surface, either forming an obtuse angle with the inner and narrower face, and an acute angle with the outer wider face, or slanting off from the middle towards each side, which latter is technically termed a *saddle-back* coping.

In both cases they are made to project over the wall, and in the projected part of the bed under the edges towards which the inclination is given a channel or groove, called a "*throat*" is cut, to intercept the water in its inclination to run inwards towards the wall.

To protect the separate stones of a coping course from the danger of being displaced by high winds or other accidental causes, and to form a chain through its whole length, the stones are linked together by cramps of copper let into them and run with lead.

Center.—In building a combination of timber beams, so disposed as to form a frame, the concave side of which, when boarded over, corresponds to the cavity of an arch; or the wooden mould used for turning an arch of stone or brick during the time of erection.

Coffer-dam.—A hollow dam, constructed of a double range of piles, with clay rammed between, for the security and convenience of the workman while digging out and building the foundation of an entrance lock to a dock or basin, or canal, when it cannot otherwise be laid dry.

Coffer-dams are made either double or single. In the double one, the space between the inner and outer rows of piles is rammed with clay; the piles are driven as closely as possible to each other by means of a pile engine, till fixed firmly into the earth; sometimes they are grooved and tongued; sometimes they are grooved in the sides, and fixed at a distance from each other with boards let into the grooves. (See Bricklaying.)

Cornice.—Any moulded projection which crowns or finishes the part to which it is affixed; thus we have the cornice of an order, of a pedestal, of a house, of a pier, of a door, of a window, etc.

Cornices should be in proper proportion to their surroundings, and when of an expensive character they should be consistent with the order of architecture on which they are formed. For ornamental plaster work cornices may be from one-fourteenth to one-twenty-fourth of that of the room; and in coved ceilings the cove may be from one-fourth to one-sixth of the height.

Crushing height of bricks and stone.—If we assume the weight of ordinary brickwork at 112 pounds per cubic foot, and that it would crush under 30 tons per square foot, then a verticle uniform column of 600 feet high would crush at its base under its own weight. Caen stone weighing 130 pounds per cubic foot, would require a column 1376 feet high to crush it. Average sandstones at 145 pounds per cubic foot would require one of 4158 feet high; and average granite at 165 pounds per cubic foot, one of 8145 feet.

But stones begin to crack and splinter at about half their ultimate crushing load, and in practice it is not considered expedient to trust them with more than $\frac{1}{8}$ to $\frac{1}{10}$ the part of it, especially in important works; inasmuch as settlements and imperfect workmanship often cause undue strains to be thrown on certain parts. The Merchants' shot tower at Baltimore is 246 feet high, and its base sustains $6\frac{1}{2}$ tons per square foot. The base of the granite pier of Saltash bridge (by Brunel), of solid masonry to the height of 96 feet, and supporting the ends of two iron spans of 455 feet each, sustains $9\frac{1}{2}$ tons per square foot. The base of a brick chimney at Glasgow, Scotland, 468 feet high, bears 9 tons per square foot; and Professor Rankin considers that in a high gale of wind, its leeward side may have to bear 15 tons. The highest pier of Rocquefavour stone aqueduct, Marseilles, is 305 feet and sustains a pressure at base of $13\frac{1}{2}$ tons per square foot.

Weight of a cubic foot of the various building materials, in pounds (approximate).

Granite	168	pounds.
Marble	165	"
Sandstone	135	"
Blue-stone	165	"
Slate	180	"
Mortar, dry	80 to 100	"
Common brick	112	"
Dry sand	100	"
Fire-brick	135	"

Cisterns.—Brick receives the preference for constructing cisterns, it being sufficiently durable, and at the same time cheap. As brickwork is not adapted to resist tensile strains, brick cisterns of any considerable size cannot withstand water pressure, by the strength of walls alone. So we put them under ground, getting the earth pressure from without to balance the water pressure from within, and at the same time protect them from the frost. The circular form is generally used, and is strong enough in itself to resist the earth pressure when the tank is empty, for this is a compressive force.

The extended application of hydraulic cement enables us to construct in almost any part of the world where commercial relations exist, an imperishable and incorruptible water tank, so far as its own materials go. But cistern water will be more or less contaminated by the accumulation of dust swept from the roof. Hence a cistern should be thoroughly cleaned from time to time as occasion may require. Every cistern intended for drinking use, should have a filter. For this purpose a chamber can be parted off on one side of the cistern, within which the suction-pipe takes the water for use, and the filtering material placed so as to pass the water through holes in this partition. Sometimes soft or half burnt brick are used for this partition, through the pores of which the water passes freely, if sufficient surface is used. If, however, it be desired to remove any dissolved impurities from the water, these mechanical filters, whether brick, gravel, sand or sponge, are useless, and recourse must be had to a charcoal or spongy iron filter, which acts chemically upon various substances in solution, burning them up, as it were, by the oxygen in the filter.

These filters, however, require such frequent cleansing for the renewal of their efficiency, that they can only be used in a portable form, and cannot therefore be built into the tank.

By applying the following table a mason can build almost any tank of a required capacity; a gallon contains 8 pounds of pure water, multiply the gallons in the following table by the number of feet in depth of cistern, and you will get the contents near enough for practice:

3	feet in diameter contains	....	$55\frac{1}{4}$	gallons.
$3\frac{1}{2}$	"	"	....	75	"
4	"	"	....	98	"
$4\frac{1}{2}$	"	"	....	$124\frac{1}{4}$	"
5	"	"	....	153	"
$5\frac{1}{2}$	"	"	....	$185\frac{1}{2}$	"
6	"	"	....	$220\frac{3}{4}$	"
7	"	"	....	$300\frac{1}{4}$	"
8	"	"	....	$392\frac{1}{2}$	"
9	"	"	....	$497\frac{1}{2}$	"
10	"	"	....	$613\frac{1}{2}$	"

Chimney-piece and mantle-piece.—"It is to be observed," says Blackburne, "that the wood chimney piece is now accepted to mean and is limited to the decoration or finish of the opening or recess in the wall constituting the fire-place. Anciently the wood chimney appears to have been used to designate a furnace, a stove, or a hearth; and in mediæval architecture, it had occasionally the same application. The chimney-piece *per se*, and divested of other adjuncts is the receptacle, or place for the fire, with the aperture, or flue, for the voidance of smoke from it. This latter was, in the first instance, a sloping and ascending cavity in the thickness of the wall; and later the flue was carried up vertically to the top of the wall, as common in the present day, and was there finished and capped in mediæval times by an almost endless variety of what are called chimney shafts and caps, with these, however, we have in connection with the immediate subject in hand, but little directly to do; our consideration is with that which these are but the subservient accessories. The chimney as viewed as above, therefore, may be taken as an opening at the level of the floor of sufficient width and height for the making of a fire, and the transmission of its heat to the apartment. This is its essential necessity and appearance, and 'thus,' says Ware, 'it appears to us in the first construction of rooms, and thus stands before the architect to be finished.' The form of this opening has had some variety, but at the present time it is usually a rectangular recess, of greater or less capacity, according to size or dignity of apartment in which it occurs; the superincumbent wall being carried over the opening upon an arch. Such is the chimney in its simple phase of utility; the chimney-piece is properly the ornamentation applied in connection with this opening, and is so distinguished among the commonly received terms for the several parts into elaborate character, technically divided. Of these terms as the A B C of explanation as regards the modern chimney it will be necessary now to speak. The main divisions are, the lower part, or opening into the room, with its floor, sides and back, the voiding course, or shaft for the smoke, which are the main useful portions, and the finish which are the decorations of the first.

The lower part is denominated the fire-place, its floor being called the *hearth*; that portion which is within the recess being designated the *inner* or *back-hearth*, and that in front of opening the outer or *front-hearth*, and sometimes *slab*, which is frequently in rich works of marble. The vertical sides of the opening are termed the *jambs*, and the term applies equally to the returned surfaces and vertical front supports of the chimney-piece. The back wall is called the *chimney-back*, and the front wall when in projection of the room, the *chimney-breast*. The conducting-shaft for the smoke is called the *flue*, and the lower part of it, which widens or tapers to accommodate the greater cavity of the chimney opening, is termed the *funnel of the flue*, the necessary contraction in the construction at this part being known as the *gathering-over*, while the junction of the funnel with the flue itself is called the *throat*. A number of these flues conjoined and carried up together is called a *chimney-stack*, and the part of them which rises above the roof, the *chimney-shaft* or shafts, their finish being the *chimney-cap* or *top*. The chimney-piece or decorative portion round the opening, is, in its more common form and according to customary language, primarily divided into mantel, jambs and shelf. The mantle, or mantle-piece, is the horizontal portion immediately above the fire-place. The jambs are the vertical additions or ornaments at the sides of the fire-place. Strictly the term applies to the return faces within the recess; but custom has established it to include the entire portions which support the mantel. The *shelf* is the flat or other projecting slab or cornice forming the covering, or crown, of the mantel. The second form is that technically described as the profile chimney, the distinction between this and the former being that, in this case, the stone work of the chimney-piece stands wholly in advance of the finish of the wall, showing a return or profile of its outer ends. The projection of these is accordant with the thickness of the stone used, and the jambs are usually formed as pilasters, with a small cap and nicking moulding under the mantel, the latter finished by the shelf, a *bed moulding* being sometimes introduced between the two. The next and third form is that what is usually called the *box-chimney*, from being constructed hollow or box-fashion. This mode of construction will be at once seen to owe its origin in economy as respects use of material, the latter being applied in thickness instead of in solid.

The box-chimney, it will be unnecessary to say, is wholly in projection; and to graater or lesser extent, according to what may be desired. In many cases, the execution of chimneys of this last description, that is to say, according to the design and projection of them in the solid, would be great waste; and it is a very general practice, therefore, to admit this mode of formation even in the best works, and are ornamented with mantel-pieces composed of marble, slate, terra-cotta and pressed brick, as well as with an iron grate or summer piece. These mantel-pieces are fastened to the wall with plaster of paris, and anchored also with wire and sheet iron.

Cement and Lime.—The calcination of statuary marble, or any other pure variety of limestone, produces quick-lime, by expelling from the carbonate of lime of which they are composed, the carbonic acid gas, water of crystallization, and organic coloring matter Lime is therefore a protoxide of calcium, or in other words, a metallic oxide. Pure lime has a specific gravity of 2.3, is amorphous, somewhat spongy, highly caustic, quite infusible, possesses great avidity for water, and, if brought in contact with it, will rapidly absorb 22 to 23 per cent of its weight, passing into the condition of hydrate of lime, in which condition it is said to be *slaked*. Lime, on account of its great affinity for moisture, and, when moist, for carbonic acid, absorbs them gradually from the atmosphere, returns somewhat to the state of carbonate of lime. To protect it against the effects of these deteriorating agents it is necessary to preserve it in close vessels; and therefore the best lime for use is the fresh burned lime.

The limestones which furnish the limes of commerce are seldom if ever pure, but usually contain, besides the carbonate of lime and the water of crystallization, variable proportions, seldom exceeding 10 per cent in the aggregate of some if not all of the following impureties, viz.: silicia, alumina, magnesia, oxide of iron, and oxide of manganese, and sometimes traces of the alkalies, the presence of which modifies to a greater or less degree the phenomena developed during the process of slaking, and renders necessary certain precautions in their manipulation and treatment when employed, for the purposes of construction, as mortars.

The striking and characteristic property of hardening under water, or when excluded from the air, conferred upon a paste lime by these foreign substances, when their aggregate amount exceeds 10 per cent of the whole, furnishes the basis for a general arrangement of all natural or artificial products suitable for mortars, into five distinct classes, as follows :

   1st. The common or fat limes.
   2d. The poor or meagre limes.
   3rd. The hydraulic limes.
   4th. The hydraulic cements.
   5th. The natural pozzuolanas, properly so called, trass or terras, the arenes, ochreous earths, schists, grauwacke and basaltic sands, and a variety of similar substances.

The common, fat or rich limes usually contain less than 10 per cent of the impurities mentioned above. In slaking they augment to form two to three and a half times that of the original mass. They will not harden under water, or even in damp localities excluded from contact with the air. In the air it hardens by the gradual formation of carbonate of lime, due to the absorption of carbonic acid gas.

The pastes of fat lime shrink in hardening to such a degree that they cannot be employed as mortar without a large dose of sand. When used alone they are unsuitable for masonry under water, or for foundations in damp soils.

Paste of fat lime may be added to a cement mortar in quantities equal to that of the cement, without material diminution of strength.

The *poor* or *meagre* limes generally contain silica (in the shape of sand), alumina, magnesia, oxide of iron, sometimes oxide of manganese, and in most cases traces of the alkalies, in relative proportions, which vary very considerably in different localities.

Their aggregate amount is seldom less than 10 per cent, or greater than 25, although in some varieties it reaches as high as 35, and even, though rarely 39 per cent of the whole. In slaking they proceed sluggishly, as compared with the rich limes, and are accompanied by a much smaller increase of volume. They dissolve in water frequently renewed, and are not adapted to be used under water or wet soil, or excluded from the atmosphere, or carbonic acid gas.

The *hydraulic limes*, including the three subdivisions of limes slightly hydraulic, hydraulic limes and limes eminently hydraulic, seldom contain an aggregate of silica, alumina, magnesia, oxide of iron, etc., exceeding 35 per cent of the whole. The proportion in the first class ranges generally between 10 and 20 per cent of the whole; in the second class between 17 and 24 per cent; while the eminently hydraulic limes contain rarely less than 20, or more than 35 per cent.

They slake still slower than the meagre limes, and with but a small augmentation of volume rarely exceeding 30 per cent of the original bulk. If mixed into a stiff paste, after being slaked, they possess the property of hardening under water; *slightly hydraulic* from 15 to 20 days; *hydraulic*, 6 to 8 days; *eminently* hydraulic, 1 to 4 day's.

The *hydraulic cements* contain a larger amount of silica, alumina, magnesia, etc., than any of the proceeding varieties of lime, though the amount rarely, if ever, exceeds 61 per cent of the whole.

They do not slake at all after calcination differing materially in this particular from the limes proper. If pulverized they can be formed into a paste with water, without any sensible increase of volume, and little, if any disengagement of heat, except in certain instances among those varieties which contain the maximum amount of lime, or border on the *intermediate limes*, for all the purposes of hydraulic construction; some of them being so energetic as to set under water at 65° F., in three to four minutes, although others require as many hours.

They do not shrink in hardening like the plaster of fat lime, and therefore make an excellent mortar for some purposes, without the addition of sand; although for the sake of economy, sand, and frequently both sand and lime are combined with them. In the United States, they are almost exclusively depended upon for hydraulic mortars.

The natural pozzuolanas.—Their principal ingredients are silica, and alumina, with a large preponderance of the former.

Most varieties contain small quantities of soda, potash, oxides of iron and manganese, and not unfrequently magnesia. None of them contain more than 10 per cent of lime. When finely pulverized without previous calcination, and combined with the paste of fat lime in suitable proportions, to supply their deficiency in that ingredient, they possess hydraulic energy to a degree that will compare favorably, in some of the varieties, with that of the *eminently hydraulic limes.*

Pozzuolana, which confers the name upon this class of substances, is of volcanic origin, and has therefore been subjected to the action of heat, whereby its constituent elements have experienced a chemical change in their primitive mode of combination. It was originally discovered at the foot of Mount Vesuvius, near the village of Pozzuoles, whence its name. Its value for the purposes of construction in combination with rich lime, has been known for many centuries, and Vitruvius and Pliny both speak of its admirable properties, as exhibited in the marine constructions of the Romans, extant in their day.

Trass or terras.—In the valley of the Rhine between Mayence and Cologne, and in various localities in Holland, a substance of volcanic origin is found, called *trass* or *terras*, which has been extensively employed throughout that region, particularly by the Dutch engineers, for the production of hydraulic mortar. It is derived from immense pits or quarries, occupying the sites of extinct volcanoes, and enjoys in nearly every particular the distinguishing properties of Italian pozzuolana, closely resembling it in its composition, and in the details of its manipulation, requiring to be pulverized and combined with rich lime, in order to render it fit for use, and to develop any of its hydraulic properties. some cements are remarkably quick in exhibiting their hydraulic property, and will loose their plastic state immersed in water at 65° F. in one or two minutes, but afterwards proceed very sluggishly in their induration. There are others, again, which, though comparatively slow in developing the first indication of hydraulic energy, yet in a few hours, greatly surpass the former in their ultimate strength and hardness, and are therefore to be preferred in all positions where a very quick induration is not specially important.

In pronouncing on the value of cements, from a comparison of their hydraulic activity, they should, therefore, be mixed with two and a half to three times their volume of sand. Even with this precaution, the result is far less reliable than some simple devise for trying the strength of the mortars, when ten or twelve days old. As an evidence of the truth of this remark, it may be stated that, although eminent hydraulic activity or quickness is not necessarily accompanied by inferior hardness and strength, and conversely, neither is a slow setting cement necessarily a strong one, still within the range of experiments, it is somewhat remarkable that the quickest cements gave the worst results, and the slowest ones the best.

Color of cement.—The color of the manufactured cement being due principally to the presence of oxide of iron, and sometimes of magnesia, or to the carbonate of these oxides, which for all practical purposes are considered to be a passive ingredient in hydraulic mortar, should be a matter of indifference to consumers, except in special cases, as in exterior stucco work or ornamentation, in pavements and fronts of houses, where a particular shade of color is sought for.

Many think that dark colored cements are the best, and many contractors encourage this belief for the reason that dark colored cements will stand a bigger dose of sand, whilst the *quickest setting* cements manufactured at the present day happen to be light colored, and the *Portland cement*, both natural and artificial, though slow setting has never been surpassed in strength and hardness by any of the natural cements of this country or Europe.

In Europe all natural cements are generally denominated Roman cements to distinguish them from Portland cements, which are artificial combinations of limestone (usually chalk) and clay.

Parker's Roman, as a facing to brick and other walls, is a composition forming an artificial stone, and being water-proof, is excellently adapted to this purpose; if the wall be previously wetted it will adhere firmly. Arch stones, cornices and ornamental parts of buildings may also be conveniently made of this material. This material when mixed with an equal quantity of sharp grit-sand, freed from impurities, and when beaten up with a due proportion of water, forms a handsome and durable covering for the outside of buildings. If the sand should have been previously moistened, the cement must be immediately used, and in no case mixed up beforehand.

To give a proper finishing to this kind of work, a mixture of 5 ounces of sulphate of iron to a gallon of water, is mixed with as much lime and cement as will produce the consistence and the color required, for a wash to be applied to the surface of the work. Sometimes the color is modified by vitrolic acid, and when the face of the work is made to imitate bonded masonry, the intersecting spaces are tinted with amber. It is generally calculated, that one bushel of cement, properly applied, will form a superficial covering of nearly four square yards. In performing this work, which is called *floating*, unceasing, *laborious* and *quick action* will be required, as the composition sets almost instantaneously.

Artificial or Roman cement.—A composition, said to be equal to Roman cement, is made by dissolving three pounds and a half of sulphate of iron (green copperas), and mixing it with a bushel of lime, and a half a bushel of fine gravel sand, previously made into mortar.

Portland cement is made from the nodules of conglomerated stones containing clay and limestone, and sometimes a small percentage of silica, found on the banks of the Medway in England, and at Boulogne in France, and on the Hudson river in this country.

These nodules are subjected to a high degree of heat in a furnace, and thereafter all foreign matter, scorified portions, etc., picked out from the mass of the proper nodules, which are then ground into a fine powder, and when mixed with water form what is known as Portland cement, and which has by far the highest reputation amongst practical men of all the cements yet introduced.

Generally speaking, the hydraulic cements require mixing with sand, but Portland cement may be used without sand. It sets with a comparative slowness so that a good quantity may be mixed at once and used, without the inconvenience of immediate or very quick hardening, and does not reach its greatest strength until years after it has been used. Iron, bricks, stone and wood must be subjected to indurating solutions for their preservation, no preparation is required on the other hand for Portland cement. In the air, in the water, and in fact under all circumstances, the possibility of using this material with success forms one of the greatest recommendations in its favor.

On account of the great demand for Portland cement, a great many manufacturers have been induced to bring out an artificial kind, and this is as much used as that made from the cement stone, and on account of it being able to stand a larger dose of sand than the common cement, it is considered by some builders to be cheaper for that reason, and is admirably adapted for the following purposes: Concrete for foundation walls, wharfs and piers. Sidewalks, garden and any outside walks. Cellar, stable, brewery and malt-house floors, and any floor for heavy traffic, mastic stucco or any outside plastering. For laying tile and marble floors, roofs, kitchen hearths, abutment of bridges, etc., etc.

Keen's cement in appearance is a great deal like plaster of paris, and is of two qualities, coarse and superfine.

When used for walls the coarse should be used with equal parts of sand for *scratch coat*, and then finished with superfine. They are almost always used for work which require a hard and beautiful finish. But in no case should they be used for outside work, or in any place where they are exposed to the action of water, as they are like all pure limes, partly soluble in water.

Parian or *Keating's* cement is said to be produced by mixing calcined and powdered gypsum with a strong solution of borax, then recalcining, grinding and mixing with a solution of alum. Thus are two qualities, *superfine* and *coarse*. Parian is said to work freer than either Kein's or Martin's cement, and is therefore preferable for large surfaces, which have to be hand-floated before troweling; but the two latter cements are fatter, and produce sharper arises and mouldings.

Martin's cement is made in a similar manner to Parian; potash carbonate (pearlash) being used instead of borax, and hydrochoric acid being sometimes added.

It is made in three different qualities: coarse, fine and superfine; the coarser kinds being of a reddish white color, and the fine a pure white. It is said to cover more surface in proportion to its bulk than any other similar material.

Metallic cement has a metallic lustre, is suitable for outside work, and is intended to dispense with coloring or painting, but is not much used. One variety is made by mixing ground slag from coppersmelting works with ordinary cement stone.

Cement for uniting stone.—A new mineral compound for imitating stone and resisting water, one that is said to be superior to hydraulic cement, is made by mixing 19 pounds of sulphur with 42 pounds of powdered glass or stone ware. Over a gentle heat the sulphur melts, and the whole is stirred till a homogeneous mass is obtained, when it may be run into molders. It melts at 248° F., and becomes hard as stone, and will resist boiling at 230° F. It may be reformed indefinitely by remelting, and used for imitating stones, etc.

A paste made of pure oxide of lead, litharge and concentrated glycerine also is used for uniting broken stone.

A strong hydraulic cement for pointing up stone stoops, etc., is made of powdered clay, 3 pounds; oxide of iron, 1 pound; and boiled oil to form a paste.

Coloring cements.—The pigments used to color hydraulic and other cements, and obtain the shades here mentioned, the following proportions are employed:

For black, pyrolusite.......................... 12 per cent.
" red, caput mortuum...................... 6 "
" green, ultramarine green .... 6 "
" blue, " blue.................. 5 "
" yellow, ochre............................ 6 "
" brown, " .... 6 "

The strength of the cement is rather increased by the addition of ultramarine pigments, but somewhat diminished by the others. The ill effects of the latter may be somewhat removed by grinding the cements again after the pigments have been added, whereby it gains in fineness, and the strength is so much increased that no difference is observable between this and the ordinary cement.

Mortars.—*Proportions sand, lime, cement.*—The proportions of one measure of quicklime, either in irregular lumps or ground, and five measures of sand, is about the average used for common mortar by good builders in our principal cities; and if both materials are well mixed or *tempered* with water, the mortar is as good as can be required for ordinary purposes as require no addition of hydraulic cement. The bulk of the mortar will usually exceed that of the dry sand about $\frac{1}{8}$ part. Allowing for the usual waste; or 20 cubic feet, or 16 bushels and and 4 cubic feet or $3\frac{2}{10}$ struck bushels of lime, will make sufficient mortar to lay in best manner 1,000 brick of the ordinary size of 8 x 4 x 2, with the coarse mortar joints usual in interior house walls, varying say from $\frac{3}{8}$ to $\frac{1}{2}$ inches thick. For mortar of fine screened gravel, for cellar walls of stone rubble, or coarse brickwork, 1 measure of lime to 6 or 8 of gravel is usual; and is good mortar.

In average rough massive rubble, as well as in brickwork, about $\frac{1}{3}$ of the mass is mortar, consequently a cubic yard will require about as much as 500 such bricks; or 10 cubic feet (8 struck bushels) of sand; and 2 cubic feet, or 1.6 bushels of quicklime. Superior, well scabled rubble carefully laid will contain but about $\frac{1}{5}$ of its bulk in mortar; or $5\frac{1}{2}$ cubic feet sand, and 1.1 cubic feet lime per cubic yard. In work exposed to dampness an addition should be made to the foregoing mortars, of a quantity of good hydraulic cement equal to about $\frac{1}{8}$ of the lime; or $\frac{1}{8}$ of the lime should be omitted, and an equal amount of cement substituted for it. If exposed to *water* the proportions of cement should be increased and that of the lime diminished.—Trautwine, C. E.

It must *ever* be remembered by the mechanic, that in the mixing of mortars an excess of water in slaking the lime swells the mortar, which remains light and porous, or *shrinks* in drying; and an excess of sand destroys the *cohesive* properities of the whole mass.

Proportions of brick and mortar in a wall.—With bricks of $8\frac{1}{4}$ x 4 x 2 inches the following are the quantities of mortar as compared with the whole mass; and the number of bricks required for a cubic yard of massive work:

Size of joint, inch.	Am't of mortar in whole mass.	No. of brick in cub. yd.	No of bricks in cub. ft.
$\frac{1}{8}$	$\frac{1}{9}$	638	23.63
$\frac{1}{4}$	$\frac{1}{7}$	574	21.26
$\frac{3}{8}$	$\frac{3}{10}$	522	19.33
$\frac{1}{2}$	$\frac{1}{3}$	475	17.60
$\frac{5}{8}$	$\frac{4}{10}$	433	16.04

[Trautwine, C. E.]

From the foregoing information the mason can easily calculate how much his mortar will cost per thousand bricks laid, and per cubic yard of stone, knowing the price of lime, sand, and cement which varies in different parts of the United States.

Concrete is admirably adapted to a variety of most important purposes, and is daily growing into more extensive use and application. For foundations in damp and yielding soils, and for subterranean and submarine masonry, almost under every combination of circumstances likely to occur in practice, it is superior to brickwork in strength, durability, and economy; and in some exceptional cases, is considered a reliable substitute for the best stone, while it is almost preferable to the poorer qualities.

For submarine masonry, concrete possesses the advantage that it may be laid without exhausting the water (which under the most favorable circumstances, is an expensive operation), and also without the aid of a diving-bell, or submarine armor. On account of its continuity and impermeability to water, it is well suited to the purpose of a substratum in soils infected with springs, for sewers and conduits, for basement and sustaining walls, for columns, piers and abutments, for pavements in areas, basements and cellars; for walls and floors of cisterns, vaults, etc. Groined and vaulted arches, and even entire bridges, dwelling houses and factories, in single monolithic masses, with moulded ornamentation of no mean character, have been constructed of this material alone. Concrete is composed of natural hydraulic cement, under circumstances requiring only a moderate degree of energy and strength, paste of fat lime is sometimes added in quantities seldom greatly exceeding that of the cement, coarse gravel and broken stone is almost invariably used as the basis of concrete, when made it is at once deposited in its allotted place, and well rammed in horizontal layers of about 6 in. in thickness, until all the coarse fragments are driven below the general surface.

The ramming should take place before the cement begins to set, and care should be taken to avoid the use of too much water in the manipulation. The mass when ready for use should appear quite coherent, containing water, however, in such quantities, that a thorough and hard ramming will produce a thin film of free water upon the surface, under the rammer, without causing in the mass a quicksand motion.

It will be found in practice that cements vary very considerably in their capacity for water, and that fresh ground cements require more than those that have become stale.

An excess of water is, however, better than a deficiency, particularly when a very energetic cement is used, as the capacity of this substance for solidifying water is great.

A too rapid desiccation of the concrete might involve a loss of cohesive strength if insufficient water be used. In the preparation of concrete the cement and sand should be thoroughly mixed first dry; then add water gradually and mix to a plastic mortar; the broken stone should be dampened by sprinkling, when all should be thoroughly incorporated and carried as quick as possible to the trench, and rammed as above described. Subjoined is an analysis of concrete used under the supervision of some of the best authorities upon the matter:

1 barrel German Portland cement (395 pounds).
$5\frac{1}{2}$ " damp and closely measured sand.
6 " gravel and pebbles.
9 " broken stone.

One batch of this concrete makes fifty cubic feet rammed concrete.

This concrete is of first rate quality, being compact, free from voids, and strong. It is richer in mortar than would be necessary for most purposes.

1 barrel Boulogne Portland cement (400 pounds).
1½ " slaked ground lime in powder.
8 " loosely measured damp sand.
16 " pebbles and gravel.
16 " broken stone (2" cu.).

One batch of this concrete will make 105 cubic feet rammed concrete, of suitable quality for most kinds of massive work. It contains the greatest admissible proportions of gravel and broken stone. The quality of this concrete would be improved by using 18 barrels of gravel and 14 barrels of broken stone, instead of 16 barrels of each. This concrete possesses a crushing strength of 220 pounds to the square inch, when two months old, the pressure being applied to 5 inch or 6 inch cubes.

1 part Portland cement, 3 parts clean sharp sand, and 5 parts broken stone, are proportions used in some of the massive works in this country. From the above practical receipts the mason can modify them to answer any practical purpose, and arrive at the cost of the same, knowing the prices of materials in the different portions of the states.

Weight of good concrete, 130 to 160 pounds per cubic foot.

Cost of concrete $5.00 to $9.00 per cubic yard if roughly deposited; and $9.00 to $13.00 if first made into blocks; depending upon the kind of cement, locality, etc.

Strength of cement.—The strength, hardness and adhesion of cement to brick and stone are much greater than in lime mortar.

The cohesion or strength to resist a pull, averages from 40 to 75 pounds per square inch; or 2 to 5 to 4 to 8 tons per square foot, in good Rosendale cement without sand; six months after being laid.

It is sometimes 30 to 50 pounds within a month. The Portland cement of Francis & White of London, when fresh and of the choicest quality, is stated to have a cohesion of of 100 pounds per square inch within seven days; and of 400 pounds within three months. Its adhesion to brick and stone seems to be far less.

Many spurious and inferior articles are sold under the name of Portland cement.

The crushing strength of cement—Of bricks made of best English Portland cement 3 and 9 months old, was found to be 243 and 385 tons per square foot. With one part of sand, 160 and 292 tons per square foot.

With 5 parts of sand, 61 and 108 tons.

The tenacity or cohesive strength of mortar, that is the resistance of it to a pull; of hardened good common lime mortar, according to careful trials by Gen. Totton of the U. S. Army, with mortar only six months, varies from 00 to 34 pounds per square inch; or from 864 to 4896 pounds, or from 39 to 2.19 tons per square foot.

About $15\frac{1}{2}$ pounds per inch is near the General's experience; and is quite as high as should be assumed in practice. It is true that his experience showed that at the end of $4\frac{1}{2}$ years, some of the mortars had acquired from 2 to 3 times greater strength; but others in that time increased but $\frac{1}{8}$ part. Moreover, in practice the working strains are generally brought upon masonry by the time that some of its mortar is not more than six months old or even less; therefore, we cannot avail ourselves of the increased strength given by time; but if such increase is needed speedily, we must add cement.

The crushing force may be taken at 50 tons per square foot; or 777 pounds per square inch.

The sliding resistance, or that which common mortar opposes to any force tending to make one course of masonry slide upon another, is stated by Roudelet to be but 5 pounds per square inch; or about $\frac{1}{3}$ tons per square foot, in mortar six months old.

Transverse strength.—Prisms six inches long, 2 inches square and 4 inches between the supports, made from equal measures of quicklime and sand, will when six months old break under a centre load of about 200 pounds. With more sand they are weaker; and with less they are stronger.

The adhesion to bricks or stones may ordinarily be assumed to be at least equal to its cohesive strength in properly executed work.

But in practice it should not be exposed to more than ⅓ part of the above loads, or strains, in any of the cases. It is the opinion of some good practical authorities that the mortar will be better if the lime is slaked to a dry powder, or made into a paste, for about a week before adding the sand. The delay gives time for the numerous small refractory particles which occur in all limes, to slack and soften, otherwise they do so after the mortar is laid some time; and thus produce in it a partial disintegration. On this account ground lime, if fresh, is preferable to lump; the grinding breaks down these particles or the mortar may be well mixed a few days before being used, and then worked. The powder of slaked lime may be kept good for several months. If closely packed in barrels, and kept dry.

The strength of all mortar depends to a much greater extent than is generally supposed, upon the thoroughness of the mixing.

In important works on a large scale, the lime should be finely ground into paste with water by a mill, and the sand and cement then added gradually, and also mixed with the paste by a mill.

Air slaked lime makes a weak mortar; and an excess of water in slaking (or what is called *drowning* the lime) is also injurious.

The best mode of slaking so far as regards the quality of the mortar, is by *sprinkling*, the loose lump or ground lime, with about ¼ to ⅓ by trial, of its own bulk of water, and then covering it with sand. Water should not be added after the lime begins to heat.

Good mortar for setting boilers and furnaces and building generally. A good mortar is a solid silicate of lime, that is, the lime unites with the silica or sand to form a silicate of lime. In ancient times those who had some conception of the way the two things united superintended their mixing; but nowadays anybody knows much about it. Dry lime and sand laid together or mixed and kept dry for a thousand years would not unite to form silicate of lime any more than acetic acid and carbonate of soda dry in a bottle would effervesce. To make silicate of lime just as good as was made by the Romans, all that is necessary is to proceed intelligently: Procure good caustic, *i. e.*, fresh burned lime, and if you find it all powder, *i. e.*, *air slacked*, don't use it; use only clear lumps; slake this (if possible in a covered vessel), *using only enough water to cause the lime to form a powder.* To this while hot add clean sand, not dirt and loam called sand, but *sand*; and with the sand add enough water to form a paste. Then let it lie where it will not become dry by evaporation, if in a cellar so much the better; for as soon as you have mixed the sand and lime as above, they begin to react one on the other, and if not stopped by being deprived by moisture will go on reacting until silicate of lime (as hard as any silicate of lime ever was), is formed. But if you take this so-called mortar as soon as made and lay bricks with it, unless the bricks are thoroughly wet you stop the formation of silicate of lime, and might as well lay your bricks in mud when used in the above work. Lime and sand, after being mixed, might lie two years with advantage, and for certain uses, such as boiler setting, or when the whole structure is to be dried, the mortar ought to be mixed for one year before use, and two would be better; but for house building, if the bricks are so wetted as not to rob the mortar of its moisture as soon as used; mortar that has been mixed a month will form good solid silicate of lime among the bricks it is laid with in ten years, and will be still harder in a hundred years. The practice of mixing mortar in the streets and using it at once is as foolish as it is ignorant, and would be no improvement.

Silicate of lime is made only by the slow action of caustic lime and sand, one on the other, under the influence of moisture. Dry they will never unite, and mixing mortar as now mixed and using it at once, so as to dry out and stop the formation that the mixing induced, is *wrong*.

And when preparing colored mortar for fronts and plastering, and as well as for tuck-pointing in their different tints for stopping, the above instruction should be followed as near as possible that the different shades sought may retain their color when in combination with lime.

A new mortar for the finish of walls, laying bricks, etc. This material is designed for application to walls and ceilings in place of sand finish, plaster of paris.

It is claimed to be greatly superior for many reasons. Among its advantages are claimed the following:

It will not chip-crack, is applied with less labor, involves no loss of material in gauging; can be painted or papered at less cost; is a non-absorbent and non-conductor; is impermeable to grease, stains or germs of disease; can be washed without injury; is pleasanter to the eye than the glaring white of ordinary finish, and does not become discolored with age, but improves in tone and cleanliness; presents the finest surface for papering in oil or water colors; and its cost compares favorably with that of any other kind of finish. It is also supplied, ready mixed, in various colors, red, blue, drab, etc. It makes a beautiful surface, and the color is permanent. The soapstone finish has been used for several years past on churches, school houses, etc. The Providence, R. I., Soapstone Co., also manufacture the Potter color mortar, which makes a close, strong joint for brickwork, and being unaffected by heat, gases or exposure to the weather, is well adapted for chimney tops and fire-places, and for laying up fire-brick, making a strong and durable joint. For this purpose it is furnished in red, black, brown and buff colors.

A cement for stopping joints, such as around chimneys, etc.—White lead ground in oil, as sold by the keg, mixed with enough pure sand to make a stiff paste that will not run. It grows hard by exposure, and resists heat, cold and water. Pieces of stone may be strongly cemented together with it, allowing a few months for proper hardening.

Litharge cement is composed of equal measures of litharge, sand and plaster of paris, made into a paste with boiled linseed oil, used for pointing up stoops, etc.

Alum and plaster.—These two materials make a very good cement for common use. The better way is to make a strong alum water, and wet the plaster of paris with it to the proper consistency.

Peio's composition for covering buildings and *colored mor-*

tars. Take the hardest and purest limestone (white marble is to be preferred), free from sand, clay or other matter; calcine it in a reverberatory furnace, pulverize and pass it through a sieve; 1 part by weight is to be mixed with two parts clay well baked and similarly pulverized, conducting the whole operation with care. This forms the first powder. The second is to be made of 1 part calcined and pulverized gypsum, to which is added 2 parts clay, baked and pulverized. These two powders are to be combined, and intimately incorporated so as to form a perfect mixture. When it is to be used, mix it with about a fourth part of its weight of water added gradually, stirring the mass well the whole time until it forms a thick paste, in which state it is to be spread like mortar upon the desirer surface. It becomes in time as hard as stone, allows no moisture to penetrate, and is not cracked by heat. When well prepared it will last a long time. When in its plastic or soft state, it may be colored any desired tint.

Higgins' stucco. —To 15 pounds of best stone lime add 14 pounds of bone ashes finely powdered, and about 95 pounds clean washed sand quite dry, either coarse or fine according to the nature of the work in hand. These ingredients must be intimately mixed, and kept from the air till wanted. When required for use, it must be mixed up into a proper consistency for working with *lime water*, and used as speedily as possible.

Ashlar work is usually set or pointed up in a putty mortar formed of lime, white lead, and a small quantity of fine sand or pulverized stone of the kind being set.

A cement which will stand a moist climate is composed of 1 bushel of lime with 15 gallons of water, and $4\frac{1}{2}$ bushels of fine gravel sand mixed with $3\frac{1}{2}$ pounds of copperas, disolved in hot water and kept stirred while being incorporated, and while being used. Sufficient should be made for the day during which it is to be used, as the color is not easily matched.

Asphalt.—The best bituminous cements are obtained from the natural asphalt. The mastic is of 3 qualities, **fine gritted, and** coarse gritted. The first being without any admixture of grit, is used in special cases for close joints in brickwork. The fine gritted is used for covering arches, lining of tanks, and as a cement for brickwork. The coarse is used for paving and flooring. These mastics being ductile and readily yielding, require a proper foundation to be prepared for them,

In melting asphalt about two pounds of mineral tar is added to every fifty-six pounds of the asphalt, but they are all inferior to the natural asphalt.

A hard cement for pointing stoops, basins and cementing stone is made of 63 parts well burnt brick, and 7 parts lithage pulverized and moistened with linseed oil. Moisten the surface to which it is to be applied.

Mastic cement.—Boettger says that these cements are mixtures of 100 parts each of sand, limestone, and litharge, with 7 parts linseed oil. These ingredients, carefully mixed and well worked together, will have the consistency of moist sand, and at first but little coherence. When pressed, however, the mixture gradually acquires the hardness of ordinary sandstone. The binding agents in such cements are the litharge and oil, the sand giving the body, and limestone or chalk filling up the interstices.

Frozen mortar.—There is risk in using common mortar in cold weather. If the cold should continue long enough to allow the frozen mortar to set well, the work may remain safe; but if a warm day should occur between the freezing and the setting of the mortar on that side, while that on the other may remain frozen hard. In that case the wall will be apt to fall; or if it does not, it will at least always be weak; for mortar that has partially set while frozen if then melted, will never regain its strength. Strong hydraulic cements seem not to be injured by freezing.

Fire wall, the finishing wall of a building or that portion which rises above and encloses the roof and should be built with cement mortar and well flashed with lead' to receive the tin covering of the roof.

Salt in mortar.—The American architect asserts that adding salt to cement mortar in cold weather to preserve it from the bad effects of freezing, has been found beneficial. It is not quite clear why the salt should act in this way, as the beneficial results of using it are visible with mortar that has certainly been frozen, and frozen salt water expands nearly as much as fresh water. But engineers and contractors who have tried it are unanimous in their opinion of its value. Many cases are seen where masonry has been laid in cement in cold weather, using a considerable amount of salt in the mixture, which, after repeated freezing and thawing, has remained in perfect condition, while work near by laid in mortar of the same kind, but without salt, has been disintegrated by the frost.

Dampness.—*Prevention of damp in buildings.*—Damp is caused in buildings by the presence of water in the atmosphere and the soil, combined with the porosity of building materials which absorb it. Its effects are to cause disintegrating of masonry, the decay of timber, the development of saltpetre on walls, and injury to the health of the inhabitants of the buildings, with damage to the decorations of walls and to furniture. Remedies to prevent and cure it may be applied to both the causes by:

1st. Employing suitable materials for cellars and other parts of buildings below or on the level of the soil; 2d, inserting damp courses to stop the upward progress of damp; 3rd, applying preparations to protect the face of the exposed wall from the weather, or to prevent damp in the wall from affecting an apartment; and 4th, adopting precautions against infiltration. Concrete covering the whole ground-area of the future building with a layer four inches thick, forms the most sanitary foundation.

Well-puddled clay is also good and inexpensive, but is not effective in old buildings. The porosity of materials has been obviated by injecting them with gas-refuse, by immersing or washing them in solutions of soap and alum successively, and by plunging them into a solution of silicate of potash, and by painting them with gas-tar. Mortars are made impervious by mixing them with cement. Ventilating bricks admit air to the interior of walls, and thus keep them dry. Under the Joument patent, ventible and perfectly dry floors and areas are made by laying the cement around pipes, which **being drawn** out, leave the foundation penetrated by **tubes.** Conduits are made with the glycometallic **liquid, or with gutta-percha.** The stone settings of windows should be made moisture proof, and leaden gutters on the inside to catch the moisture that drops from the glass, will be of service. Finally, drains from closets should be furnished with ventilating pipes.

Damp courses..—In structures used for domestic purposes, it is scarcely necessary to say that it is of the utmost importance that the walls be kept dry and free from damp; the drainage of the site is of the utmost importance that this may be attained.

It is usual, in order to keep the walls dry, to have near the ground level a course, which is called a damp-proof course, and for this purpose asphalt may be used, or a double course of slate bedded in Portland cement. A course of hard stone as well should be laid along the *grade-line* to prevent moisture from the exterior.

The asphalt should be spread about $\frac{1}{2}$ inch thick (and sprinkled with coarse sand) and of the best quality, and there may be no fear as to the compressibility of the asphalt of that thickness from the heat of the sun in the summer-time, on account of the proximity of the soil, and the alternation of temperature of day and night. And there can be no question that the construction of masonry below the ground line of buildings should be done in hydraulic cement mortar, as an effectual means of preventing the ascent of humidity in buildings.

Dampness is said to prevail most in buildings finished hastily; because the materials which compose the walls having never been dry, conform themselves to the humidity rising, in a regular current, by capillary attraction, never allows the possibility of the walls afterwards becoming dry. And the precaution should be taken as explained under damp-proof course.

Mr. F. Ransome of London claims to render stone and brick **walls water proof by** coating **them** to saturation with a solution **of silicate of soda,** which is superficially decomposed **by the further** application **of** chloride of calcium.

The surface thus obtained consists of silicate of lime, which is perfectly insoluble, and therefore water-tight, while it does not alter the appearance of the wall.

Dentils.—A row of similar and equal solids in a cornice, disposed at equal parts each presenting four equal sides of a rectangular prism; in setting a dentil course the line should always be placed at the under side of the dentil course.

Dwarf-walls are low walls of less height than the story of a building. Sometimes the joists of a ground floor rests upon them; and the enclosures of courts are frequently formed by them with an railing of iron on their top; any low wall used as a fence may be termed a dwarf-wall.

Darby.—In plastering a two handed float, about $3\frac{1}{2}$ feet long and 4 inches wide, used by the plasterer to fetch his *browning* coat to an even surface.

Diamond-work.—Reticulated work formed by courses of lozenge-shaped stones, very common in ancient times.

Discharging-arch.—An arch built above a lintel to take the superincumbent pressure therefrom.

Dots.—Nails driven into a wall to a certain depth, so that their protruding heads form a gage of depth in laying on a coat of plastic.

Drove.—A broad-edged chisel used by stone masons.

Dry arch.—An arch sometimes employed in the foundation of buildings for the purpose of keeping them dry

Dead man.—A term generally used by the bricklayer for a temporary constructed pier to guide his line when racking up a wall.

Derrick.—A form of hoisting machine. The peculiar feature of a derrick, which distinguishes it from some other forms of hoisting machines, is that it has a boom stayed from a central point, which may be anchored, but is usually stayed by guys. A derrick has one leg, a *shears* two, and a *gin* three. A crane has a post and jib.

A whin or whim has a vertical axis on which a rope winds. The capstan has a vertical drum for the rope, and is volated by bars. The *windlass* has a horizontal barrel, and is volated by hand-spikes. The *winch* has a horizontal barrel, and is frequently the means of winding up the tackle-rope of the derrick; it is volated by cranks. The *crab* is a portable winch and has cranks. The derrick is commonly used in the United States, and has attained what appears to be maximum effectiveness with a given weight. Two spars, three guys, and two sets of tackle, one for the jib and one for the load, complete the apparatus, except the winch, crab, or capstan for hoisting.

Deafening.—The process of filling between the floor joists of floors with mortar and saw-dust, to prevent the vibration of sound. Usually from 2 to 6 in depth.

Dowel-pin.—A pin or peg uniting two stones together; their size is regulated in accordance to the weight of the stone.

Draft.—The chisel-dressing at the angles of stones, serving as a guide for the leveling of the surface.

Drip-stone.—A corona or projecting table or moulding over the heads of doorways, windows, arch-ways, niches, etc.

Discoloration of brick walls.—Brick buildings in almost all of our cities are from time to time disfigured by streaks and patches of white. Mr. Trautwine's observations are eminently worthy of the attention of masons and builders in localities where this disfiguration makes its appearance. The evil, he says, is most noticeable in dry weather on parts of walls subjected to dampness, and on entire walls after rain storms have soaked them.

The white coating is derived primarily from both the bricks and the mortar. In some instances it undoubtedly comes from the bricks; here the white substance is dissolved by moisture from the bricks even before they are built into the walls. He has found it in bricks just from the kiln.

It has a peculiar taste, that of sulphate of magnesia; but besides this salt the bricks also contain sulphate of lime. The theory is that the silicates of magnesia and lime in bricks are converted into sulphates by the sulphuric acid evolved from the sulphide of iron and iron pyrites contained in the coal, which is employed in the kilns.

Now, sulphate of magnesia effloresces in dry air, and sulphate of lime is dissolved by moisture and appears on the surface of bricks. Hence, plainly, one mode of preventing the incrustation is the employment of only wood, or of coke free from sulphur in the kilns, at least this might be done in the manufacture of pressed bricks for house-fronts.

As for the incrustations having their origin in the mortar, comes from the fact that sulphate of magnesia is largely produced by the decomposition of mortar. The observations on this head have special applications to vicinities where most of the lime used in buildings are from magnesia limestone.

The resulting mixture of limestone and magnesia, when slaked and made into mortar, is very susceptible to the influence of sulphurous fumes in the atmosphere, which produces in the mortar sulphates of lime and magnesia.

The great solubility of sulphate of magnesia facilitates its diffusion; sulphate of lime is comparatively insoluble, and does not cause so much disfigurment. Of course, mortar made from magnesia limestone quickly, decomposes, and the bricks it was intended to cement become loose.

The remedy for this is the employment of lime from nonmagnesia limestone. The remedy also offered for this evil is the addition of a small quantity of baryta to the water used for tempering the brick clay. The baryta, having a strong affinity for the free acid, would seize upon it, and with it form insoluble sulphate of baryta. A like addition of baryta to mortar, after it is prepared for use, may reasonably be expected to check the tendency to efflorescence, except of course, when the mortar, as in chimneys, is continuously exposed to the action of sulphurous vapors. It is a fact that soda in one of its forms is the cause; simple water dissolves it; and, next, linseed oil as a coating is an excellent treatment. The best success has been attained when dilute muriatic acid has cleansed the pores in the bricks, and thus permitted the oil to penetrate further into the bricks and keeping the wall dry. (See Washes.)

Dilute muriatic acid.—Mix 4 troy ounces muriatic acid with distilled water to make a pint. The specific gravity of the diluted acid is 1.038. (U. S. Ph.)

Drains.—The general principles are that each day's influx should be promptly passed out by natural flow or flushing, and not allowed to deposit sediment. The alignment should be good, especially at the bottom; the descent should be uniform, and the interior surface smooth, so as to reduce friction and not to cause clogging; the walls should be absolutely impervious, and the suction such as will cause the most rapid possible flow with a minimum of sewage. Rapid flow being essential, smooth interior walls should be provided; mortar projecting from the joints of a brick sewer markedly impedes the flow and arrests putrefiable matter. A flat-bottomed form is the worst form as regards the velocity of the flow; a circular bottom is better; an egged-shaped section, with the point downward, permits of a minimum current flushing and cleansing the bottom. In brick sewers the mortar constantly moist; must sooner or later succumb to the disintegrating action of the matters passed through it, and the whole line gradually passes into the form of a seive, allowing the liquid portions of the sewage to pass through it, and to saturate the subsoil, but retaining the solids. From the consequent saturation of the soil result contagious fevers. Hence *vitrified* clay pipes are now almost universally employed. The *slip* glazing is applied to these pipes resists the severest chemical action of sewage matter. The *slip* glaze is produced by dipping the unbaked clay into a mixture of *slip* clay, or Albany earth, and water, which under a white heat continued from twelve to thirty hours, produces a vitreous and very durable silicious surface upon the wares. These pipes are very cheap and are manufactured in almost all the States. From every water pipe carrying off rain water from the roof of a building, as well as from every sink and water closet, a small drain leads into a greater one, the former of which is called a branch drain, whilst the latter is called the main drain of the building. In all small drains, excepting those for clean water only, it is necessary to have cesspools somewhat larger and deeper than the drains to which they belong. These cesspools, being covered with an iron grating, receive the surface water which is accompanied with much sand

and earth washed down, prevent the drains from being choked up; and when the cesspools themselves are near full the grating can be removed and the cesspools emptied. Besides these cesspools, it is usual to form one of a different description, termed stink-traps, within the building to prevent offensive smells from passing into the water pipes from the sinks of the building. They are made (generally of tile) by forming part of a bottom of a drain at a lower level, so that water must necessarily stand in it all times. Care should be taken in arranging the small drains of a building that nothing but clean water drains shall have any possible communication with the tanks or cisterns for receiving rain water from the roof when such are used. The slope of a drain for clean water may be from $1\frac{1}{2}$ to 2 inches in 10 feet; the slope of a drain carrying down other sewerage should be much more when such a slope can be commanded.

All drains should be well considered before commenced, and should be about the first things executed about a building. A level should be taken from the bottom of the sewer in the street back to the furthest part of starting in the rear, and a computation taken to find how much fall can be had to a foot; drains should not be cut too abruptly in their course, and all branch drains should not enter the main drain at right angles, but should, when possible, be slanted a little to favour the direction in which the water is to flow. All joints of drains should be well cemented together to prevent the escape of sewer gas.

All brick drains should be built of the hardest burned brick, and laid in a strong hydraulic cement mortar, and the closest possible joint to render them absolutely impervious to water; it is a simple enough matter for any practical mechanic to estimate upon the drains for a building; but those of a public character which are constructed for cities and water ways are naturally followed with considerable risk, not in regards ascertaining the quantity of material to be used, but the difficulty encountered to perform the work, which arises from rains and caving in of the embankment, quicksand, etc., as well the general nature of the soil to be met with, which necessitates a percentage to be added for all kinds of such work for *risk* unseen, which is known to the judgment of the practical man acquainted with the difficulties once met with. Of course the general principles of construction must be followed in any case, and one who is acquainted with the difficulties encountered in dealing with unreliable soils and rock, may from his knowledge of such work knows what percentage to add to this kind of work.

Encaustic tile.—The art of putting together small tubes or tesseræ of different substances, so as to form patterns and figures either in monochrome or in various colors, was very ancient, being known to the Egyptians, Assyrians and Babylonians.

Mosaic was applied to the decoration of walls and pavements and was extensively used, especially for the latter purpose, by the Greeks and Romans; but Mosaic took its chief development after the spread of Christianity, and in the decoration of Christian edifices, and may, therefore, be called a Christian art. Although the chief merit of the Mosaic must depend upon the designer of the cartoon, yet much depends upon the judgment and the skill of the mason who executes it.

Encaustic tiles are those in which colored devices are introduced, the colors being burnt in during the process of manufacture.

For ornamental tiling the whole surface to be paved is *screeded* perfectly level with Portland cement mixed with sand, and when sufficiently hard the tiles are laid with a thin bed of pure Portland cement, according to a design at hand; by frequently applying the straight-edge the work will be brought to a uniform surface.

Entabliture.—Is that part of an order which is supported by the columns and forms the covering or shelter to the edifice. It consists of three principal divisions, viz., the architrave which rests upon the capitals of the columns; the frieze immediately above it; and the cornice at the summit.

Excavating.—The mason is often called upon to estimate on excavating, digging, etc., and he should be acquainted somewhat with this manner of work for that purpose. There is a difference of opinion in regard of costs and amounts of labor in this work among civil engineers' writings, which, I suppose, may be accounted for in the different manner in which the work is managed. Mr. Trautwine says that "The aggregate cost of excavating and removing earth is made up by the following items: 1st, as an ordinary average loosening by the plough, from 200 to 400 cubic yards per day, 10 hours. By the pick, 14 yards of stiff pure clay, or of cemented gravel, 25 yards of strong heavy soils; 40 yards of common loam; 60 yards of light sandy soils, all measured in place.

2d. *Shovelling the loose earth into carts.* Much of this work depends upon the weight of the material, and the proportioning the number of pickers and carts to that of shovellers; but as an average 24 yards of light sandy soils; 20 yards of loam $17\frac{2}{5}$ of the heavy soils, measured in place, per days work of man.

3rd. *Hauling away the earth;* dumping, or *emptying* and *returning* to *reload.*

The average speed of horses in hauling, is about $2\frac{1}{2}$ miles per hour, or 200 ft. per minute; which is equal to 100 ft. of trip each way; or 100 ft. of lead, as the distance to which the earth is hauled is technically called.

Besides this, there is a loss of about 4 minutes in each trip, either long or short, in waiting to load, dumping, turning, etc. Hence every trip will occupy as many minutes as there are lengths of 100 ft. each in the lead; and four minutes besides. Therefor, to find the number of trips per day over any given average land, we divide the number of minutes in a working day by the sum of 4 added to the number of 100 ft. lengths contained in the distance to which the earth has to be removed; that is:—*The number of minutes in a working day (600)* ÷ (4 + the number of 100 ft. lengths in the lead) = The number of trips, or loads removed per day, per cart. And since $\frac{1}{3}$ of a cubic yard measured before being loosened, makes an average cart load, the number of loads, divided by 3, will give the number of cubic yards removed per day by each cart; and the cubic yards divided into the total expense of a cart per day, will give the cost per cubic yard for hauling. When removing loose rock, which requires more time for loading, say :— No. of minutes (600) in a working day ÷ (6 + No. of 100 ft. lengths of lead)= Number of loads removed per day, per cart.

4th. *Spreading* or *leveling* of the earth into thin layers on the embankment. A bankman will spread from 50 to 100 cubic yards of either common loam, or any of the heavier soils, clays, etc., per day, depending upon their dryness.

5th. *Keeping the cart road* in good order, for hauling. Say $\frac{1}{10}$ of a cent per cubic yard, per 100 ft. of lead.

6th. *Wear, sharpening, and depreciating of picks and shovels.*—Experience shows that about ¼ of a cent per cubic yard will cover this item.

7th. *Superintendance and water carriers*, trimming up etc., about 2 cent per cubic yard.

8th. *Profit to contractor.*—Out of this item is generally paid clerks, storekeepers, etc., and is generally put down from 6 to 15 per cent. according to the magnitude of the work.

Cost of excavating by barrows.—The cost by barrows may be estimated in the same manner as by carts. Men in wheeling move at about the same average rate as horses do in hauling, that is 2½ miles an hour, or 200 feet per minute, or 1 minute per every 100 feet length of lead. The time occupied in loading, emptying, etc. (when, as is usual, the wheeler loads his own barrow), is about 1.25 minutes, without regard to length of lead; besides which, the time lost in occasional short rests, in adjusting the wheeling plank, and in other incidental causes, amounts to about $\frac{1}{10}$ part of his whole time; so that in practice we must consider him as actually working but 9 hours out of his 10 working ones, at the rate of 1.25 minutes per 100 feet of lead. To find then the number of barrow loads he can remove in a day, multiply the number of minutes (60) in a working hour by 9 and divide the product by the sum of 1.25 added to the number of 100 feet lengths in the lead;

that is: *The number of minutes in a working day of* 9 *hours* = 1.25 × the **number** of trips of lead.

The **number of trips** or loads removed per day per **barrow**. The number of loads divided by 14 will give the number of cubic yards, since a cubic yard measured in place averages about 14 barrow loads.

For rock, which requires more time for loading, say *number of minutes in a working day* =1.6 × *number of lengths of lead*; number of loads removed per day per barrow.

Removing rock excavating by wheel barrows.—A solid cubic yard of granite or sand stone when broken up by blasting for removal by carts or barrows will occupy a space of about 1.8 or 1⅛ cubic yards; whereas, average earth when loosened swells to about 1.2 or 1⅕ of its original bulk in place; although after being made into embankment, it eventually shrinks into less than its original bulk. In estimating for earth, it is assumed that $\frac{1}{14}$ cubic yard in place is a fair load for a wheel barrow. Such a cubic yard will weigh on an average 2,430 lbs., or 1.09 tons; therefore, $\frac{2430}{14}$ = 174 lbs. is the weight of a barrow load on 2.31 cubic feet of loose earth. Assuming that a barrow of loose rock would weigh about the same as one of earth, we may take it at $\frac{1}{27}$ of a cubic yard; which gives $\frac{2430}{27}$·$\frac{18}{10}$ = 177 lbs. per load of loose rock, occupying 2 cubic feet of space.

Ample experience shows that when labor is $1 per day, 45 cts. per cubic yard, in place is a sufficiently liberal allowance for loosening hard rock under all ordinary circumstances. In practice it will generally range from 30 to 60 cts.; depending upon the position of the strata, hardness, toughness, water and other considerations. Soft shales, and other allied rocks, may frequently be loosened by pick and plow, as low as from 15 to 20 cents; while on the other hand, shallow cuttings of very tough rock, with an unfavorable position of strata, especially in the bottoms of excavations, may cost $1 or even considerable more. These are exceptional cases of comparatively rare occurrence. The quarrying of average hard rock requires about ¼ to ½ lb. of powder per cubic yard in place; but the nature of the rock and the position of the strata, etc., may increase it to

½lb. or more. Soft rock frequently requires more powder than hard. A good churn-driller will drill 8 to 12 feet in depth, of holes about 2½ feet deep, and two inches in diameter, per day, in average hard rock, at from 12 to 18 cents per foot; drillers receive higher wages than common laborers.

Float Stone.—A rubbing stone used by the bricklayer for smoothing compass-bricks. It takes out the axe marks acquired in roughly dressing to shape.

Floors for cellars and walks.—The following will be found to make a hard and durable floor or sidewalk: Mix well together, dry, 3 parts of broken stones or brick bats and 2 parts of coarse gravel and 1 of Portland cement. Then add the water by sprinkling, and spread from 3 to 6 inches thick, well pounded, and before it is thoroughly set another coat is put on of 2 inches thick, of 1 part of cement and 2 of sand, *screeded* with a straight edge and well *troweled* to a smooth and hand surface. This preparation can be colored to suit the taste with lampblack and ochres, as desired, and explained in this work for that purpose.

Hair.—This is a very necessary material used by the plasterer. It should be long (the longer the better), sound, free from grease and dirt, thoroughly separated, beaten up, or switched with a lath, so as to separate the hairs, and thoroughly dried.

Grounds.—Pieces of wood nailed on by the carpenter as guides for the plastering which comes flush with the surface of the *grounds*.

Grout.—A thin coarse hydraulic mortar used to run into crevices or joints between the stones or bricks of a wall. All walls or foundations, where strength is the main object to be attained, should be grouted.

Hawk.—Is a wooden tool used by the plasterer in plastering. It is generally made of pine, thin on the edges, being bevelled from the centre on the under side to each of the four edges; and is made from 11 to 13 inches square; the handle should be about 6 inches long and about 1½ inches in diameter.

Impost.—The upper member of a pillar column, or entablature, upon which an arch or superstructure rests.

Incrustation.—A facing or covering to a wall of a different material from which it is mainly built, such as marble or stone.

Jack arch.—An arch of only one brick in thickness.

Jointer.—In bricklaying, a crooked piece of iron, forming two courses of contrary flexure by its edges on each side, used for drawing the coursing and vertical joints by the edge of the jointing rule, in which way the work is prepared for the painter for penciling.

Level.—An instrument used by mechanics for ascertaining levels. The most convenient kind of levels is the *spirit level*, which is more accurate than any other, and is most extensively used. This instrument consists of a cylindrical glass tube filled with spirits of wine, except leaving in it a small bubble of air; its end being sealed to keep in the fluid. This bubble being the lightest of the contents of the tube, will always run towards that end of the tube which is most elevated; but when the tube is perfectly horizontal the bubble will have no tendency towards either end.

Lintel.—A stone or beam of timber over an aperture; for sustaining the superincumbent part above.

Ledger.—In scaffolding for brick buildings, the horizontal pieces of timber or poles parallel to the wall, fastened by chords in order to support the put-logs, on which are laid the boards for working upon.

Masonry.—The art of arranging stone together for the formation of walls, in the construction of buildings. The early Greeks constructed their walls, particularly those which surrounded their cities, of rough stones of an immense size; such were those of Mycenea and Tiryns. The interstices that were left between these shapeless blocks, were filled up with small stones. According to the report of travelers, there still exist in the isles of Gozzo and Malta circular edifices of this construction. When the ancients began to cut their stones, they did not cut them rectangular, but gave them an irregular figure of three, four or six sides, but fitted them together, so that, when in their places, they left no interstices between them. The ruins of the ancient wall about the city of Cora, near Velletri, are an example of this mode of building. Winckelmann makes the same remark on the walls of Corinth; on those of Eretria, in Eubœa; and of Ostia, in Cyprus.

We also find in the ancient Lesbos, now called Mateling, and in different parts of Greece and Asia Minor, vestiges of similar walls. Chandler gives to this construction, the name of *incertum*, and takes it, without doubt, for the *incertum* of Vitruvius. But the mode of building which the Roman architect speaks of under that name, is of a very different character. The ancients next employed stones cut at right angles, and of an oblong form, but their size was not uniform. We find the remains of such walls in Greek and Etruscan buildings. The stones are generally from nine to twenty-two feet long, and from two to six high, in the walls of Volatarra, Cortona and Pestum; those of the latter city have been restored by the Romans. Sometimes they gave to the exterior of these stones the form of a rombus or lozenge, as we see in the ancient walls in the isle of Syra, and in Samos. As by degrees the Greeks brought their architecture to perfection, they constructed their buildings in a manner more agreeable, more regular and less gigantic. There were three different modes of building: The *isodomon*, which was formed of ranges of large stones of equal height, and which gave to the buildings in which it was employed a handsome appearance, and was, therefore, chiefly employed in the construction of temples; the *pseudisodomon*, which consisted of ranges of stones of unequal height; and the *emplecton*, which was employed when it was requisite to give a thickness greater than ordinary to the walls, and in which the outside only of the walls was built up of regular hewn stones, and the interior part filled with rough stones and mortar. For the sake of greater solidity, they placed with care at certain distances cross-stones, which served to bind the two outer faces.

The Romans at first imitated the Etruscans in their manner of building. But in later times, independent of the use of bricks and hewn stones, the Romans had two modes of building, which they called *reticulatum* and *incertum* or *antiquum*. The *incertum* consisted in employing the stones just as they came from the quarries, ranged in any order, as they could best fit them together. What was called *reticulatum opus*, was a wall composed of square stones, which were not placed in a horizontal direction, but in such a manner that the junctures lay in a horizontal line, which gave the wall the appearance of net work, which it received the name of *reticulatum*, and was called by the Greeks *dictyotheton*. Vitruvius assures us, that in his time this was the mode of building most commonly practiced. Many edifices of this construction still remain. The Romans imitated the *emplecton* of the Greeks, but they did not execute with the same care or the same solidity. They employed also stone and brick at the same time; and the order and symmetry, which is observed in walls of this construction lead us to conclude, that their aim was to adorn and embellish them.

The walls of Armaira, in Persia, are described by Sir R. K. Porter: Some of the towers are of prodigious magnitude, and exhibit the finest specimens of the ancient high-finished armaira masonry, being composed of white and reddish stones, joined in the nicest art. The common thickness of Grecian walls was seven or eight feet. Those of the Acropolis of Pharsalia are fifteen and a half feet thick. They are constructed sometimes with one single row of blocks, but more generally with a double row, united without any space in the middle. Those at Pharsalia and other places, where they are of an unusual thickness, are lined on both sides with large blocks while the interstices are filled up with smaller stones, and earth and mortar, the *emplecton* of Vitruvius. The ancient Cyclopean walls were an exception, being twenty-five feet thick at Tiryns, and solid throughout. The walls of Platara, which in some parts are in a high state of preservation, exhibit the mode of building walls in Greece, in the age of Alexander, when they were rebuilt. They are in general composed of regular masonry, with some irregularity in the size of the stones, which does not appear to be symmetric. They are about eight feet thick, and are fortified by square towers, with a few of a circular form. The foregoing remarks will be found interesting to those who will have use for this book; as will the following remarks on masonry of "modern times."

"HEWN ASHLAR MASONRY. If set stone and stone, or with thin beds of mortar, and the face work is either backed up with rubble or brick, must be weak. Neither *science* or care can make such hybrid work *strong*, or preserve it true in line, or face, vertically, or horizontally; the backing will shrink and *draw* the face work. I do not believe a straight cornice line can be found in any binding of any length and height, unless there are numerous inner and cross walls to counteract the shrinking and building actions named." Masonry may be defined as the art of constructing with stone upon a plan or system calculated to insure durability. The structure may be a single fence wall of dry random rubble; or it may be the most complicated and elaborately carved cathedral. Betwixt these extremes their are many varieties of masonry.

ROUGH RUBBLE MASONRY.

This class of work, whether set dry or in mortar, consists of stones of small dimensions, on which no labor has been bestowed, other than that necessary to raise them from the earth or quarry. No stone should be larger than one man can lift; and a skillful worker always finds a place for each stone after he has once taken it in hand. As defined by Johnson, 'A mason that makes a wall meets a stone that needs no cutting, and places in his work.'

"ROUGH OR RANDOM RUBBLE MASONRY may be set dry, or it may be set in mortar; but dry, it forms fence walls, retaining walls, and backing, to prevent the earth coming in contact with masonry or brick work—as behind retaining walls of rubble set in mortar, of coursed wall stone, or ashlar; or to protect foundation walls from clay, marl, or wet earth. *Rough rubble* masonry consists of : 1. *Random rubble* set dry, as in moor and field fence walls. 2. *Random rubble* set in mortar,—as fence walls, house walls, and other structures. 3. *Coursed rubble* set in mortar,—as rubble stone, leveled up in courses, generally the depth of ashlar, or single quoins. *Snecked rubble* set in mortar,—as rubble stone having the faces *snecked*, that is, the rough taken off so as to present a more even surface, the beds remaining undressed.

"Rubble masonry is also used as backing to many varieties of masonry; the face of a wall, bridge and abutment, or other structure, may be of *wall stone*, of *block in course*, or of ashlar, and the backing may be of rubble; or there may be two faces, with a filling or *hearting* of rubble.

"Although *random rubble* forms work "of the rudest class, it is not certain that untutored men would construct it, as considerable experience and skill are required to wall small unhewn stone in line on face and in form."

"CYCLOPEAN MASONRY.—This form of masonry seems to have been adopted for military and for religious purposes by the aborigines of countries wide apart. There are remains of Cyclopean construction older than written history Most known examples blend with myths, and are to be found in the deserts of India, of Asia, of Central America, and in Druidical remains spread over Europe.

"Cyclopean masonry is essentially barbaric, whether the stone be rough and unhewn, or hewn and squared, or hewn and fitted in angles and irregular forms. The temples of Egypt, of Palmyra and Greece may be exceptions; but like many exceptions confirm the rule. Masonry, in its highest branches, consists in the art of constructing with small stones—as the best abbeys and cathedrals.

"Mr. Sharp states that few stones in the grand and elaborate structures exceed a cubic of two feet square; most of the stones are of less dimensions, or such as a man could carry.

"The newest forms of masonry most in use for modern purposes may be specified as: *Random rubble* set dry; *random rubble* set in mortar; *random rubble* set with quoins, joints and architraves and levelled in courses; *snecked rubble*, generally set in courses; *rubble with ashlar binders*;

rubble in alternate courses with bricks or with tiles; *flint rubble,* whole or cut; *boulder,* or *pebble rubble,* whole or cut. Flint and pebbles are generally used with brick, tile, or stone quoins and courses. *Slate rubble,* this is set in horizontal beds having an angle of 45°, or at any intermediate angle, and examples may be found vertical. *Herring-bone rubble,* where flat-headed stones are found, this example of masonry may be seen. The Romans frequently used it, not only for face work, but to back squared wall stone, or to form the *hearting* to their military walls. Intermediate betwixt true rubble and regular coursed wall stone, or ashlar, there are forms of masonry in which stones are set irregularly, labor being required to produce irregularity. Much of this kind of work has neither economy, beauty or strength to recommend it.

" *Wall stone squared and bedded; coursed wall stone* set dry; *coursed wall stone* set in mortar; *rough faced wall stone; pitch faced wall stone; scabbled wall stone; punched wall stone; skutched wall stone; bousted wall stone.* There are other forms of finish for the face of coursed wall stones, and the beds and joints generally rise in finish to accord with the faces; that is, *rough faced,* or *pitch faced, punched,* or *skutched off wall stones* have a higher finish on the face; will have clean bousted beds and joints. Coursed wall stones vary in depth up to nine inches.

" BLOCK IN COURSE.—This form of masonry may have all the varieties as named for *coursed wall stone,* the difference consisting in dimensions alone. *Block in course* may commence from 9 ins. (the depth of each course), upwards until it verges into *rough ashlar.* The engineer or architect should, however, in all cases, specify the dimensions for coursed wall-stone and block in course, as also that which is to constitute the difference betwixt these and ashlar; and all the other varieties of masonry should be defined."

STONES WITH TWO FACES.—Parpoints may consist of wall-stone, block in course, or ashlar. Stones of this denomination are used in walls such as *battlements* or *parapets* to bridges. The faces may be rough, or rubbed, or of any intermediate grain of workmanship.

ASHLAR.—Ashlar forms the main feature in true masonry. The stones are always set in true courses, and the depth may be from 12 inches to any available thickness. The beds and joints should always be chiseled dressed; that is, drafted and bousted off. The varieties of finish for the face of ashlar are too numerous to describe. The work may be *rough faced, frosted, sparrow pecked, rock faced, drafted and pecked,* or *punched,* in a variety of ways, or *diamoned,* or *reticulated,* or *rowed,* either *horizontally, diagonally,* or *herring bone.* There are varieties of *drafted* and *bousted work, randomed tooled* and *stroked tooling,* as also *rubbed* or *polished faces.* Ashlar may also have all the varieties of rustic, from a plain chamfer to the compound of fillet and segment.

When the stones which compose the ashlar facing are quite smooth, and exhibit none of the marks of the tools by which the stones were cut, it is called *plane ashlar.* When wrought in a regular manner, so that the surface has the appearance of parallel flutes, placed perpendicularly in the building, it is called *tooled ashlar.* When the surfaces of stones are cut with a broad tool, without care or regularity, it is said to be *random tooled.* When wrought with a narrowed tool, *chiselled* or *boasted;* when cut with very narrow tools it said to be *pointed;* and when the stones project from the joints, with either smooth or broken surfaces, the ashlar is said to be *rusticated.* In the construction of ashlar the mason is called upon to use a great deal of skill, especially in the smaller towns and villages throughout the states, as then he is supposed to be able to both lay and cut stone to a certain extent.

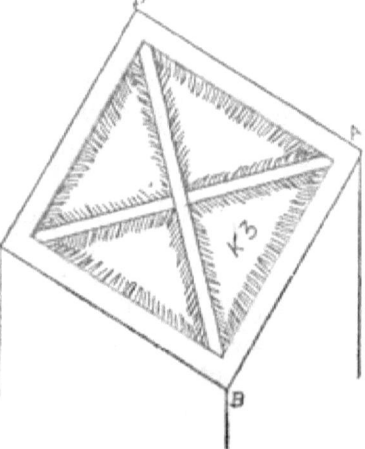

To form a plane surface on a stone the mason first knocks off the superfluous stone along one edge of the block a. b. until it coincides with a straight edge throughout its whole length; this is called a *chisel draught*.

Another draught is then made along one of the adjacent edges, as b. c., and the ends of the two are connected by another draught, as a. c.; a fourth draught is then sunk across the last as b. d., which gives another angle point d, in the same plane with a, b, and c, by which the draught d, a, and a, c, can be formed; and the stone is then knocked off between the outside drafts until a straight edge coincides with its surface in every part. The cutting that the mason is principally called upon to perform at the present time is the rusticated or *rock-faced* and *broken ashlar* or *block in course;* he must fetch his stone first to a rectangular form; the edges are simply cut about one-half or two-thirds of an inch round the margin, so as to be in the plane of the wall, or parallel to it; and the intermediate part is broken with the hammer, so that the protuberant parts may project generally about an inch or more beyond the margin. *Rustic chamfered* is that class of work in which the faces of the stones are beveled at an angle of 135° with the surface of the wall, and as the joints are at right angles to the faces, the margins will also be at 135° with the joints, so that when two rustics come together the bevelling or chamfering, will form an internal right angle, as in cut A, which shows the rectangular, and cut B that

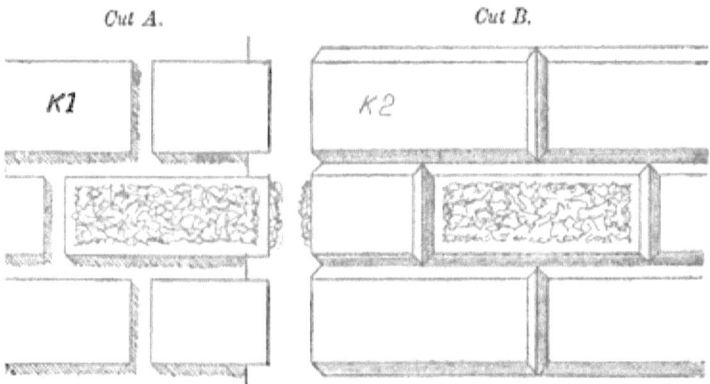

Cut A.   Cut B.

shows the chamfered joint. Both the chamfered and other kinds of rusticuted stone work have other distinctions in the nature of the work or ornamentation on the surface of the projecting part of the stone, the cutting of which is generally within the province of the stonecutter, or those whose knowledge of character and peculiarities of execution in the ornamentation of different periods of the art, and mechanical skill in the representation of the same, a satisfactory result in the production is, to a very large extent, if not wholly dependent, of these.

Rustic work frosted is that in which the margins are reduced to a plane parallel to the plane of the wall, and where the intermediate part has the effect of ice with an irregular surface in protuberant parts.

Rustic work vermiculated is that where the margins are reduced to a plane parallel to the plane of the wall, and where the intermediate part of the stone or general surface is so formed as to have the effect of being eaten by worms.

BLOCK-IN-COURSE.

Differs from coursed rubble in that no course in *line* comes up to the same level, but a continuation of the bond on the face is carried into the upper and lower course; and thus carried throughout the whole surface of the wall.

(*A*) *Block in Course.*

Masons throughout the states call this workmanship also *broken ashlar* or *double binding* and it taxes the skill of the mason in constructing it in a regular manner. As a general thing he usually starts this *bond* all right, but before he goes far, runs somewhat at random, and should be guided by a sketch or plan similar to the one here given, according to the dimensions of the pier or wall to be constructed, and by referring to it from time to time he will be enabled to have his work appear in an uniform and regular manner and a center joint carried plumb throughout; bearing in mind always for a first class job that the *rises* of this work, or as near as possible to them should run 4, 8 and 12 inches, and 8, 16 and 24 inches in their lengths, and he should work his stone to the best advantage for that purpose. Blocks of stone of a rectangular form look best in this style of work, and those of a square surface should be avoided as much as possible. Much of this work is performed in the rock-faced style, and looks well if properly performed. The beds of every stone should be worked quite straight and not *dished* or *hollowed out*, which masons are too apt to do, with the view of making a fine joint. This practice cannot be too severely depreciated, as stones which have been thus worked, or dished out, are liable to flush or break off at the angles.

Ashlar is commonly set in fine mortar or putty, and before the mortar hardens the joints are raked out about a quarter of an inch, to be tuck-pointed (when the work is cleaned down), with a putty mortar in imitation of the color of the stone put on with a *tuck pointer*.

In setting ashlar, both the upper and lower beds of a stone, as well as the vertical joints, should be at right angles to the face of the stone, and the face, bed and vertical joints at right angles to the beds. In an ashlar facing, where the stones run nearly of the same thickness, it is of some advantage, in respect of bond, that the back of the stone should be inclined to the face, and that all the backs thus inclined should run in the same direction, as this gives a small degree of lap in the setting of the next course;

whereas, if the backs were parallel to the fronts, there could be no lap where the stones run of an even length in the thickness of the wall. It is of great advantage likewise to select stones so that a thinner and thicker one may follow each other alternately. The disposition of the stones in each course should follow in the same order as those in the course below, and every vertical joint should follow as nearly as possible in the middle of the stone below. All ashlar should be properly anchored in the backing up, with anchors. The brickwork on the back of ashlaring should be laid in the most substantial manner of hard brick, and lime and cement mortar; as the joints in brickwork being more numerous, are more liable to be compressed, and consequently that portion of the wall is liable to settle more than the stone front of the wall, it is prudent never to hurry the brickwork, but to carry it regularly all around the building, and where there are piers with ashlar facing to keep them well stayed as the work progresses.

When backing up light-colored ashlar, and even granite, it is prudent to use lime mortar against the immediate back of the ashlar, as it has been found that some cements penetrate and discolor the front.

To tie in ashlaring to brick walls cramps are used either of cast iron, wrought iron, copper or bronze. The two latter, of course, are the best; the former exfoliating by air or damp, and splitting the stone unless perfectly secured. When iron anchors are used, they should be put in the holes hot, and surrounded with asphalt. By this proceeding the iron is forever preserved from oxidation; it has proved the best system, because the application of mortar, gypsum, sulphur and lead have all failed. Anchors are also set in Portland cement. With reference to the modern practice of cramping, dowelling, joggling and tying, etc., it will be found that the terms are frequently used indifferently to denote the same processes. A cramp may, however, be properly distinguished, perhaps, as a vertical or horizontal bar of iron or other metal, caulked or bent at either end, inserted in the beds or courses of stones, to connect or tie the same together, or in various other forms to attach ashlar facings to the main work of walls, etc. Dowelling, properly, may be taken as the application of vertical or horizontal plugs of wood, stone or metal to connect and prevent a longitudinal or other slip or separation of the material, as in the case of the stone courses of a column, the boarding of a floor, etc. Joggling is the uniting of two pieces of stone by means of a projection formed in the vertical section of the edge of one, called the male joggle, and a corresponding recess or groove in that of the other, called the female joggle; as in the case of landing of stairs, balconies, or other surfaces formed of slab stone. Tying, it is, perhaps, hardly necessary to add, is an introduction of iron, or other metal, in lengths to act against outward thrust and to connect opposite and distinct points, or to preserve connection under settlement. Iron, chain-bound, hoop iron, and other such like contrivances, are used in foundations, domes, etc. Lead, in connection with iron, should never be admitted where there is exposure to the air, or at all, if it can possibly be avoided. It is better to expend time, patience, and extra expense in good fitting, and to bed the metal in first-class cement. If, however, it is unavoidable, as in harbors, light-houses, and other such heavy works, cast iron should be adopted in preference to wrought, and the metal should be heated slightly and coated with oil previous to being inserted, and the lead then run in. It may be questioned, nevertheless, whether the harder kinds of wood and stone might not be used with advantage in all cases, due care being taken, however, with respect to the former, that it is thoroughly seasoned, and placed in a situation where moisture or wet cannot reach it. It should also be accepted as an axiom, that thoroughly good fitting is essential in every of the above methods, to render the work sound and permanent. Iron should be used with caution, and only in such situations as will allow of all exclusion of the air from contact with the metal so employed. Sir Christopher Wren urges this latter point strongly, and says that in "Cramping of stones no iron should be within nine inches of air, if possible;" and he advocates the employment of strong mortar as the fixing medium, "seeing," he says, "that it has been observed in taking out cramps from stonework at least four hundred years old, which were so crusted in mortar that the air was perfectly excluded, the iron appeared as fresh as from the forge."

With *Buttresses, Water-tables, String courses and mouldings*, generally, the mason has to set, fit and construct, in reference to which Mr. Blackburne says: "as portions of constructive masonry, though of themselves in a measure simple are matters, executively speaking, requiring some consideration on the part of the mason. As features adding much to the proper and effective character of the outline in a building, it is of no little consequence that the latter should be fully alive to the spirit and character of the detail desired to be exhibited by the architect designing the same. It is not sufficient that he should confine himself solely to the manipulation, according as it is to be obtained from the drawing or section, of such furnished to him.

There is something beyond this essential to the perfect realization, in many cases, of the architect's desire and intention, in aid of which the manual capability possessed by the mason is to be assisted by a knowledge of the theoretic and artistic principles which he has to put in a material shape. It is vain to expect, without the existence and possession of this in him, that the most perfect design can be properly carried out; and the maxim applies not only to the mere ornamental features or enrichments of stone work, but equally to every part of the wrought or chiselled portions. Dependence, on the part of the architect, upon the mason's correct appreciation of the proper form of a particular moulding, exists here almost to the same extent as it does in the case of the more elaborate operations of the carver; and as it often happens in the carrying out of a work, points arise unforeseen, and, consequently, unexpressed when the design is prepared, it cannot be questioned but that something more than the mere *manual-labor knowledge of his work is necessary to be known*, to enable the mason to properly carry out that which is set before him. It has often been objected that the operator is employed to work, and not to think. The general admission of this would paralyze correct expression in all art. Fortunately, however, this would appear to be less likely than those who advocate this theory could wish, since, for the education of the art workman, many facilities are now afforded which did not formerly exist, and which it should be the object of all who are interested in its progress to aid and assist. The *art-workman* should be thought-tutored as well as *hand-practiced*, until which time, the hand is largely a fittual hand, not only as respects the exposition of his own, such as they may be, but of the ideas of others who may seek his executive *aid*."

The above remarks, though fully applicable to the portion of masonry under consideration, may apply also to other portions of this work where examples and illustration other than of a practical manual character have been given, to show to the mind and judgment of the industrious worker, either in stone, brick, or mortar, the knowledge he should possess in regard to the art and science of masonry, to be considered a true and proficient mechanic, and to be in accord with the advance stride which scientific construction has assumed within the past few years in many of our cities throughout the states. Proceeding then with buttresses, the plainer or ordinary forms of which no particular constructive consideration present themselves. The work is for the most part usual wall work, the outer and inner angles of the projections, etc., of free stone disposed alternately, each with a long and short return in reversed position, so as to break joint; and this is the case generally, whether the main bulk of the buttress is ashlar-faced, or formed, as is very commonly the case of rubble or random, or coursed stone-work, of less free working nature. The buttress tables are generally each slope of one stone, but in works of large proportions the breadth of face frequently precludes this, and the same contain more than one piece in each course. The joints of these are of course perpendicular to the horizon, or at right angles to the beds, and it is of importance here, as in all other stonework, that the stone should be laid to bed as it does naturally in the quarry. A good tailing in of the buttress slopes is also of some consequence constructively, as well as artistically speaking. The various separations or jointings of the parts are usually, or should be so, shown on the working drawings furnished by the architect; the setting of the various forms of tablings, strings, and corbellings, etc., as connected with buttresses, and with other projections formed by varying thicknesses in different parts, usually called set-offs, or by overhanging portions of walls, require, as respects their proper treatment and formation, a due attention on the part of the operative mason. In regard to the setting and construction of the flying arch it is performed on the ordinary arch principal, the same radiating to a common center. The stones at either end, that is to say, at the respond and at the buttress forming portion of it; and upon the accuracy of position, and true arrangement of these stones, the efficiency of the action of the latter materially depends. This is particularly the case with that part which is constructed with and derives support from the buttress itself. This is the main butment, and the connection should be such that while the courses bond horizontally together, the thrust or pressure of the arch should be directed to, and thrown as vertically as possible upon the body of the buttress; the shaft and pinnacle being designed to act for constructive purposes as a superincumbent weight or resistance at the haunch of the arch.

The mason should make himself familiar and handy in the rigging of derricks and the handling of them with care, before he raises a stone to its place, be sure that it is the right one for its position in the structure, have its bed dampened, and the mortar spread just in time to receive it, lower the stone first upon one or more strips of wood as near as possible to its true position, and then by the aid of *pinch bars* it may be moved one way or the other while the mortar is damp, and truly *plumbed* and *leveled*. In using bars and rollers in handling cut stone the mason should be careful and protect the material by old carpet, etc.

In constructing rock-faced work the *line* is carried above it, and care must be taken that it is kept plumb with the cut margins of the corners and angles. All projecting courses, sills, lintels, etc., should be covered as the work progresses, and clean from all mortar stains, and other injury. A pailful of clean water should be at hand when setting cut stone, and when any fresh mortar comes in contact with the face of the work, immediately cleaned off with it. The cut stone work may be cleaned down with soap and water, or boil 1 pound of pipe clay, a quart of water, and a quart of sour beer, and put in a bit of stone blue. Wash with this mixture and when dry, rub the stone with flannel and a brush. The following remarks from an essay on "*Modern Masonary,*" will be instructive to the mechanic:

"All masonry ought to depend upon gravity for stability."

Rustics, rough faces, rock work, and other analogous forms of masonry, are not necessarily any stronger, because of the mass on the face beyond the bed bearing lines.

"Acute angles, either in beds or in joints, are not allowable. Any angle more acute than a right one tends to weakness."

"Bent heads in arch stones, or in masonry generally, must be weak."

"Mitre joints are not legitimate masonry, all mouldings must be returned. The mouldings will mitre; the bed or the joint square."

"Weight over spaces tends to weakness. Pyramidal formed arches are objectionable."

"Ashlar should have harmonious proportions. On face 1, 3, 5, on bed never less than the depth of the face, and square full to the back of the ashlar; slab *veneering* is *false* masonry."

"Arch stones should have a just proportion to the openings, and to the ashlar generally in which they are set."

"Projecting stones, bearing weight on acute angles are weak, and this mode of construction is false in masonry."

"The springing line in arches must be the line of greatest strength. Pyamids do not stand on their apex."

"Combination of **rustic** and of moulded masonry are incompatible with **strength or with** beauty."

"Single stone architraves, **mullions and groins are a cause of** weakness."

The bedding of the **courses should** be carried throughout.

"Single **stone columns** are weak, especially those **of** laminar sandstones or **of limestones.** Built columns, **like those** of the Madeleine in Paris, are **better masonry.**

"Moulding **ought** to accord **with the stone in which they are cut.** Classic **mouldings cannot be cut in sandstones so as** to show **and endure.**

"Buildings constructed **out of the stones of the district** are most in **keeping with the landscape.**

"Ashlar **faced walls should not be backed with brickwork, or with rubble, without precautions** to prevent shrinking or **separation of the parts.**

"Deep quoins **and their courses produce weak work,** especially **in towers and in spires.**

"Notched **and broken coursed masonry is only allowable** where the **stone of a district is unsuitable for a more regular form of masonry.** To spoil good stone for the sake of such imitation **is false in masonry and** extravagant in architecture. **Put every stone to its best use** in the best form and not **in the worst form.**

"Horizontal **openings cannot be spanned** with **vertical jointed** masonry; columns, architraves, and piers must be **covered** with single stones or with an arch; **joggles, dowels, and cramps** cannot **make such work good** masonry.

"All building stones which have had an aqueous formation, **such as stratified sandstones and** limestones, should **rest on their natural beds.**

"Combinations of brickwork and stones for face work are allowable **under certain conditions. Perfect courses of** bricks **may alternate with courses of stone.** Combinations of various **kinds of stone are allowable. Perfect** courses of stone **may alternate in variety."**

The tools used by the mason for cutting stone consists of the *mallet* and *chisels* of **various sizes.** The mason's mallet **differs from that used by** any other artisan, **being** similar **to a dome in contour,** excepting **a** portion of the broadest **part, which is rather** cylindrical; the handle is short, being only sufficiently long to enable it to be firmly grasped; the *point*, which is the smallest chisel, only about ¼ inch broad on the cutting edge; the *inch tool;* the *boster*, which is 2 inches wide; and the *broad tool*, the cutting edge of which is 3½ inches wide. Besides the above cutting tools the mason uses the *banker, straight edges, squares, bevels,* and *templets,* for making the shapes of the blocks, and for trying the surfaces as the work proceeds. A templet is a pattern for cutting a block to any particular shape; when the work is moulded, the templet is called a *mould;* and are commonly made of sheet zinc, carefully cut to the profile of the mouldings with shears and files. For setting his work in place he uses the *trowel, lines* and *pins,* the *square, level, plumb* and *battering rules.* In setting heavy masonry the mason uses the derrick. In hoisting blocks of stone they are attached to the tackle by means of a simple contrivance called a *lewis*.

Cost of Masonry.—The following estimates are from the best authorities obtainable on the subject: Every item composing the total cost is liable to much variation; therefore we can merely give an example to show the general principal upon which an approximate estimate may be made; assuming the wages of a common laborer to be $2.00 per day for 8 hours working, and $3.50 per day for a mason:

Cost of Ashlar Facing Masonry.—The average size of the stones, say 5 feet long, 2 feet wide and 1 foot 4 inches thick, or two such stones to a cubic yard. Then supposing the stone to be granite or gneiss, the cost per cubic yard of masonry will be:

Getting out the stone from the quarry by blasting, allowing ¼ for waste in dressing, 1¼ cub. yd. at $3..	$4 00
Dressing 14 ft. of face at 35 cts..................	4 90
Dressing 52 ft. of beds and joints at 18 cts........	9 36
Hauling, say one mile; loading and unloading.....	1 20
Mortar, say...	40
Laying, including scaffolding, hoisting machinery, etc...	2 00
Net cost..	21 86

Profit, say 15 per cent, to contractor............ 3 28

Total cost............................... $25 14

Dressing will cost more if the faces are to be rounded, or moulded. If the stones are smaller than we have assumed there will be more square feet per cubic yard to be dressed, etc. If, in the foregoing case, the stones be perfectly well dressed on all sides, including the back, the cost per cubic yard will be increased about $10; and if some of the sides be curved, as in arch stones, say $12 or $14; and if the blocks are carefully wedged out to given dimensions, $16 or $18, thus making the net cost of the dressed stone at the quarry, say $36 to $38 per cubic yard. The item of laying will be much increased if the stones are to be raised to great heights; or if it has to be much handled; as when carried in scows, or to be deposited in water piers, etc.

Almost every large work presents certain modifying peculiarities, which must be left to the judgment of the contractor.

Cost of large scabbled granite rubble, such as is usually used for the foregoing ashlar; stones average about ½ cubic yard each.

At the above rates of wages:

Getting out the stone from the quarry by blasting, allowing ⅛ for waste in scabbling; 1¼ cubic yards at $3.00 .... $3 43
Hauling one mile, loading and unloading.......... 1 20
Mortar, 2 cubic feet, or 1. 6 struck bushels of quicklime, either in lump or ground, and 10 cub. ft. or 8 struck bushels of sand or gravel, including mixing... 1 50
Scabbling, laying, including scaffold, hoisting machinery, etc..................................... 2 50

Net cost....................................... $8 63
Profit to contractor, say 15 per ct................. 1 29

Total cost............................. $9 92

Common rubble of small stones, the average size being such as two men can handle, costs to get out at the quarry about 80 cents per yard of pile; or to allow for waste, say $1.00; hauling one mile, $1.00. It can be roughly scabbled and laid for $1.20 more; mortar as foregoing, $1.50. Total net cost, $4.70; or with 15 per ct. profit, $5.40, at the rate of wages herein stated.

With smaller stones, such as one man can handle, we may say stone, 70 cents; hauling, $1.00; laying, and scaffold, tools, etc , $1.00; mortar, $1.50, making the net cost, $4.20; or with 15 per cent profit, $4.83.

Neat scabbled irregular range work cost from $2 to $3 per yard more than the common rubble, according to the character of the stone, etc.

The laying of thin walls cost more than that of thick ones, such as abutments, etc.

Cost of ashlar facing masonry. If the stone be sand stone, with good natural beds, the getting out may be put at $3 per cubic yard.

Face dressing at 26 cents per square foot, say $3.64 per cubic yard. Bends and joints, 13 cents per square foot, say $6.76 per cubic yard. The neat cost laid $17, instead of $21.86 per cubic yard for granite; and the total cost $19.55, instead of the $25.14 for granite.

And the total cost of large well scabbled ranged sandstone masonry including mortar may be taken at about $10 per cubic yard, at the stated cost for wages. When dressed ashlar facing is backed up by rubble the expenses per cubic yard of the entire mass will of course vary according to the proportion of the two.

Thus if ashlar at $12 be backed up by an equal thickness of rubble at $5, the mean cost will be $\frac{\$12 + \$5}{2} = \$8.50$, or if the rubble be twice as thick as the ashlar, then $\frac{\$12 + 5 + 5}{3}$

= $7.33, etc. At the above prices, cellar and other walls of rough rubble are generally estimated at from $5 to $6 per perch of 22 cubic feet of wall. Outside walls with a facing of broken range rock-work of sandstone (as common in

Gothic chuches), is generally estimated at \$8 to \$10 per 22 feet in wall including everything. A perch of stone work, in walls or foundations, measure $24\frac{3}{4}$ cubic feet. (Trautwine, C. E).

Dressing stone.—A stone cutter will first take out of wind and then fairly patent hammer dress, 8 to 10 feet of plain face in hard granite, in a day of 8 hours working or twice as much of such inferior dressing as is generally bestowed on the beds and joints; and generally on the faces of bridge masonry, etc., when a very fine finish is not required. In good sandstone and marble he can do about one-fourth more than in granite. Of *finest* hammer finish, of granite 4 to 5 feet.

A cubic yard of solid stone broken up and thrown together in a pile will measure about $1\frac{9}{10}$ yards of pieces; when a yard of pieces are built in a wall, adding the space which the mortar occupies, they will measure up about 22 cubic feet of wall.

Hauling by Horses.—When working all day, say 10 working hours, the average rate at which a horse walks while hauling a load, and while returning with empty vehicles, is about 2 to $2\frac{1}{4}$ miles per hour; but to allow for stoppages to rest, etc., it is safest to take it at $1\frac{8}{10}$ miles per hour, or 160 feet per minute.

The time lost in each trip, in loading and unloading, may usually be taken at about 15 minutes. Therefore, to find the number of loads that can be hauled to any given distance, first find the time required in minutes in hauling one load and returning empty. Thus: Divide the number of feet in the round trip by 160 feet. The quotient is the number of minutes the horse is in motion during each trip. To this quotient add 15 minutes lost each trip by loading and unloading; the sum is the total time in minutes occupied in each trip. Divide the number of minutes (600) in a working day by the number of minutes required in the round trip, the quotient will be the number of loads hauled per day.

In estimating rough quarry stone for buildings, etc., bear in mind that each cubic yard of common, scabbled, rough masonry requires the hauling of about $1\frac{2}{10}$ cubic yards of the stone as usually piled up for sale in the quarry, or otherwise; or about $\frac{3}{4}$ of a cubic yard of the original rock in place. A *cubic yard of solid stone*, when broken up into pieces, *usually occupies about* $1\frac{2}{10}$ *cubic yards perfectly loose*; or about $1\frac{3}{4}$ yards when piled up. A strong cart for stone hauling will weigh about $\frac{3}{4}$ tons, or 1500 lbs., and will hold stone enough for a perch of rubble masonry; or $1\frac{2}{10}$ pers. of the rough stone in piles. The average weight of a good working horse is about $\frac{1}{2}$ ton. (Trautwine, C. E.)

Stone.—In selection of building stones for the exterior walls of a building, *color, texture* and *durability* are objects of the first importance; and all of these should be combined to render the structure perfect. Too little attention has been given to the subject of building stones; and while on the one hand we are largely using a brown stone, which gives a somber, cheerless aspect to the structure, the opposite extreme has been sought in the white marble, or that which is more nearly white in color. In a few eastern towns we find the light gray granites now used in preference to the brown free stone, the white marble, or the dark granite which have been much in use in the past years. No one can fail to experience the sensation of relief afforded by the structures, of light, colored granites in the city of Boston, or those of the buff or dove colored limestones in the city of Chicago, or of the light, gray free-stone of many buildings in Cleveland and other places, and of the buff colored brick of Milwaukee. In these cases we have not the excessive reflection of light, or the glare which comes from white buildings whether of marble or painted brick; nor the somber, cheerless expression of the darker stone, caused by its great absorption of light. In many cases where the rock is homogeneous throughout and the color uniform and satisfactory, it is only to be inquired whether the coloring material is such as will produce decay or disintegration of the particles. When the general color is produced by the aggregation of different materials of distinct coloration, the character of each one is considered, and its effects upon the whole; and it is important to have such material comparatively fine grained, and the different parts as uniformly mingled together as posssble. As a general rule, it is only in the darker stones that the coloring matters has any tendency to disintegrate the mass. In the selection of building stones the simple presentation of a sample is not enough. The rock in place should be examined in the outset; for in its material outcrops it has been exposed to the action of the weather, in all its influences, for many thousands of years. One of the principles taught in elementary geology is that the soft and decomposing rocks appear in low rounded and flattened exposures, or entirely covered by the soil of their own debris, forming no conspicuous feature in the country; while on the contrary the harder rocks stand out in relief, producing marked and distinguishing features in the landscape.

It is true, however, that no artificial structure or position will ever subject the stone to the same degree of weathering influence to which it is exposed in its natural position, but the same changes in degree will supervene upon any freshly exposed surfaces In its natural position the bed has been encased in ice, washed by currents, saturated with rains and melting snows, frozen and thawed, and exposed to the extreme of summer heat without mitigation.

The rock which has withstood these influences is quite equal to withstand the exposures of a few centuries in an artificial structure. Yet there are occasionally modifying influences and conditions which have sometimes subdued the permanence of a building stone, and given preference to others less durable. It therefore becomes necessary to carefully examine all these conditions, and to determine not only from the rock in place, but also from its physical constitution, whether it will meet the requirements of the structure proposed. It not infrequently happens, in working a quarry, that layers are reached which have not been exposed to the weather, and it is then necessary to test the strength and power of endurance of the stone.

This may be done by repeated exposure of freezing and thawing, by testing the strength or power of resistance to pressure, etc. The exposure to freezing and thawing will not only determine its power of resisting the action of the weather, but will determine also whether such foreign ingredients as iron pyrites may exist in the mass.

Chemical analysis may be resorted to, for the purpose of comparison with specimens of known composition and durability; but chemical analysis alone cannot determine, without other testing experiments, the strength or power of endurance of stone. In some countries, and in certain localities in our own country, the evidence obtained from ancient structures is available in determining the durability of the stone which has been used. Yet it would seem that this information has been of little avail in many places, when the rebuilding of edifices is repeated every century. Experience in many cases does not teach the lesson anticipated; and when a dilapidated structure is pointed out, the argument is made that "these stones are not well selected" or they were obtained "at the first opening of the quarry, and were not as good as now furnished."

And, again, there are few cases where parties are permitted to select the material without prejudice, the influence of interest, or the absence of important information. Examples are everywhere before us of the improper selection of materials for buildings, and these examples do not deter from their use in the erection of others. When good material is abundant and accessible, it will be used; in other situations, comparatively few durable structures are likely to be erected. The rock or varieties of rock offered in nature, and from which we are compelled to make our selections, may be named under the following heads:

1. *Granite, Sienite, Geneiss, etc.*
2. *Marbles*, or *Matamorphic crystalline limestones.*
3. *Limestones.*
4. *Sandstones*, or *Freestones*; and all the stones used in building under whatever names they may be known, are composed of a few essential elementary minerals. These are: 1. **Silica** or **Quartz**; 2. *Alumina-Clay*, or *Argillaceous matter;* 3. **Carbonate of lime;** 4. *Carbonate of magnesia.*

Beyond these, except in crystalline rocks, the presence of other materials is almost non-essential or advantageous, and usually injurious to the integrity of the mass. The ultimate chemical composition of a stone has little to do, as a general rule, with its character for durability, nor will a chemical analysis determine the value of a stone for building purposes.

Manner of laying.—Sandstones or Freestones and all varieties of argillaceous sandstones should be laid in the building according to the natural bedding of the rock, so that the wear of the elements may act upon the exposed edges of the laminæ. Since it is impossible to have any great thickness of stratified stone, especially sandstone, entirely uniform and homogenous in texture, or without interlamination, it follows that by turning the blocks upon their edges, we shall in one case have the face of a harder or coarser layer, and in another of a softer layer of the same rock, thus exposing the wall to unequal weathering. Not infrequently the face of the stone is the line of the soft shaley parting, and the effects of this practice may often be seen in the scaling off of an entire surface of a block of ashlar for several feet square in extent.

Such examples may be seen in some of our buildings, which have been erected within the past twenty-five years. Had these blocks been laid in an opposite direction, the edges of the shapely seams only would have been exposed, and their destruction would have been comparatively slow. The sandstones separate usually with great freedom along the line of bedding, and thus offer great facilities for dressing the surface in the direction of the laminæ; and from this course, and a desire to present as large a surface as practicable in each block, has arisen the practice of setting them upon their edges. A block of stone may, however, be split in the same direction, through one of its more sandy layers, and the objections urged may not be so palpable. An equally reprehensible practice is the cutting of step stones from blocks with distinct shaley partings, which produce exfoliation and consequently inequality of the surface.

Mode of dressing.—In the use of argillaceous sandstones, as well as some other rocks, there are some considerations as to the mode of dressing which should not be forgotten. There are some stones which, if dressed elaborately, disintegrate rapidly upon the surface.

This comes from the crushing of the material under the tool (called by the workmen *deadening*); the natural texture and cohesion of the particles being broken up, it absorbs more water, and on freezing decays rapidly and becomes unsightly. Many stones that are unfit for finely dressed work are nevertheless quite durable if rough dressed; that is, by dressing the joints close and a smooth space along the edge, while the greater part of the face is left roughly broken without tool work of any kind. During wet weather, the moisture will collect at the numerous projecting points or edges, and much of it drops off, which would be absorbed by a smooth dressed face stone. The effect of freezing is much less destructive under such conditions. Moreover, a moderate degree of weather wearing on such surface is less conspicuous than on finely dressed stone.

Durability of Building Stone.—Dr. Alexander A. Julien has made examinations of buildings of various ages and of tombstones of the older grave yards around New York city to assist in determining the durability of the various stones used in buildings in this country. The coarse brown stone, which is largely employed, appears to be one of the most perishable materials in use, so that many builders are returning to brick, although the firm varieties of brown stone are better and compare favorably with other materials. Among the causes of decay of this stone are mentioned, erection on bed of lamination, the heat of the sun on exposed sides, and imperfect pointing with poor mortar, which falls away and leaves the joints exposed to the weather. The presence of sea salt in the atmosphere has exerted no appreciable effect, and lichens growing on the stone do not appear to have occasioned any decay or corrosion. The light-colored Nova Scotia sandstones have been too recently introduced to show marked defect, but evidences of exfoliation and of slight moldering in damp spots have begun to appear.

Buildings constructed of the Amherst (Ohio) sandstone show little decay, only discoloration; and that is regarded as a favorable sign rather than otherwise, for it indicates durability, while a stone that cleans itself does so by disintegration of its surface, the grains dropping out and carrying away the dirt. The coarse fossiliferous limestone from Lockport has disintegrated rapidly within the last ten years, chiefly on account of careless arrangement in masonry. The oölitic stone from Ellettsville, Indiana, shows an almost immediate and irregular discoloration, said to be produced by exudation of oil. The oölitic from Caen, France, has shown decay in several instances where it was not protected with paints. The dolomitic marble from Westchester county, N. Y., has decayed considerably after sixty years of use, but much of this is owing to the stone having been improperly laid. Often marbles of various kinds in tombstones are in fairly good conditions Horizontal slabs show a tendency to bend. The frequent obliteration of inscriptions, the general and often rapid granulation of the surface, and the occasional fissuring of slabs, show that the decay of marble—in the varieties hitherto long used in New York city—is steady, inevitable, and but a question of time; and if unprotected, this material is likely to prove unsuitable for out of door use, at least for decorative purposes or cemetery records, within the atmosphere of a city.

A blue stone or gray wacke is yearly coming into more general use, and though somewhat sombre in tone and difficult to dress, seems likely to prove a material of remarkable durability. The bluish Quincy granite has been used in many buildings, and rarely shows as yet many signs of decay. A fine grained granite from Concord, New Hampshire, also promises to be durable. The light colored and fine grained granite of Hallowell, Maine, in which the white feldspar predominates, has shown some exfoliation, but in the single building in which this is remarked, the stones appear to have been set on edge, and as their structure is laminated, that is an important matter. The weathering of granite does not proceed by a merely superficial wear, which can be measured or limited by fractions of an inch, but by a deep insinuation along the lines of weakness, between grains, through cleavage-planes, and into latent fissures. Thus, long before the surface has become much corroded or removed, a deep disintegration has taken place by which large fragments are ready for separation by frost, from the edges and angles of a block.

When directly exposed to the heat of the sun, an additional agency of destruction is involved, and the stone is suddenly found ready to exfoliate, layer after layer, concentrically. The following is an approximative estimate of the *life* of different kinds of stone, signifying by the term life, without regard to discoloration or other objectionable qualities, merely the period after which incipient decay of the variety becomes sufficiently offensive to the eye to demand repair or renewal: Coarse brown stone, *five to fifteen years;* laminated fine brown stone, *one hundred* to *two hundred* years; blue stone, untried, probably *centuries;* Nova Scotia stone, untried, perhaps *fifty* to *two hundred years;* Ohio sandstone (best siliceous variety), perhaps from *one* to many *centuries;* coarse fossiliferous limestone, *twenty* to *forty* years; fine oolitic (American) limestone, untried, coarse dolomite marble, *forty years;* fine dolomite marble, *sixty* to *eighty* years; fine marble, *fifty* to *two hundred years;* granite, *seventy-five* to two hundred years; gneiss, *fifty years* to many centuries.

Many of the best building stones in the country have never been brought to the city. In this country the endurance of stone in a great measure depends to a great extent on its power to resist the action of frost, as we may easily satisfy ourselves by an inspection of the walls of buildings all around us. The determination of the power to resist this action is accomplished by soaking the stone in a strong solution of sulphate of soda, and then permitting the salt to crystalize in its pores; repeating the operation a few times, the stone soon begins to show effects, which are measured by weighing the particles that are broken off. Another method of estimating the same disintegrating action is that proposed by Professor J. C. Draper, of alternately heating and then quenching it in cold water, and weighing the detached particles.

The Preservation of Building Stones.—The following abstract is taken from a paper read before the American Institute of Architects at their eighteenth annual meeting, Albany, N. Y., October, 1884, by Dr. R. Ogden Doremus: He mentioned many well known buildings that were crumbling away, such as Girard College, the College of New York, Trinity Church, N. Y. He had dined with Gorridge soon after the obelisk was put up in Central Park, and the subject of the weathering of the obelisk was suggested. Gorridge said that it had stood 4,000 years, and would stand 4,000 years more. But, in fact, the obelisk is crumbling away. He showed several vials full of chippings collected at the foot of it; also specimens of stone found peeled off from inside the new capitol during the visit of the institute to it in the afternoon. A simple remedy was suggested, and one that has been extensively applied in St. Louis, and to some extent in New York, namely, an application of paraffin mixed with a little creosote.

The building is heated by a small furnace, and when there is ornamental work a blow pipe is sometimes required to heat depressions.

The paraffine is then applied in a melted condition, and sinks in about a quarter of an inch, giving a beautiful and indestructible glossy finish, and rendering the material absolutely water proof and air tight.

In reply to a question about fire, he said that a fire would only drive it in a little.

It costs on an average about 50 cents a yard, and never needs to be applied a second time, as no chemical agent in the air or in the rain affects it at all. Even caustic potash does not unite with it.

If the application is made to marble that has been weather beaten the marble should first be cleaned with steel brushes.

Marble thus cleaned, however, unless treated with paraffine soon becomes covered with a yellow stain, as appears in the building 50 Wall St., N. Y. Some of the buildings in New York, which have been treated with paraffine are St. Mark's Memorial Church, houses 124-6 South Fifth Ave., and other buildings in New York.

The paraffine method is confidently commended by Dr. Doremus as the very best used. Kuhlman's process consists in coating the surface of stone to be preserved with a solution of potash or soda silicate. The hardening of the surface is due to the decomposition of potash or soda silicate. If the material operated upon be a limestone, potash carbonate, lime silicio-carbonate, and silica will be deposited; besides which the carbonic acid in the air will combine with some of the potash, causing an efflorescence on the surface which will eventually disappear. When applied to lime sulphate, crystallization takes place, which disintegrates the surface. In order to correct the discoloration of stone sometimes produced by the application of preservation solutions, Kuhlmann proposed that the surfaces should be colored. Surfaces that are too light may be darkened by treatment with a durable manganese and potash silicate.

Those that are too dark may be made lighter by adding baryta sulphate to the silicious solutions. By introducing the iron, copper, and manganese sulphate he obtained reddish-brown, green and brown colors. Among other processes which have been tried are: Solution of baryta followed by solution of ferro-silicate acid so as to fill the pores of the stone with an insoluble ferro-silicate of baryta; solution of baryta followed by solution of superposphate of lime producing an insoluble lime phosphate and baryta phosphate. Soluble alumina oxalate applied to lime stones produces insoluble lime and alumina oxalate. These three processes last alluded to possess the advantage of producing by the changes they undergo within the structure of the stone an insoluble substance, without at the same time giving rise to the formation of soluble salt likely to cause efflorescence which necessarily attends the use of alkaline silicates.

Ultimate average crushing loads in tons per square foot for stones, etc. The stones are supposed to be on *bed*, and the height to be not less than two or three times the least *side*. Stones generally begin to crack or split under about one-half of their crushing loads. In practice, according to some authorities, neither stone or brickwork, should be trusted with more than $\frac{1}{10}$ to $\frac{1}{8}$ of the crushing load, according to circumstances and some authorities:

	Tons sq. ft.	Av. tons.
Granites and Syenites	300 to 1200	750
Limestones and Marbles		700
Oolites, good	100 to 250	175
Sandstones for building	150 to 250	
Sandstone, red of Connecticut and New Jersey		200
Brick	50 to 300	175
Brickwork, ordinary cracks with	20 to 30	25
Brickwork, first rate in cement	50 to 70	60
Brickwork, good in cement	30 to 40	35
Slate	400 to 800	600
Caen stone	100 to 200	150
Caen stone to crack	20 to 30	25
Plaster of Paris, 1 day old		40
Concrete, lime 1 part, gravel 3 parts, 3 weeks old	30 to 50	**40**
Portland hydraulic cement, English. pure, 6 weeks' old	80 to 160	120
Portland cement, 1 part, 1 part sand		80
Portland cement, 1 part, 3 part sand		40

	Av. tons.
Portland cement, 10 splts shingle......	18
Roman hydraulic cement, English pure.	50
Roman, 1 part cement, 2 parts sand...	5
Sheppy & Atkinson's cement, pure.....	80

Mensuration.—Every mason should understand how to estimate the quantity of superficial feet contained within any form or figure, as well as its solid contents. From an ignorance alone of these simple rules of mensuration, many an honest and capable mechanic has been left in the rut, and struggled on for a life-time as a wage-worker for men, generally as found, less skillful than himself as a mechanic. I, therefore, urge upon every mason the necessity of making himself familiar with these simple rules, and to carry them every day with him and apply them in a practical manner with his work, and after a short while he will begin to understand them to his advantage. *Masonry*, in a word, is nothing more or less than *practical mensuration*, and, therefore, every mason should thoroughly understand it.

I will take it for granted, that every mason is acquainted with the elementary principels of arithmetic, that may be learned in a primary school book, and if he is the examples which are here given, or the principels on which they are computed, may be applied when estimating upon work from the proportions of the smallest hut to the most embellished cathedral.

The meaning of the *signs* and *marks:*

+ plus, or more; the sign of addition: as 5 + 6 = 11. ——
minus, or less; the sign of substraction: as 20 — 5 = 15.
× multiply by; the sign of multiplication: as 8 × 9 = 72.
÷ divide by; the sign of division: as 16 ÷ 4 = 4. == equal to; the sign of equality: as 27 cubic feet = 1 cubic yard.
:: proportion; the sign of proportion: as 3 : 6 :: 8 : 16. $\frac{1}{4}$ fraction. '√ square root. '√ cube root. ' feet. " inches.

The following **table** of **measurement is used for stone and brickwork in many** places:

1 Perch, mason's or quarrymen's measure,

16½ feet long, ⎫
16 inches wide, ⎬ = 22 cubic feet; to be measured in **wall**.
12 inches high, ⎭

16½ feet long, ⎫
18 inches wide, ⎬ = 24.75 cubic feet; to be measured in pile.
12 inches high, ⎭

1 cubic yard = 3 feet × 3 feet × 3 feet = 27 cubic feet.

The cubic yard has become the standard for all contract work of late years. Stone walls less than 16 inches thick count as if 16 inches thick to mason; over 16 inches thick, each inch additional is measured.

The following number of brick also are allowed for each square foot of face of wall in measuring brickwork when laid by the thousand by the mason in some places:

Thickness of wall.		No. brick.
4 inches		7½
8 "		15
12 "		22½
16 "		30
20 "		37½
24 "		46
28 "		52½
32 "		60
36 "		67½
42 "		75

Cubic yard = 600 bricks in wall.
Perch (22 cubic feet) = 500 brick in wall.
To pave 1 sq. yard on flat requires 48 brick.
To pave 1 sq. yard on edge requires 68 brick.
Square yard = 3 feet × 3 feet = 9 square feet.

We will now proceed to the various forms of plain surfaces, and the methods of measuring them, and beginning with the *square*, which has four equal sides, and four right angles, as A, B, C, D. *Rule:* Multiply the given side by itself, and the product is the area required.

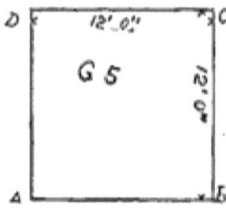

Ex. 12 × 12' = 144'.

The next figure will be a *parallelogram*, or oblong square.
Rule: Multiply the length by the breadth and the product gives the area.
Ex. 18′ 0″ × 6′ 0″ = 108′ 0″.

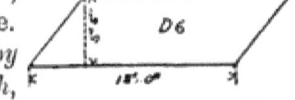

The next figure will be a *rombus*, which has four sides all equal but not right angle.
Rule: Multiply the base by the perpendicular height and the product is the area.
Ex. 16′ 0″ × 14′ 0′ = 224′ 0″.

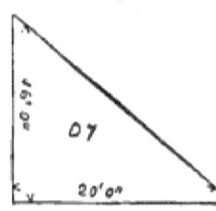

The next figure will be the *rhomboid*, which has its two sides *equal* and *parallel*, but no *right angle*; it is a long square pushed aside.
Rule: Multiply the longer side by the perpendicular height, or breadth, and the product is the area. Ex. 18′ 0″ × 5′ 6″ = 99′ 0″.

The next figure will be a right-angled triangle, having one of its angles a true square; or just 90 degrees. *Rule: Multiply one of the legs forming the right angle by half the other;* the product is the area. Ex. 16′ 0″ ÷ 2 = 8′ × 20′ 0″ = 160′.

The next figure will be a tri-angle. *Rule: Multiply the longest side by one-half the perpendicular, and the product is the content.*
Ex. 14′ 0″ ÷ 2 = 7′ 0″ × 24′ 0″ = 168′ 0″; area required tri-angle.

The next figure will be the tra-pezium, which consists of four unequal angles; it is, indeed, two triangles, and may be measured at twice, as shown in the preceding triangle, or by this *Rule: Multiply the diagonal by one-half the sum of the two perpendiculars.* Ex. 8′ 0″ + 4′ 0 = 12′ 0″ ÷ 2 = 6′ 0″ × 20′ 0″ = 120′ 0″; the area required.

The next figure will be the area of a circle. *Rule: Square the diameter, and multiply that product by* ·7854, a decimal, and the product will be the content.

Ex. 12′ 0″ × 12′ 0″ = 144′ 0″ × .7854 = 113.0976.

The next diagram will be a segment, or part of a section of a circle; to measure this: *Multiply* **half** *the sum of the two arches by one of the ends*, and the product will give the area. Ex. 24′ 0″ + 18′ 0″ = 42′ 0″ ÷ 2 = 21′ 0″ × 2′ 0″ = 42′ 0″, is the area required.

Where the figure is found of the shape annexed, with two right angles, and the sides not parallel, instead of dividing it and measuring it as a parallelogram and an angle, take the *mean* of the two perpendiculars and *multiply* by the *length;* the product will be the area required. Ex. 12′ 0″ + 8′ 0″ = 20′ 0″ ÷ 2 = 10′ 0″ × 32′ 0″ = 320; area.

It is now necessary to take into consideration the methods of measuring solid or cubic bodies; for example, to begin, viz.: a solid bounded by **six square sides,** similar to a die. *Rule: Multiply the side by itself,* and that product by the *side again;* the **last** product will be the **solid** content. Ex. 6′ 0″ × 6′ 0″ × = 36′ 0″ × 6′ 0″ = 216′ 0″, cubic feet.

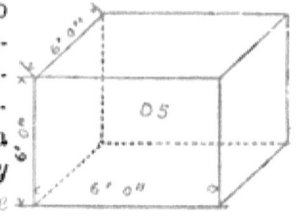

The next is the *parallelopipedon,* or *oblong cube. Rule: Multiply the breadth* by the *depth* and the product by the *length;* this last product will be the content of it.

Next proceed to the prism, to meas-

ure which find the area at the end, multiply that by the length, and that product is the content. Ex. The perpendicular height, 6' 0" ÷ 2 = 3' 0" × 12' 0" = 36' 0" × 32' 0" = 1152' 0".

The inclined plane and *wedge* may be measured by the same *rule* as the prism.

The next figure is a square pyramid, and the one-half of which is a very prominent formation in banks, and is measured by *multiplying* the *area* of the *base* by *one-third* the *height* or *length*. Ex. 6' 0" × 6' 0" = 36' 0" × 6' 0" 216' 0"; content.

Arriving now at the cylinder, this is measured by *multiplying* the *area* of the *base*, or *end*, by the *length*. Ex. 12' 0" × 12' 0" = 144' 0" × .7854 = 113, 0976 × 20' 0" = 2260 0".

The cone is also measured by *multiplying* the *area* of the *base* by *one-third* the *perpendicular height*. Ex. 12' 0" × 12' 0" = 144' 0" × .7854 = 113' 0" × 6' 8" = 753' 4".

The next figure is the *frustum* of a square *pyramid*, which also is a form peculiar in embankments and cuttings. *Rule :* To *four times* the *area* of the *mean* base add the area of each end, which divide by 6; multiply the product by the length, you will find the contents. Ex. 4' 0" + 6' 0" = 10' 0" ÷ 2 = 5' 0", the *mean* height of the base, or thickness, will be 5' 0"; 5' 0" × 5' 0" = 25' 0" × 4' 0" = 100' 0" + 36' 0" = 136' 0" + 16' 0" = 152' 0" ; 152' 0" ÷ 6' 0" = 25' 4" × 20' 0" = 506' 8", contents.

The same rule applies to the *frustum* of a cone. I know of no quantity of excavating, **masonry, brickwork** or plastering, pertaining to a structure, **that may not be** estimated by applying the rules given in calculating the superficial and solid measurement of the above plain examples. And, any mason that will thoroughly make himself familiar with the items in respect to the *labour*, as given in their several branches of this work—as excavating, masonry, bricklaying and plastering, etc.—and ascertaining the local prices of the different materials, may consider himself competent to estimate upon any structure in an intelligent manner.

Gauging.—Gauging is the art of measuring the capacity of casks and vessels of any form. To gauge accurately use the following general rule: Having taken the necessary linear measurements, compute by the rules of mensuration given, the volum of the inside of the cask or vessel in cubic inches. Divide this by 2150.42 for the measurement in bushels, by 282 for beer gallons, by 231 for wine gallons.

Plain and ornamental brickwork.—The art of erecting edifices or walls of brick cemented together with mortar. I will therefore treat the subject in a general manner, so as to give the mechanic a thorough understanding of the different parts he often is called upon to exercise his skill in the erection of a building. For the business of a bricklayer or mason not only consists in the performance of all kinds of brickwork and stonework, but he is often called upon to take charge of the erection of an edifice, and works of construction and to carry them on to a successful termination; and he should, therefore, be familiar with all the knowledge necessary to that end, for those who have the reputation of possessing such knowledge, their employment is more anxiously sought for by those who carry on the business of erecting buildings, as well as by the public generally who have work of a private character to be done; we have, therefore, not only in this portion of our book, but in every other part of it, endeavored to place before the mind of the practical mason that knowledge which we deem essential for him to possess to be in harmony with the advanced stage of construction that is being advocated in many parts of our country at the present time.

In preparing for the erection of any building the first

thing the mechanic should make himself familiar with is the plan, elevation and section of the proposed edifice (see plans and drawings), and upon which too much care cannot be bestowed, so that he may get them thoroughly impressed upon his mind, for by so doing very many mistakes will be prevented.

The determination of the exact position of an intended building being sometimes difficult to accomplish, a few remarks on the subject may be acceptable.

The setting out of the leading lines are simple enough on level ground, when nothing occurs to interrupt the view, or to prevent the direct measurement of the required distances; but to perform this operation at the bottom of a foundation trench when the surrounding ground is blocked up with brick and stone and other material, requires a degree of skill and patience not always to be met with. Before, therefore, the excavation is begun it is necessary to establish the centre and main front lines by driving proper stakes a sufficient distance from the excavation that they may not be disturbed and are accessible at any time to draw lines from, which the mason with the use of a plummet is enabled to locate at the bottom of the trench or cellar, as the case may be, those lines being fixed, it is then easy enough to measure from them all the rest or side lines. It is also necesrary that he establish in the middle of the cellar a proper guide to regulate him in carrying his work up to its several heights, as drains, areas, door sills and lintels, window sills and lintels, all slots and chimney starting points, height of floor joists, etc. This is accomplished by erecting a smooth broad board in the middle of the cellar, or works, and marking upon it the grade line which must be transferred from the surveyor's stake, or one established by the parties interested, this being done, mark from it the several distances downward as they are shown upon the section plan of the building; resource can be had from time to time to this until the walls are up to receive the first tier of timbers, which will guide him thereafter. This is a very simple and practicable manner to engineer a foundation out of the excavation, and saves time in not being compelled to refer continually to the plans. When the excavations have been made, the ground must be tried by the repeated blows of a rammer, or by driving into it an iron bar, and working it backwards and forwards, in order to ascertain whether it be sufficiently firm to sustain the proposed weight of the building. If it be not sufficiently firm, it must be piled and planked, or sleepered and planked as the case may require. Or a layer of concrete may be put down under the walls, which is the common way of dealing with unreliable soils at the present time. The operation of piling consists in driving large piles of wood, tapered at one end, and shod with iron, into the earth, till they extend the whole width of the footings; and then, at any distance, not exceeding 5 feet, drive another course; and so in continuation throughout the whole length of the walling.

This operation being completed, the ground between the different courses of piles, in the longitudinal direction of the wall, is well rammed and made good. Planks of wood called sleepers, are then laid on the heads of the piles, in a transverse direction to the length of the building; and other planks are laid in the opposite direction, that is, with their length extending in the direction of the length of the wall, resting partly on the sleepers, and partly on the ground which has been made good. Sleepered and planked consists in placing planks of wood in a similar direction to the above, without having recourse to piling. When the intended walling is to be, for instance 2 feet thick, the sleepers and plank should extend about 2 feet on each side of the wall that is the sleepers should be 6 feet in length. When the soil in general proves firm, but has in one or more places loose earth, the parts that are loose must be excavated, until the bricklayer arrives at a part that is sufficiently firm to sustain a pier or piers.

These piers, similarly to the walls of a building, must have footings; and must be carried up until they are on an exact level with the first course of the footings of the wall, of which thickness the piers must terminate at the top. Sometimes, when not very loose, the ground may be made firm, by ramming into it large stones, after the manner of paviors, which stones are close packed together, and are of a breadth at the bottom proportional to the intended insisting weight.

Foundation trenches also in good soils may here and there present bad parts of a yielding or compressible nature, the bad parts may be removed until good soil is met with, filling up the holes thus made with sharp sand.

Perhaps there is no part of the building business in which the skill and judgment of the mechanic is taxed more than the successful dealing with compressible soils in the erection of an edifice; in fact, the public look upon the operation with caution, and are not satisfied unless the work is entrusted to men of practical experience, and reputed care and judgment in the successful performance of such work. We have, therefore, subjoined extracts from reports of engineers to Congress upon such work, and of the successful operation of the building of foundations generally, that the mechanic's mind may be enlarged upon the subject, and, if his judgment be sought in regard to such matters, he may be enabled to pass it with intelligence based upon the experience of the past.

Foundations in compressible soils. Hollow iron cylinders sunk by atmospheric pressure in very compressible soils.—The principle was applied by Mr. Hughes in sinking the piles at Rochester bridge, England. With his modifications it has entirely superseded the ordinary diving bell for foundations in deep water.

Compressed air is made to free a hollow pile from the water within it after it has been placed in its situation (the bed of the river or other place), there used as a diving-bell, without again being drawn up, and remains as a part of the permanent structure. Mr. McAlpine has used it with success for a bridge over the Harlem river, N. Y., in a muddy and sandy soil. The draw piece of this bridge was composed of one central, and ten circumscribing iron columns, each 6 feet in diameter and 50 feet in height, the water being 20 feet in the deepest part. These piles were sunk by the pneumatic process (both plenum and vacuum).

It had been decided to fill the columns with concrete; and it was suggested to extend this masonry below the bottom of the iron cylinders (as the men could work in water), undermining the adjacent earth as far as practicable, and to extend the concrete into the space thus undermined. This was done in sections of about 2 feet in width; and, when the rim had been completed, it was found that the column was virtually extended, and that the crater would readily sink under the pneumatic pressure, to a level with the bottom of the concrete, so that the sand within it was easily removed, and the space filled with concrete to a depth, generally, of 4 feet or more.

The cement set with greater rapidity under the pneumatic pressure, than in the open air. The last column was driven from 16 to 20 feet in from 3 to 6 days, in sand and porous material, free from obstruction, 12 men, all told, were sufficient to do the work, including engine-drivers, stevedores, and foremen. The metal in the columns was $1\frac{1}{4}$ in thick. No ill effects were experienced by the workmen from a pressure of $2\frac{1}{2}$ atmospheres. This system is perfectly reliable in all cases where the compressible soil can be removed and a hard bottom reached on which to found the contemplated structure.

Pile foundations.—The next system for consideration is that of piles driven into the ground on which the superstructure rests directly, or through the intervention of a floor of wood or masonry.

The most extensive and oldest application of pile driving for foundations to which instructive reference can be made is in the city of Amsterdam, Europe. The original site of this city was a salt marsh. All the buildings (28,000) for a population of 224,000 souls in 1850, covering a surface of 900 acres, are supported on piles of from 50 to 60 feet in length. After passing through a mixture of peat and sand of little consistence, at a depth of about 40 feet, they enter a bed of firm clay. The ends of the piles are sawed level and covered with thick plank on which the masonry is constructed. Though the houses have declined from the perpendicular, they are considered to be quite secure against falling; yet such a contingency occurred in 1882 by the sinking and total ruin of a large block of ware-houses heavily filled with corn—wheat in bulk that shifted the weight. The palace built in 1648 is supported on 13,659 piles. It is 282 feet long, 253 feet wide, and 116 feet in height, exclusive of a cupola of 41 feet.

The labors of engineers in the valley of the Thames river at and about London, give much useful information in the construction of ancient as well as modern pile foundations.

Old London bridge was commenced in 1176, and finished about 83 years thereafter. The piers rested on piles driven only around the outside of the pier, so placed as to carry the whole weight. They were of elm, and at the expiration of 600 years on being drawn up, remained without material decay. A part of this bridge fell about 100 years after it was finished, and the whole structure was removed to give place to the new bridge in 1825.

Old Westminster bridge was built between 1733 and 1747. Piles were used under one pier only. Its piers (with one exception) were constructed in caissons or flat-bottomed boats. Each caisson contained as much timber as a forty gun frigate. They were 80 feet long by 30 feet wide. These foundations failed; the caisson bottoms or floors sunk in the middle; the sides and ends projecting beyond the stone work broke off and bent upwards. The sinking of the bearing area of the sub-stratum, under the partial and unequal pressure of the floors of the caissons, has had more to do with the failure than any other defect.

Waterloo bridge, built between 1809 and 1817. The foundations of the piers of this bridge are built in coffer-dams or caissons; the floors of which rest on piles, about 3 feet apart, under the entire base of the pier, penetrating the clay about 18 feet. The foundation is arranged with plank, concrete and stones, as in the New London bridge.

The estimated pressure per foot on the head of each pile is, in this case, about 68 tons. The arches are 120 foot span, and weigh about 2,500 tons each.

New London bridge, built between 1825 and 1831. The foundation of the piers under the entire area of the bases of the piers, the piles are about 20 feet long and 3 feet apart, penetrating the clay 18 to 19 feet. On the heads of the piles were laid sleepers; the loose earth between the heads of the piles is replaced with rubble concrete, on which blocks of stone and brick work filled up the spaces between the pile heads, and immediately the platform of oak planking which carried the first course of granite.

The pressure upon each pile is 80 tons, or 5 tons per square foot of the entire area of the pier. Each pier of this bridge settled from 6 to 10 inches towards the down stream. No further settlement is apprehended.

New Westminster bridge, built in 1858 and since. The arches of this bridge are of wrought and cast iron. Elm piles 32 feet long are driven in alternate rows of 3 and 5 ft. each, to the number of 145 in each pier, and 18 to 20 feet into the London clay, each tested to a bearing weight of 60 tons. Circumscribing the area into which the elm piles are driven, hollow cast iron 15 inch diameter, 25 feet long, are driven 4 feet apart, and between these, in grooves cast on hollow piles, flat iron piles are driven to nearly the same depth, forming a coffer-dam, within which all the soil overlaying the gravel bed is excavated, and concrete filled in to the top of the piles, which are cut off 6 inches below low water. On the heads of the elm piles is a course of stone covering two or three piles alternately, upon this the bottom course of granite of large size is laid. The bearing piles are 14 inches square driven at intervals of 1 foot 9 inches from centre to centre, to an average depth of 20 feet in the clay. It will thus be noticed that the solid stone piers sustaining the iron arches, rest upon the heads of the wooden piles, which stand a considerable height above the bed of the river; that these piles are within an enclosure of cast iron and granite slabs; and around the piles and filling up the casing or enclosure there is a solid bed of concrete as good as rock.

From the above, the conclusion arrived at by the English engineers is that the compressibility of volitic and tutiary clays can *only be overcome by piling* deep sinking, heavy ramming, or heavy weighting.

The point of **bearing** must be carried below the *possibility of upward reaction*. *The depth of a foundation in compressible* **ground** ought not to be less than *one-fourth* the intended *height* of the building above ground—that is, for a shaft of 200 feet the foundation should be made secure to a depth of 50 feet by piling or well sinking and concrete. Masses of concrete, brick or stone, placed on a compressible substratum, however cramped and bound, may prove *unsafe*. *Solidity from a considerable depth can alone be relied upon*. Mere *enlargement of a base* may not in itself be sufficient. The following weights supported by the foundations of the piers of several of the remarkable and heaviest structures in pounds per square foot :

Dome of St. Peter's, Rome...................... 35,254
" St. Paul's, London...................... 41,713
" Invalids, Paris...................... 31,862
" the Pantheon, Paris...................... 43,440
Column of the Basilica of St. Paul........ 42,950
Steeple of the Church of St. Mary's.............. 63,325

Practice and experience of **United States** *engineers* in the construction of foundations in different localities and in compressible soils :

The dry dock at the Brooklyn Navy Yard, New York, was commenced in 1841 and completed in 1851. It contains 13.837 cubic yards of masonry, resting upon 38,532 cubic feet of pile timber. The soil was found to be chiefly vegetable decomposition to the depth of 10 feet, and below this almost impalpable quick sand, containing a large proportion of mica. When confined and not mixed with water, it is very firm and unyielding, presenting a strong resistance to penetration. When saturated with water it becomes a *semi-fluid*, and moved by the slightest current of water passing over or through it. Small veins of course sand were also occasionally encountered, through which flowed springs of fresh water.

Borings were made to the depth of 80 feet and brought up sand, clay and fresh water. There is a small proportion of clay in any part of the foundation. The borings extended 40 feet below the foundation of the dock. The foundations for the superstructure of this dry-dock were placed 37 feet below mean tide and 52 feet below the surface of the ground.

Black mica overlaid the quicksand under the coffer-dam; 3504 piles were driven, averaging 39 feet in length by 15 inches square. The earth above low water was removed before the coffer-dam was formed, and about 10 feet was removed by dredging. The *semi-fluid* state in which the material was found, after the water was pumped out of the pit, was very difficult to remove. It was so fluid as to require tubs for its removal. Bottom springs of fresh water were found in about 6 feet of the required depth of the foundation; the largest discharged 10 gallons per minute. When flowing from a level of 26 feet below low water it discharged 38 gallons per minute, containing 27 ounces of sand; at a level of 22 feet it discharged 33 gallons per minute, containing 17 ounces of sand; and at a level of 17 feet it discharged 10 gallons per minute unmixed with sand. These springs presented great difficulties in laying the foundations from the flowing of the water, which as it came up brought large quantities of sand, which, if continued to flow, would soon have endangered the surrounding work.

The pressure of the water was so great as to raise the foundation however heavily it could be loaded. The settling of the piles supporting the pump well was the first evidence of undermining of one of these springs. The site of the well was changed but the spring followed, and compelled another change of the well. This spring was driven out of the old well by driving piles until it was filled up, but it immediately burst up among the *foundation piles* of the dock near by.

In a single day it made a cavity in which a pole was run down 20 feet below the foundation timber; 150 feet of stone were thrown into this hole, which settled 10 feet during the night, and 50 feet more were thrown in the following day, which drove the spring to another place where it undermined and burst up through a bed of concrete 2 feet thick. This new cavity was repeatedly filled with concrete leaving a tube for the water to flow through; but in a few days it burst up through a heavy body of concrete in a place 14 feet distant, where it soon undermined the concrete, and even the foundation piles, which settled from 1 to 8 inches, although 33 feet long and driven by a hammer of 2,200 pounds falling 35 feet at the least, blow not moving the pile ½ inch. It was then determined to drive as many additional piles into the space by means of followers to force those already driven as deep as possible. The old concrete was then removed to a depth of 20 inches below the top of the piles. An area of about 1,000 square feet around the spring was then planked, on which a floor of brick was laid in dry cement, and on that another layer of brick set in mortar. The space was next filled with concrete and the foundation completed over all. Several vent holes were left through the floor and foundation. After a few days, wnen the cement had well set, the spring was forced up to a level of about 10 feet above the former outlet at which it flowed clear without sand. Two other of these springs were closed by freezing in 1848 and forced up in one case 800, and in the other 1,200 square feet of the foundations. This took place between the lower timbers and the planking lifting also the first *course of the stone floor; which was from 12 to 15 inches thick.*

The whole number of bearing piles in the foundation is 6,549. They are chiefly round spruce timber 25 to 40 feet long, averaging 14 in diameter at the head. The average length of all the piles driven was 32 feet 7 inches. The piles were originally driven three feet from centres. Afterwards as many piles were driven as could be placed into the earth. Whenever a hammer of 2,000 pounds weight, falling 35 feet, drove the pile for the last few blows, exceeding 3 inches per blow, another and larger pile was driven alongside. With the exception of 541, all these piles were driven by hammers from 2,000 to 4,500 pounds each, falling from 35 to 40 feet. The average number of blows per pile was 151 with the small hammers and fifty blows only with the large hammers. The 541 piles were driven with a Nasmyth steam pile engine.

The foundation was mostly laid as follows : The excavation being completed to the proper depth, and piles cut off to a uniform level, 2 feet in thickness of *concrete was rammed between the bearing piles*. These piles were capped with 12 and 14 inch yellow pine timber, laid transversely with the axis of the dock, and *tre-nailed* to each pile. The concrete was then raised to the top of these timbers and a light flooring of 3 inch yellow pine plank was laid upon and spiked thereon. Another course of similar timber was then placed upon this floor, breaking joints with those below, to which they were *tre-nailed*. The intervals were next filled with concrete, and another floor of 3 inch plank spiked down; which completed the foundation. The support of this foundation is derived mainly from the cohesion of the material into which the piles were driven and slightly from their sectional area. It was ascertained that it required a weight of 122 tons to draw up one of these piles, or rather start or put it in motion, when driven 33 feet to the point of ultimate resistance with a ram of one ton falling 30 feet at the least blow.

The piles average 12 inches in diameter in the middle, making at least a support of 100 tons per square foot of foundation.

The railroad bridge at Havre de Grace, on the Susquehanna river, was commenced in October, 1862, and finished in November, 1866.

The foundation of the piers of this bridge are referred to as examples of piles driven in the compressible bed of the river, supporting an iron caisson on a grillage of timber resting on the piles, and a caisson lowered to solid rock through 15 feet of compressible soil. In 1863 piles were driven and sawed off 40 feet below the surface of the water for the foundation of pier No. 3; a platform or grillage of timber, strongly ironed, upon which the pier was to rest, was constructed near the site of the work and floated over the site of the foundation under which the piles had been driven.

This platform was placed between two substantial construction piers of timber; lowering screws, 6 in number, of

3½ inch diameter, were attached by hooks to the platform; and to the construction piers a section of an iron caisson was constructed, resting upon the wooden platform thus suspended. The masonry was then built within the caisson, lowered by means of the screws, as it approached the top of the section, when a second section of the iron caisson was added, built within and lowered by the screws in like manner as the preceding, and thus continued until the platform or grillage rested upon the heads of the piles. Another pier (No. 7) was founded on the rocky bed of the river underlaying the compressible bed of the stream for a depth of of 15 feet. This latter had been displaced in several places by the spring freshets of 1865, rendering piling impracticable; all the earth was in consequence, removed down to the surface of the rock. At the site of the pier the rock bed was 18 feet below the original undisturbed bed of the river. To remove this earth a wrought iron foundation caisson, averaging 8 feet square, was lowered so as to enclose the site of the pier. This was gradually depressed to the rock by removing the earth within it by means mainly of powerful pumps, aided by the constant exertions of skilled divers. The masonry was then laid within the tank upon the solid rock, and being brought to a level some feet below the top of the foundation caisson; the caisson of the pier resting upon the platform of timbers was lowered and built upon. The foundation of this pier was 36 feet below low water.

The soil of part of the foundation of Fort Richmond, now Fort Wadsworth, on being excavated to low water level, was found to be very compressible, discharging large quantities of water. The scarps and counter scarps of the southern half of the land front and face of the adjacent bastion of the water front were situated on such a soil, resembling that of the dry dock at Brooklyn.

The weight to be sustained was a granite casement battery of four tiers of 8 and 10 inch guns, with the shot, shell and other munitions therefor. The scarps, piers and arches are all of granite. Piles were in this case resorted to, and no settlement has since been noticed. The work was commenced in 1856, and finished to receive its armament in

1861. The piles were 30 feet long, 12 inches square at the head, and not less than 10 inches at the small end. They were driven by a hammer of 1,800 pounds weight, with blows in quick succession, the last blow of the hammer being from a height of 45 feet. They were cut off level with the surface of the ground and capped with large flat stone, covering the heads of from three to five piles, the joints being filled with concrete, well rammed. A second layer of large flat stone breaking joint with the first, on which the masonry of the granite scarpe was commenced. It will be noticed that there was no timber grillage covering the heads of these piles. *The formula* deduced by engineer, Mr. McAlpine, from his labors at the Brooklyn navy yard, applicable to rams of 6,000 to 3,000 pounds, falling from 20 to 30 feet, was — $X = 80 (W + .0228 \sqrt{F} - 1)$. In which X was the supporting power of a pile driven by the ram W, falling a distance F; X and W being in tons and F in feet, and that not more than $\frac{1}{3}$ of the result given by this experience should be borne or relied upon for any pile.

Major Studers' formula deduced from his experience in driving piles at Fort Delaware with a ram of 3,500 pounds, falling 3½ feet, driving a pile 4 feet 2 inches, is

$$\frac{r}{8} \times \frac{h + b}{} = \frac{3,500 \times 42 + 4.2}{8} = \frac{3,500}{8}$$ —the 4,375 lbs. weight the pile would bear with safety.

Grillage Foundations.—Third system of foundations for compressible soils is that of *grillage*, resting on the natural formation on the surface or at any selected depth. The following are examples of this character by engineers who have constructed many edifices on this principal in the United States: The earliest structure of this character, of which the writer has information, is a building at the Balize Bayou of the Mississippi river, near the site of the pilot houses. It is built of brick masonry, constructed by the Spaniards or French during the early settlement of the country, and apparently for a magazine. It had settled so deep up to the year 1829 as to make it impracticable at that time to ascertain the uses to which it may have been applied. From the practice of the inhabitants of the country it is inferred, in the absence of positive knowledge, that a grillage was used in this case. The foundations of Fort Pike, on the Rigolets, were commenced about the year 1820. The soil is very similar to that at the mouth of the Mississippi, the surface being mostly vegetable matter underlaid by a combination of vegetable earths and dry clay. The foundations of the scarps and piers of the casements were all laid on a grillage of round pine logs, side by side, resting on the excavated soil and crossed on top at right angles by similar logs of from 10 to 12 inches diameter, and about 2 feet apart in the clear. The masonry of the piers was built in, and thus united to the masonry of the scarps. The work was finished about the year 1828. The foundations are about 6 feet below the level of the waters of Lake Pontchartrain, and the ground below that level is saturated with water. The work settled irregularly. The masonry of the casement piers broke from the scarps, making cracks about 4 inches wide. The timber grillage in this case failed to overcome the compressibility of the subsoil or to preserve uniformity of settlement. The St. Charles Hotel in the city of New Orleans was commenced in 1836 and finished in 1837. The foundations were of brick masonry, on a grillage of flat-boat gunwales of 60 to 80 feet in length, 20 to 30 inches wide, and 6 to 12 inches thick, and laid about 6 feet below the sidewalk. This building settled 2 feet in twelve to fourteen years.

The present hotel was commenced in 1850 on top of the old foundations and finished in 1853. It has settled over 12 inches more (in addition to the settlement of the former building), making a total compressibility of the subsoil since 1837 of over 3 feet.

In this case grillage has failed to secure the desired object. The First Presbyterian Church in New Orleans was commenced in 1846 and finished in 1857. The main tower is 20 feet square and 115 feet high, surmounted with a wooden spire. The foundations were built of brick masonry, laid in cement mortar, on a grillage of two thickness of flat-boat gunwales of 45 feet in length, crossing one another. The excavation was 12 feet below the surface of the street. The bottom was a hard, stiff, blue clay, the best ever seen, after a practice of thirty years of an architect in New Orleans. It settled 5½ inches in eleven years.

Custom House, New Orleans, was commenced in 1848, and progressed from time to time to 1860. It is founded upon a flooring of plank laid on the excavation seven feet below the street pavement. On this floor a timber grillage is laid of 12 inch logs, *side and side*, over which similar logs are placed transversely, distant from each 2 to 3 feet in the clear. The space between the timbers is filled with concrete, which is continued over the whole grillage for a depth of one foot. Counter arches 1½ bricks thick support the walls of the interior subdivisions of the building, thus throwing the weight of the building upon the entire surface within the outline of the building.

As a concrete and grillage foundation to support this heavy building, no greater surface, to resist the weight and pressure of the walls, could well be attained.

The walls of 2 feet 6 inches thick rest on grillage timbers 10 feet wide. Walls of 4 feet thick on grillage timbers 15 feet wide, walls of 9 feet thick on grillage timbers 20 feet wide.

In 1860 the granite walls of this building had been carried 75 feet above the concrete base to the architrave line of the enlablature, and all the iron floor beams of the fourth story finished. The exterior walls are 4 feet thick, exclusive of projections; 2½ feet of which is of brick masonry, 1½ feet of stone masonry. In 1851 a commission reported that borings at the custom house, and at a point not far removed from it, indicated different degrees of compressibilty. It is situated upon the firmest, dryest and most reliable ground in or about New Orleans. The maximum settlement of the building in any one point, up to 1860, was 2 feet six inches. This compressibility of the soil beneath the grillage was very variable. The line of the exterior walls in 1864, on which the temporary roof rested, varied in the level 3 feet. This grillage covers a surface of about 300 feet square, and although well constructed, and with great care it has failed in its object.

We know the following account will be interesting and instructive as the greatest achievement of mankind in carrying constructive masonry to its highest altitude in the past or present time.

Washington's Monument.—Mr. Wm. A. Eddy, in a treatise on the highest structure in the world, says: A tower about 1,000 feet in height was first thought of during the organization of the Centennial Exposition at Philadelphia in 1876, and its possible construction was discussed at the time. But consultation with engineers and architects probably resulted in the conviction that the scheme was impracticable, and the expense beyond the value of the investment, especially if masonry were used. Aside from the question of outlay, a serious difficulty in the construction of any kind of material to such an altitude, there are questions of pressure and danger that daunt experienced engineers. M. G. Eiffel, constructor of some of the greatest works in France, notably the trestle work viaduct at Garabil, 407 feet high, concluded that the building of such a tower had not been attempted in ancient times, so far as known, because iron then lacked the lightness, strength and adaptability seen in modern work. The enormous weight of masonry in so great a mass would not only imperil, by its tremendous pressure, the courses of stone near the ground, but would cause an irregular settling of the foundations, as in the well known instance of the Leaning Tower of Pisa. In modern work, a pressure of 66 pounds for each square centimetre is considered dangerous. (A square centimetre is about 2·5 of an inch on a side.) It is admitted that 55 pounds in this proportion is too extreme for safety, although owing to peculiarities of construction, this has been exceeded in some of the following instances cited by M. Navier:

Pillars of the dome of the Invalides, Paris... 32.55 pounds
Pillars of St. Peter's, Rome.................. 36.08 "
Pillars of St. Paul's, London................. 42.70 "

Columns of St. Paul-horo-leo-Murs, Rome.. 48.58 pounds
Pillars of the tower of St. Merri, Paris...... 64.85 "
Pillars of the dome of the Pantheon, Paris.. 64.94 "

M. Navier includes an estimate of 99.25 pounds for the church of La Toussant a' Angers, which is in ruins, and so not a convincing example. It thus appears that the resistence in some daring structures is from 33 to 44 pounds, and only rises to nearly 65 in two instances. M. Eiffel cites Washington Monument, which in its simplicity and boldness he considers remarkable. In M. Navier's estimates given for the greatest feats of architectural engineering in the Old World, this huge obelisk stands high on the list of wonderful structures, the pressure at its base amounting to 58.35 pounds in the proportion above given. With the exception of the Eiffel tower, it is easily a bolder undertaking than any other of its kind known in the world, because it stands upon a relatively small base, with no side support, with a weight upon its foundations of 45,000 tons. This immense square shaft, about 55 feet on a side, served as an illustration of the danger in attempting to carry masonry to a greater height than before achieved. Fortunately, the foundation settled evenly, but to prevent probable demolition part of the base was reconstructed and filled in with concrete. Meantime the structure began to lean to an extent that caused great uneasiness, and finally the suspension of the work. The construction was began in 1848, and in 1854, when it reached a height of 152 feet, its dangerous condition became somewhat marked. Its originally intended altitude of 600 feet was then reduced to 500.

In 1880, after great difficulties, the base had been widened and the foundation enlarged and deepened. Work was then recommenced, and the masonry continued upward at the rate of about 100 feet yearly, until the topmost stone was laid December 6, 1884, 555 feet high at the greatest altitude ever achieved in masonry by man. An additional source of peril in the use of masonry, not included in the danger of settling, as in the Washington Monument, is the insufficient adherence of modern mortar to great masses of stone, **causing** serious crumbling, and a reputation for danger **much to be** dreaded. An attempt to extend **stonework** to **a height of 1,000 feet would cause an** expense **too great for the end attained, and the danger of** fracture **would be incessant and unavoidable.** It seems that we can excel the ancients very little in the treatment of masonry. There is no easily discovered evidence that they built any such structure higher than the great Pyramid of Cheops, originally 480 feet in height. They had good reasons for this caution. If the foundations are solid, the stone may disintegrate, owing to the unequal distribution of the enormous weight, due to the limited power of the mortar to act as a cushion to equalize the force. The Egyptian and other ancient builders constructed some masonry without mortar by polishing and closely fitting the stone, but it is not probable that they **tried to carry such work to a** very great height. **In some modern buildings** it **is found** that the resistance **of very hard stone increases** that **of the** mortar. **Stone or brickwork might reach a** higher point than **the Eiffel tower by the invention of** cements more efficient **than any now known.**

The pressure upon the base of the Eiffel **tower is not** more **than nine pounds for each** square centimetre, **while** in the **case of the Washington Monument it** is, **as we have seen, more than 58 pounds in like proportion.**

Height of the greatest structures in the word of **masonry:**

Washington Monument .... 555 feet.
Cathedral of Cologne........................... 522 "
Old St. Paul's, London (destroyed by fire)........ 520 "
Cathedral **of Rouen**............................ 492 "
Pyramid **of** Cheops .... 480 "
Cathedral **of** Strasbourg....................... 465 "
Cathedral of Vienna............................ 453 "
St. Peter's, Rome .... 432 "
Present St. Paul's, London.................... 404 "

The idea **of** a tower **1,000** feet high first assumed definite form, it will be remembered, in the United States, **and it** remained for a man of constructive genius in another and newer republic to crystallize it into an accomplished fact.

To determine the resistance of stone piers Gen. Smith had a pier of Lemont stone nine feet high and one foot square, composed of six stones with carefully dressed beds, laid up with only a wash of Portland cement mortar, and its crushing strength was 800,000 *pounds*.

James M. White in *Architecture and Building*, April 4, 1892, says that Gen. Wm. Sooy Smith lectured before the students of the Engineering College of Illinois March 31st on the " Engineering Problems of Tall Building Construction." He advocated a new method of construction which does not employ steel in either foundation or superstructure. For foundations, he recommends piers extending to bed rock when possible, or piles driven to bed rock, then cut off well below water level and masonry piers built upon them. This method was designed particularly to suit conditions such as those found in Chicago. He would substitute stone piers for iron and steel columns, and the floor construction is a modification of the Guastavino method, brick arches with steel tie rods being used instead of steel beams to support the tile vault. The fire-proofing is a plaster composed of one part talc and three of plaster of Paris.

Foundations in Quicksand.—Mr. McAlpine, the eminent engineer, has adopted many expedients in dealing with foundations in quicksand. One of these was a method employed at Albany, N. Y., in the preparation of the foundation for the Capitol. The ground on which the edifice is built consists of a rather soft blue clay, which suffers considerable compression from any heavy weight placed upon it. To obviate any disturbance from this cause Mr. McAlpine first proposed to bore holes at equal distances in the clay, and to fill them up with sand, forming thereby sand piles, which were practically incompressible; but on further consideration it appeared to him that these piles might be dispensed with by taking the precaution to make the area of the foundation for every wall in the structure strictly proportionate to the weight which such foundation would have to sustain, so that the pressure per square inch of the foundation would be equal in every part. In such a case it was clear that though the building would sink somewhat, it would all sink equally, and so no damage would be done by the unequal settlement of the parts. This was the plan that was practically carried out, and it has been found to be in all respects successful.

A new form of foundations for buildings has been made the subject of some recent experiments. Trenches were cut down to the hard pan and then filled with water. Sand was then sifted into the water till the trenches were filled with the mingled sand and water, and when the sand had settled into a compact mass concrete was spread over it, and on this the walls were erected, and no better plan could be adopted for a *base-course* to buildings of a firm substratum.

Thus we have at some length given the manner of forming some of the principal and artificial foundations in the United States and Europe, from which the mason can derive sufficient knowledge to guide him in any ordinary building; ever keeping in his mind the object to be attained in the construction of any foundation is to form such a solid base for the superstructure that no movement shall take place after its erection. We must bear in mind that all structures built of coursed masonry (whether brick or stone) will *settle* to a certain extent, and that, however trifling its character, all soils more or less, will become compressed under the weight of a building. *Our aim, therefore should be not so much to attempt to prevent settlement as to insure against inequality of settlement and lateral escape of the supporting material, that it should be uniform, so that the building should remain without crack or flaw.* In building upon a natural bottom, the only precaution necessary is to level the foundation trenches so that the masonry may start from a level bed.

If it is necessary that some parts of the foundation should start from a lower level than others. Care must be taken to keep the mortar joints as close as possible, or to execute the lower parts of the work in cement or the work will settle at those points where the greatest number of joints are.

Strong gravel may be considered as one of the best soils to build upon, as it is almost incompressible; sand, as well, forms an excellent foundation, so long as it can be kept from escaping; but as it has no cohesion, and acts like a fluid when exposed to running water, it must be looked upon with suspicion and treated with *caution*. Another necessary precaution which we must never fail to observe in *all foundations*, is the keeping of the excavations perfectly *dry*. The drainage of the site of a building, therefore, is of the utmost importance, and should be thoroughly carried out.

The use of timber is objectionable where it cannot be kept constantly wet, as alternations of dryness and moisture soon cause it to rot, and for this reason concrete is very extensively used in situations where timber would be liable to decay. To prevent the lateral escape of the supporting material this is especially necessary when building in running sand, or soft, buttery clay, which would ooze out from below the work and allow the superstructure to sink. In soils of this kind, in addition to protecting the surface with planking, concrete, or timber, the whole area of the foundation must be inclosed with piles driven close together. When concrete is used, it should be tipped over from a barrow into the trenches, and not thrown from a height, as was formerly the practice, as the materials are then apt to separate. Particular care should be taken in excavating the trenches no wider than is absolutely necessary to take the concrete, in order that there may be an undiminished lateral support. Particular care also should be taken in pounding this concrete; after it is spread out evenly of about six inches deep at a time, it should be tamped until the water oozes on top, which is sufficient evidence that the concrete is thoroughly saturated alike. Concrete may, under ordinary circumstances, be from two to four feet in depth, and about one and a half to twice the width of the lower course of footings; but as the material has little transverse strength, the depth should be proportional to the width. When brick footings are used on concrete they should all be of whole brick, the hardest and best burnt being selected. The bottom courses should be double, and no brick joints be allowed beyond the face of upper work, except in double courses, the projections also being kept very slight ($2\frac{1}{4}$ inches to $4\frac{1}{4}$ inches), or fracture of the footings, or consequent settlement of the wall, will probably occur. Mortar should be sparingly used; and sometimes footings are laid dry. There are various building acts in the States for the width of footings and walls that the mechanic must follow.

In building where wells or cesspools are to be sunk, it would be well to have them made previously to the sinking of the foundations, as they answer two purposes; first, that of ascertaining the nature of the ground on which the building is to be erected; and secondly, that of supplying water, in many cases, for the mason to slaken his lime. In building upon an inclined plane, where the length of the wall is to be very great, and the inclination of the plane is very rapid, the bottoms of the trenches should form a series of level steps; the extent of each of the levels being decided by the number of courses of brickwork that is necessary to bring the height of the first level with that of the second, and that of the second, to a height of that of the third, and so on progressively. The number of courses of brickwork necessary to this purpose should never exceed four.

In building upon an inclined plane, where there is to be a range of buildings separated by party-walls into distinct houses, as is frequently the case in forming the streets of large towns and cities, it would be as well, and perhaps better, to make the steps extend from party-wall to party-wall, which will make the distance the extent of the frontage of each house.

Footings.—The stones for footings should be chosen as large as can be conveniently obtained, and square stones are not so good as those which are rectangular in plan. It is not essential that the courses should be all of the same thickness; but it is essential, in order to prevent unequal settlement, that all the stones of the same course should be of the same thickness. The length of the stones should be such, if possible, that they will reach across the full breadth of the footings, and should be laid without mortar for the first course, well packed together, and pounded down level. (With buildings in general it is a rule to make the foundation course twice the thickness of the wall.) The joints of this course should be well *chinked* up and *grouted* with cement, and if there be the second course of footings care should be taken that the joints of the first course are broken with them, and they diminish equally on both sides, and the *set-off* in each course should not exceed 3 to 4 inches. The outward and interior walls of a building *should* rise from the *same level*.

Inverted Circles.—In places where the soil is loose, and often even in good foundations, over which it is intended to place the apertures of the intended building, as the doors, windows, etc., while the parts on which the piers are to be constructed are firm, the best plan is to turn an inverted arch under each of the intended apertures, as then the piers in sinking will carry with them the inverted arch, and by compressing the ground compel it to act against the under sides of the arch, which, if closely jointed, so far from yielding will, with the abutting piers, operate as one solid body. But, on the contrary, if this expedient of the inverted arch be not adopted, the part of the wall which is under the aperture, being of less height, and consequently of less weight, than the piers, will give away to the resistance of the soil acting on its base, and not only injure the brickwork between the openings, but fracture the window heads and sills. In constructing so essential a part as the arch, great attention must be paid to its curvature, and where there is great weight depending, we strongly recommend the parabolic curve as the best adapted for this purpose; but if, in consequence of its depth, this cannot be conveniently introduced, the arch should never be made less than a semicircle. The bed of the piers should be as uniform as possible; for, though the bottom of the trench be very firm, it will, in some degree, yield to the great weight that is upon it; and if the soil be softer in one part than in an other, that part which is the softest will of course yield more to the pressure and cause a fracture. If the solid parts of the trench happen to be under the intended apertures, and the softer parts where the piers are wanted, the reverse of the above practice must be resorted to; that is, the piers must be built on the firm parts, and have an arch that is not inverted between them. In performing this, attention must be paid to ascertain whether the insisting pier will cover the arch, for if the middle of the pier rest over the middle of the summit of the arch, the narrower the pier is, the greater should be the curvature of the arch at its apex. When suspended arches are used, the intrados should be kept clear of the ground, that the arch may have its due effect. Inverted arches are of great utility in giving stability to buildings, as they distribute the weight over the whole length of the foundation.

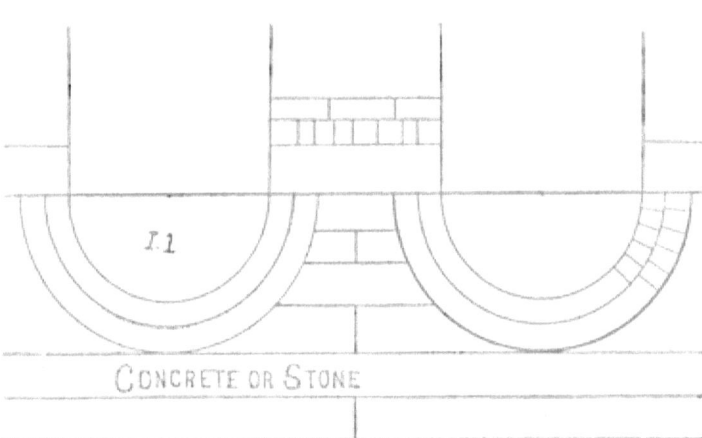

When the radius of curvature of an inverted arch is small, that is to say, when it is under or not exceeding three or four feet, the best arrangement is to build two or more four-inch concentric brick arches as shown in figure; each of these successive rings being built as an independent arch, laid close and in the strongest cement mortar.

One matter also requires particular attention in constructing inverted arches. They should never be used unless there is a strong *abutment* for them on *both* sides, as any settlement will tend to force the side wall out of the perpendicular. For the same reason, when arches are turned over apertures near angles, the outward thrust should be counteracted by means of one or more iron bars turned up at the ends.

Generally upon the footings the rubble masonry is started, and rough in appearance as this manner of wall is, nevertheless, there is no mode of construction that requires more care or caution on account of the weight it generally has to support, and should always be built with both exterior lines, and these lines should be leveled off every 12 or 16 inches of the rise of the wall, and on these levels binding courses should be laid.

Rubble masonry built below the surface of the ground should be laid in a strong hydraulic cement mortar; and as there are more joints in this irregular mode of masonry than any other, the stone should be laid in the closest possible manner, the mason repeatedly striking the stone with his hammer, and all the spaces properly *flushed up*. Care should be taken that the several heights to which this work is to drop off should be reached accurately to receive the cut stone or brick work, which we will now proceed to consider.

First in importance in brick-laying is that it be perfectly plumb or vertical, and that every course be perfectly level, both longitudinally and transversely. The lowest course in footings of a brick wall should be laid with the strictest attention to this particular; for, the bricks being of equal thickness throughout, the slightest irregularity or incorrectness in that will be carried into the upper imposing courses, and can only be rectified by using a greater or less quanity of mortar in one part or another; so that the wall will, of course, yield unequally to the superincumbent weight, as the work goes on, and perpetuate the infirmity. To insure correct work, the brick-layer, on clearing the footings of a wall, builds up 6 or 8 courses at the external angles, which he carefully plumbs and levels across, and from one to the other.

These form a gauge for the intervening parts of the courses, a line being tightly strained from one end to another, resting on the upper and outer angles of the gauge bricks of the next course to be laid, and with this he makes his work range. If, however, the length be great, the line will, of course, sag, and it must, therefore, be carefully set and propped at sufficient intervals. Having carried up 3 or 4 courses to a level, for the guidance of the line, the work should be proved with the level and plumb rule, and particularly with the latter at the corners and reveals as well as on the face. A smart tap with the end of the handle of the trowel will generally suffice to make a brick yield what little it may be out while the work is so green, and not injure it. Good workmen, however, take a pride in showing how correctly their work will plumb without tapping.

To work which is circular in the plan, both the level and the plumb rule must be used, together with a guage mould or a ranging trammel, to every course; as it must be evident that the line cannot be applied to such in the manner just described. (See bond.)

Fire-places, chimney-breasts, flues, etc. — The mason should see to it on the start, that the fire-places and flues are properly formed. The fuel in open fire-places is consumed in an iron grate of various degrees of ornamentation, this being enclosed in a brick, stone or slate mantle piece, and the whole termed a chimney-breast. The brickwork of the flues does not rest simply upon the joists or beams of the floor, but upon parts projecting from the wall

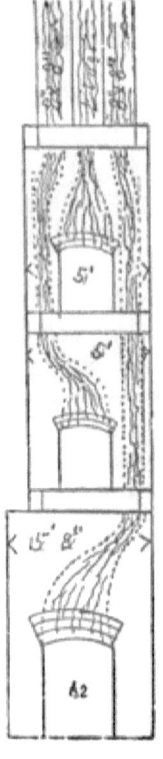

called *jambs*, and are generally started in the cellar or foundation.

These *jambs* serve the important purpose of continuing the flues, by which the smoke is conveyed from the fire-place to the open air. These flues are generally formed above the arch covering the fire-place opening to the *dimension* of the jambs, before the height of the chimney-breast reaches the next floor joists, leaving in the middle of the breast the same space to form the fire-place for the next story.

In the case of a single fire-place the flue is a simple matter; but in the case of a house with several stories, and several apartments in each story, the arrangements of the flues become a much more complicated affair and requires no small degree of care and skill. In the cut we give a rough sketch of a chimney-breast for a three-story house, the kitchen chimney-breast is generally larger than the other stories, to allow for a stove or range; in this case it is 5 feet 8 inches, and the two other stories 5 feet and *tops out* 3 feet 4 inches; but in cases when there are more than three stories the breast must be larger or it is necessary to corbel out for the extra flue or flues as the case may be.

In the case of floors where timber joists are used, in order to prevent accidents arising from the communication of the heat of the fire-place to the wood-work, a flat stone, called a hearth stone, is placed immediately below the grate; and still further to prevent accidents, this hearth

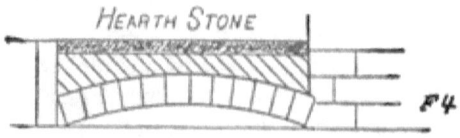

stone does not rest upon the joists, but upon a brick arch called a *trimmer arch*, which springs above the ceiling line of the story below from the chimney breast, and finishes against the *trimmer joist* enough below the floor line to admit the hearth stone.

All the joints of the flues should be properly filled on the inside, or the joints of the brick *struck* to prevent smoke from escaping and to insure them a good draft, the capacity of any flue should be continued throughout of the *same proportion* that it was started with; generally for ordinary houses the size is 64 square inches.

In carrying up a building, the walling should be carried up as regular as convenience will permit, and ought never to be carried more than 4 feet out of level at any time without having its contingent parts added to it. This is a very necessary precaution, for as all walls shrink immediately after building, the part which is first brought up will settle before the adjacent part is brought up to it, and when the adjoining part is raised to the same height, a shrink or settling will take place and separate the former from the latter, and cause a crack which will show more and more evident as the work proceeds. Nothing but absolute necessity can justify the work being carried higher in any particular part than one scaffold, for whenever it is done the workman is certainly answerable for all the evil which may arise from such error.

If, for any reason, one part is carried up above another during the progress of the works, it should not be toothed to take the remainder, but be racked, or sloped back at each end, and such racking should be well wet, if in warm weather when the adjoining wall is being built. All the internal joints of a wall should be flushed up with mortar, and for heavy cement walls the interior joints should be grouted with liquid cement mortar; if walls are built otherwise they are *weak and hollow* and the *damp penetrates* to the interior; this matter is often neglected from the joints not being seen, and for the purpose of saving the mortar and the time that it would take in the using of it. Angles and junctions of return walls require very sound construction, and piers are useful as well in adding to the strength of walls as increasing the base on which they stand. *Sets-off*, or diminutions in thickness of walls, are best made equally on both sides because of the greater stability thus insured. *Corbelling* is carrying out brick work to support flues, fire-places, cornices, etc. In the soundest construction joists should not be built into the walls on account of the cutting up of the bond, the decay often induced at the ends, and the unequal bearing, unless strong plates are used; it is preferrable to set out the the plates, supporting them on brick or stone corbelling, or strong irons. Where there are heavy timbers or iron girders they should be laid on large pieces of hard stone. thus distributing the weight; this end being also promoted by introducing stones above, and the opening left facilitates the circulation of air, of value in preserving the ends of timbers from effects of damp, as it is at the ends that decay generally commences. Trimmer walls in basements are used to carry slabs of fire-places. Mortar joints should be as thin as possible, and the mortar of a kind that sets quickly, in order that it may not be unequally pressed closely at varying times. Where walls are faced with stones, the latter should be properly squared to sizes that will bond securely with the brick work, or the materials will be very liable to separate.

When there is a continuation of walling or great weight of brickwork over a window or other opening, it is a good practice to turn an arch above the lintel in the interior face of the wall, correspondent to that in the exterior face. Arches may also be advantageously turned above the lintels in partition walls, as also above the lintels in chimney breasts. Each of these arches should consist of three distinct courses of brick, by means of which an advantage will be gained, should at any time the door or chimney breast be required to be raised, it can very easily be effected by taking away the first and second courses of the arches.

The mason should be ever watchful and see that the walls are properly anchored and stay-lathed, as the work progresses the walls of a building can never be safely said to be secure from storms until the roof is on and the flooring is laid. Walls that are faced with stone or pressed brick, and backed up with an inferior kind of work should be stayed and watched until the work is dry and the building inclosed.

The following from *Carpentry and Building* will be of interest to bricklayers in regard to *flushing up* their walls:

In some of the ruder kinds of early masonry bricks were often used as mere lacing or string courses, to bind together at varying heights the whole of the underlying constituent parts of the masonry. When so used in the construction of arches in combination with stone, the object of their use with the builders seems to have been to obtain even and equal bedding planes here and there throughout the arch by the insertion, as it were, of bricks or brick courses, irregularly alternating with the rough, unworked, or rudely scraped stones of uneven beds, chiefly composing the body of the arch.

Bricks are still sometimes so employed, says the *Building News*, and as inclosures to flint diaper work, but more in the capacity of ornamentation, and as units or scales of a known dimension to aid the eye in the realization of the extent and effect of the composition as a whole, than as parts of construction necessity. In modern work some of the greatest achievements of engineering skill have been carried out chiefly in brickwork, and in some instances almost to the entire exclusion of stone. This being so, it will not be out of place to consider the essential conditions of what is now universally accepted as being worthy the name of good brickwork. In the first place, brickwork has made rapid and well-marked strides in the last quarter of a century, or since the decadence of the stuccoed front, and the revival and use of pressed brick and terra-cotta under the sympathetic and able advocacy of our architects and masters of modern refined thought as applied to architecture. Prior to the time mentioned, the *shuff*, the *grizzle* and rough stock were mostly in demand, but which are now happily supplanted by bricks of a better class and quality, except in the erection of suburban villas and other *jerry-built structures*. One of the recommending advantages of the use of bricks over stone is the thorough and perfect bonding which may be obtained throughout the mass of the work; the ease and certainty of obtaining solid and homogeneous bedding of the bricks when laid by skilled bricklayers working under the recognized conditions essential to the production of good work. Also the imperishable nature of the material as compared with most of the building stones in use, even the *granites;* and the ease with which they lend themselves to the construction and production of complex forms and outlines under a skilled treatment as compared with the vastly greater expenditure of labor and material required to bring about similar results in stone. Of the importance and necessity of solidly bedding the bricks and effectually flushing up the interior joints (known as cross joint and wall joints), no one is so fully alive as the civil or municipal engineer, long experienced in the construction or personal superintendence of sewers, water works, and hydraulic works generally. The sewers built recently in a *western* suburb afford a good instance—a case in which the brick-work is so badly executed that to connect the house drains to the sewers "would be," said the reporting engineers "nothing less than converting the whole of the inhabited area into a hot-bed of *typhoid fever* The question of *flushing up* as applied to a building, differs in degree of importance as applied to a sewer or similar work. Apart from flushing up the brick-work, as a means of obtaining the maximum amount of tensile strength, in addition to that obtained by good transverse and longitudinal bonding, to carry the loads to which most walls are subjected, and to provide against the possible lateral movement of any of the constituent parts when the whole is under strain, the question has its sanitary aspect also; and by reference to most of the published engineers' pocketbooks will be found formulæ to find the amount of air in cubic feet, which will in a given time, under certain conditions stated, pass through walls of various thickness built of different kinds of material. The walls of dwelling houses defectively flushed up are, therefore, admittedly air filters on a large scale. They are liable to be receptacles of damp driven in by storms, and induced by the hollow, or partially hollow, state of the brick-work, **leading** up to **disease, and in some cases** probably **to fatal consequences.**

The seemingly **paradoxical aphorism that "wet** building makes **a dry house" is worthy of all acceptance.** Walls built wholly of **dry or insufficiently wetted bricks will be found wanting in two chief characteristics of good work, viz., solidity, and a firm and binding adhesion of the bricks and mortar.** This is nowhere better exemplified, on the one hand than in old brick footings and walls in situations subjected to the continuous presence of adjacent moisture—many retaining walls, for instance, supporting an undrained or badly drained bank of nonporous earth—in which case the chemical action set up between the sand grains and the lime, has gone on so uninterruptedly that the mortar has crystallized and attained that condition known to practical men as water bound brickwork. In this condition the mortar, though set, is not hard and could easily be reduced to a plastic pulp by heating, yet the adhesion between the bricks and mortar is so firm that to separate them is no easy task, the mortar very frequently tearing away with it portions of the bricks at the line of separation, the separation being generally effected by steel-pointed wedges driven by sledge hammers. The extreme opposite case is that of building walls with dry bricks in the height of summer. The dust coating the bricks is unremoved, forming a separating medium or layer between the bricks and the mortar, and so preventing *adhesion*.

And where dust is not present the moisture of the mortar is taken up with such avidity by the dry bricks that very little or no adhesion is the result, and the mortar, by examination when dry, is found to be little better than a cake of slightly moistened *compressed dust*. On the other hand, the bricks should not be wetted to the degree of *saturation*, or they will be incapable of absorbing the finer particles of the mortar into their body which they should do, forming so **many** threads **binding the** bricks and the mortar together. **Unless the** bricks **be well** wetted to induce the **mortar into the cross** joints and wall joint during the *modus* **operandi of flushing up every** course, the work should be *grouted*. But under any conditions and circumstances the bricks should be *wetted before use*, except in *winter* or *frosty weather*, when the air is generally so humid as to reduce the absorbant power of the bricks. It is then advisable to forego the risk of wetting the bricks, especially if the work is in exposed situations.

All brick work should be built as level as practiceable, as it rises in its different courses; the workmen frequently comparing their several heights of corners with the floor joint line as the work progresses, that both may come to their requisite *heights* in the same number of courses from said line or level. In building in dry and warm weather, the brick must be well wetted or dipped in water, as they are laid, to cause them to adhere to the mortar, which they would not do so well if laid dry; for the dry, sandy nature of brick would absorvb the moisture from the mortar and prevent adhesion. In the winter and frosty weather the brick should be kept perfectly dry, and for work that must be accomplished at this time of the year cement mortar should be used immediately as made, but the use of frozen mortar tempered up cannot be too much deprecated, as well as brick that have been wet and frozen and laid in that condition. We know that good results have been attained with brick work in frosty weather when the lime has been slaked and immediately made into mortar and used in a warm condition, for the dry nature of the brick absorbs the water that may be in the mortar, and cohesion takes place before the frost can accomplish much injury; and the *Deutsche Bauzeitung* says that at "Christiana, in Norway, building operations are successfully carried on at temperatures as low as 12 degrees Farenheit, and that the work executed under these conditions compares favorably with summer work. In fact the Christiana builders maintain that it is superior. The secret of successful work under these conditions is said to be in the use of unslacked lime in mixing the mortar in small quantities at a time, being made up immediately before use. The mortar must be put in place before it loses the heat due to the slacking of the lime. The lower the temperature the larger the quantity of lime required, so that below 12 degrees Farenheit the work cannot be carried on profitably."—*Engineering, London.*

In the winter it is very necessary to preserve the unfinished walls from the alternate effects of rain and frost; for it be exposed, the rain will penetrate into the bricks and mortar, and by being converted into ice will expand and burst, or crumble the material in which it is contained; consequently, as soon as the stormy weather and frost set in, the unfinished walls should be covered either with straw or weather boarding, and the trenches around the foundation well filled in with stable manure.

Front work in pressed brick.—There is perhaps no branch of the bricklayer's art which requires more attention, and to be thoroughly understood, than that of pressed brick face work, which is becoming more and more in demand in the United States. Mr. Fergusson says: "Sublimity is not perhaps to be attained in brick-work; the parts are too small; and if splendor is aimed at, it may require some larger and costly material to produce the desired effect; but, there is no *beauty* of *detail* or of *design* on a small scale that may not be *obtained* by the moulded bricks, and they are in themselves far more *durable*, and, if carefully burnt, retain their sharpness of outline longer, than most kinds of stone.

Burnt clay may be moulded into shape as *elegant* and artistic, as can be carved in stone; and the various colors which it is easy to impart to bricks may be used to form mosaics of the most beautiful patterns, but to carry out all this with success requires a genuine love of art, and an energy in the prosecution of it, which will not easily be satisfied. Without this the facilities of brick architecture are such that it can be executed by the *commonest workman.*" A mason, therefore, to be considered a proficient workman at the present time, should study, and cultivate a taste for ornamental brick-work, and when an occssion is opportune for him to practice this branch of his art, he may do so in a skillful manner, and not to *slur* it over; it takes time, and those who wish to have it done, should see that it is done in a thorough workman-like **manner**; by so doing this branch **of** the trade might be extended still further; for there are many qualities of front brick manufactured in this country that will outlast stone for the exterior face of buildings; and when the workmanship is wisely and accurately executed, they will stand as representatives of skill and laborious industry of the workmen who erected them. The Romans fully appreciated the elegancies of architecture in granite and marble; but underneath the marble there was a substratum of brick. Among the hundreds of temples, palaces, porticoes, and triumphal arches which old Rome ever boasted, only a few shattered and blackened fragments survive, but the bricks in Roman edifices contiue to hold their own beauty to this day. The Coliseum has been peeled and stripped and flayed of its last layer of cuticle; but the brick shell and the brick foundations for the seats remain, laughing stone to scorn. All over Europe are to be found the remains of Roman walls *in brick*, and they seem to grow tougher every day. We should remember—always without vanity—that we *can build* in modern times as good as they ever did in the old, and that Flemish bond and old English, in brick, may outlast all the stones of Venice and all the Pentelican marbles. The friezes of the Pantheon preserved in the British Museum, are still very beautiful to look upon, but they exhibit in many portions evidences of decay, and even of disintegration. So it is of the columns of the Pantheon at Rome. The foliated capitals have been worn perfectly smooth by the attrition of atmospheric Time; whereas there are extant thousands of works of antiquity in terra-cotta—and what is terra cotta, but moulded brick? as sharp to-day in every touch and every outline as they were two thousand years ago. And many people ask to-day, "What is the use of building stone mansions if the stone is to crumble away in rapid decay?

Far better would it be to abide by the homely, but durable product of the kiln, than to use many of the stones that we see disintegating in many of our buildings. If the chisel plays us *false*, let us pin our faith to the *trowel* and the *brick*. Fine specimens of ornamental brickwork may be seen now in many of our city buildings. Good effects may be had by brick *corbelling out*, and the use of terra cotta, and the employment of moulded bricks in *strings*, lintels and cornices, and jambs of doors and windows, etc., and some evenly well burnt brick such as the Caliamore brick may be carved, and in panels and strings will have an exceedingly harmonious contrast if nothing but brick be used. This is now being largely done in England. The carving has to be well studied in low relief to adapt itself to the material, the brickwork being built up with ordinary jointing like the other work, and carved when the mortar is set. This carved brickwork may be seen in N. Y. City. There should be more of it. Its beauty is in its shades and color which the wood cut cannot give. In pointing the brickwork it is most desirable of a dark color, and may be readily formed either with black Munich cement or Indian red pigments mixed with mortar. Also the dark moulding sand obtained from iron founders, if mixed with a good cement, produces a very pleasing, dark colored durable mortar that harmonizes well with most of the red bricks used. They are using colored mortars at the present time in Boston, New York and Philadelphia, of almost any required tint, a small amount answers for the front of a dwelling, which harmonizes well with the light-colored brick of New York, Ohio and New Jersey; and none can fail to remark the extent to which the use of these materials has effected construction in many of our cities within the past few years.

There are manufactured also brick of various designs and shapes, sizes, colors and shades; as red, buff, brown, drab, old gold, obsinian, pink, black, white, garnet, blood-stone, onyx, mottled, drused, marbled, Roman, ashlar, etc.

Cheerful edifices faced with these brick, having their cornices, string courses, and other decorative details formed in moulded and cut brickwork now meet the eye in all directions; evincing to the mind of the practiced mason the appreciation which the public regard this manner of construction in which he is himself particularly interested as it raises his work from the old and plain manner of brickwork as generally executed in the States for front work to that of the artistic, the performance of which any industrious and intelligent mechanic may accomplish who has the skill and desire to perform all of his inferior branches of the trade in a thorough and workmanlike manner.

And for the apprentice, we advise him to pay strict attention to his older worker in the trade, whose advice and handiwork in the mechanical arrangements of his art has taken years of practice and study. While he is learning the constructive portion of his trade on the building, he should pass his leisure time in the exercise of mechanical drawing at home, with the reading and study of works on sound constructive principles, that his mind may be stored with sufficient and useful knowledge to direct his hands in after life. And it requires study, for we are fast passing away in this country many of the rude forms of construction and returning to the older and more genuine practices of our forefathers in the old; for it must be remembered that ornamental brickwork is by no means a modern introduction. The Chinese have long excelled in its application. Terra-cotta cornices and bas-reliefs were used in ancient Greece. In ancient Rome the ornamental parts of many edifices, even Corinthian capitals, were carved in brickwork. An edifice still exists near the grotto of Egeria, in which cornices, modillions, dentils, and other features are cut in yellow bricks closely cemented together. As Mr. Hope remarks: "Wherever they found clay more abundant, or easier to work than stone, they used it plentifully, both in regular layers throughout the body in walls, as we do, and in an external reticulated coating, from the firmness of its texture and the firmness of its joints as durable as stone itself. Indeed, far from considering brick only as a material fit for the rough and most indispensable ground-work of architecture, they regarded it as equally fit for the elegancies of ornamental form, all the details of rich architraves, capitals, friezes, cornices, and other embellishments. Sometimes it owed to the mould its various forms, and at others, as at the Amphitheatrum Castrense and the temple of the god Ridiculus, to the chisel."—*Essay on Architecture.*

A matter of importance in connection with press brick work is *finishing*, commonly called *striking* the joints, a matter which has undergone during the last twenty years, more or less, a complete transformation of character in style of work, skill displayed, and mode of execution. The style called *white work*, or pressed brick laid in white mortar, requires a great deal of skill and experience on the part of the mechanic, and when properly executed excels all other methods of face work, both in regard to appearance and durability. The brick are laid in a close joint, and for a first class job should not exceed $\frac{1}{8}$ of an inch thick, and set with an imperceptible batter in themselves, which may not be perceived when looking at the work direct, but gives the joint a prominent feature and the work a good appearance. It can therefore be plainly seen that the brick must be gauged with great care and exactness, that the joints may appear all alike. However, as it is almost impossible to have a large amount of them, all of the same thickness, but they can be utilized by using those of the same thickness, within a certain *rise* of the work, which must be carefully looked after. The *bond* used for the face of the wall is called by the American bricklayer the *running bond;* every seventh course the brick are *clipped* in the back, and a binder placed transversely therein when backing up to hold the front. The cross joints in this work are supposed to be kept plumb from the bottom to the top, and are usually put in when the front is being cleaned down, but for durability they should be put in as the work progresses. The mortar is composed of white sand, which must be washed from salt, and fine putty lime previously run through a sieve before mixed with the sand. The mason when using this mortar carefully spreads, or *butters* it on the bed of the brick which is to be laid, in such a way that when the brick is set, the mortar will protrude about a half an inch from the face of the wall. When there are a number laid, and before the mortar becomes too hard, the joint or mortar that protrudes is cut off flush with the wall, the joint struck in a downward direction, and the upper and lower edges of the joint cut in an neat manner with a knife guided by a small straight edge. When the front is built, the whole is cleaned down with a solution of muriatic acid and water, not too strong, and oiled with linseed oil cut with turpentine and applied with a flat brush. After the front is thoroughly cleaned with the muriatic acid solution, or that portion which is being cleaned at the time, and before the oil is applied, give the work a wash of clean water to remove all remains of the acid solution.

Red Work is performed similar to white, the red mortar, when for a fine job is composed of the same lime and sand as are used for the white work, but colored with Indian red, Spanish brown and venetian red, and sometimes a small portion of vegetable black, and to add to the *staying* qualities of this mortar incorporate a dilution of copperas with it, not too strong and when the liquid is cold.

When colored mortars of this kind are required, the lime and sand should be previously mixed, that is made into mortar, at least ten days ahead, before the colored pigments are added to it, and they should be well soaked in water before being added to the mortar.

Enough mortar should be made at one time to complete the front or building, and before starting lay a few brick in the mortar, and let the joint dry in the sun, and if too dark or light, you may arrive at the tint required by adding to a sufficient amount of the above ingredients.

Of course red work does not require the same amount of cleaning down as that of white, but to give the front an uniformity of color and appearance it should be brushed down with a light solution of muriatic acid and water with a small portion of the pigment used in the mortar; if the front is to be oiled the same as in white work, apply it after the above wash; the acid solution cleans the pores of the brick at the time and readily admits the oil to penetrate into them, and prevents dampness in the wall, and often the discoloration appearing on this work.

Black mortar work is executed in about the same way as white, but still more care is required in using the mortar, which, if it comes in contact with the face of the brick, stains them, and can hardly ever be taken off in a satisfactory manner, therefore this mortar must be used in a very careful way; as little water should be used as possible that the mortar may remain always in a *plastic state*, while being used, and free from stains of any kind, as this work cannot be washed down like the *white*. The black mortar should never be stained with *lamp-black, foundry sand* or *forge blowers*, but procure from a powder manufactory a refuse called *green charge*; when it can be obtained it is in a wet state like mortar, very cheap and a little will go a long way. It should be thoroughly mixed with the white sand and putty when the mortar is being made up, so as to avoid different shades of color when the work becomes dry.

Another style of front work is that when the bricks are laid in a similar manner to the above, though the joints may not be quite so tight, say $\frac{3}{16}$ of an inch thick, is called *white-skale jointed work* or *groove joint*.

The brick may be laid eitheir in red, white or black mortar, the cross joints being put in as the work progresses, the mortar used and allowed to protrude as in the foregoing and before it gets hard cut off flush and the jointer ran through the joint guided with a straight edge. This jointer has a face the same width as the intended joint, and leaves its impress upon the material, the superfluous margins being cut or dragged off by the *Frenchman*, the same as before. This *Frenchman* is simply an old dinner knife ground to a point, the top of which is turned down square to form a hook, the hook being intended for cleaning off the superfluous mortar cut by the edge of the knife as it passed along the straight edge.

Weather joint.—Another special noticeable change has taken place in the form of the joints, whether struck in the first place or pointed afterwards. This is brought about by the adoption of what called the *weather joint*. Now it is one of the conditions of the weather joint that the face shall be bevelled inwards, thus leaving the bottom arris of the bricks above bare and undercut; and that the lower edge of the joint may have some pretence to a straight line, it is usual for the bricklayers to cut it, in which case the top arris of the bricks beneath is to a certain extent undercut also. So there are two open *furrows* or channels to every joint laid open to receive any amount of moisture. With the old and legitimate system of pointing it would not be so, because (alwaying providing the work is skillfully done), the whole surface of the joint would be *struck* flush to the face of the bricks, and completely scaled at both edges to the arrises of the course above and below, with no undercutting whatever. We cannot say that this new style of work has any advantage over the old in respect to weather, and surely it has none in regard to the general appearance.

There is another description of front work where the brick are laid as for tuck-pointing. The pointing mortar is generally laid on with a jointer guided by a straight edge and and trimmed by the Frenchman.

This kind of work is preferrable to tuck-pointing for much exposed work, inasmuch as it is capable of being made sound and durable, especially if the original joints have previously and effectually been raked out; also the mortar may contain a greater proportion of grit, and need not contain any coloring matter to depreciate its setting qualities, if for white work. It can also be pressed into the natural joints with greater effect, thereby insuring stability, and finished flush with the face, which will be a nearer approach in appearance to work legitimately struck off the trowel.

There are many reasons why, during the winter months, face brick-work should be left rough for after pointing. We all know what even one night's hard frost will do in the way of injury to the finished joints which have not had time to get sufficiently hard or dry to resist it. Nor would this pointing business be so bad if the joints were raked out effectually, so as to give a sufficient *key*, and the material of a proper description and quality; judiciously mixed, and beaten to the necessary state of consistency, used by an efficient workman with handy tools, and a reasonable allowance of time for execution; for then there would be some guarantee for future stability, and also some possibility of mitigating the evil offects of slovenly brick-laying.

To perform front work in cold weather great caution is required; in the first place, the bricks, previous to using, should be kept dry, the mortar made up under cover with fresh lime (kept fresh in a weather-tight shed), which, if not ground in a mill, should be dry-slaked, and only sufficient water used in the mixing to bring it into a fit state of consistency; the top and face of all walls, so soon as built, completely and effectually covered up, and during the building to be covered every night; the covering to remain until the danger is past, or only uncovered to meet the exigencies of the work. Pressed brick should be well wet a day or two before using on the fronts, but should be at time of using in a damp condition for summer work. On account of the closeness of the joint and the waste in cutting, the finest kind of pressed brickwork should be estimated at nine brick per square superficial foot, and for cut arches not less than ten brick per square foot. In measuring the workmanship of front work it is generally rulable to allow the workman all the openings on account of building corners, jambs, pointing up, etc.

Brick Mouldings.—As a general thing now arch brick and moulded brick are manufactured, but there are instances where the mason has to depend upon his own skill for the production of this kind of work; and it is accomplished by simply making a template the form of the brick required, and marking the brick on both sides, and then cutting or rubbing it down to these marks. But for moulding birds' mouth, splays, bulls' noses, and, in fact, almost any kind of work, it will be found much better if a box is made that will hold three or four bricks, either flat or on edge, as they may be required, taking care that the ends are both alike, and the exact shape of the brick required. The boxes for this purpose are usually covered with sheet iron to protect the wood from wear while cutting the bricks and keeping the mould in its true form.

Tuck pointing.—This is an important branch of work

which the mason has to deal with and is getting more in practice at the present time than heretofore, and if properly executed, will answer all the purposes of *front work*, especially where the work is protected by eaves as in villas, etc. It is classed under the following heads: *Tucked and Stained, White, Black and Red Tuck-pointing.*

As a general rule all brickwork for *tuck-work*, is laid with the ordinary common brick mortar, the *bond* properly laid out and *kept* plumb, and before the mortar is set, *raked out* of the joints about ½ inch deep. When there is not to be much ornamental brickwork on the front of a building, the brickwork may be laid *overhanded*, and then *tucked* from a swinging scaffold.

Tucked and stained.—In common brick when the brick used are of an inferior kind, that is, not pressed and of a uniform color; it becomes necessary to stain the entire face of the work, because some of the bricks are much darker than others, and therefore have a bad appearance when finished. The first thing to be done in preparing for all kinds of tuck-pointing, is the *cleaning down* or *washing* of the front, free from all mortar stains and dirt, with a solution of muriatic acid and water, use one pint of the acid to a pailful of water. That the acid might not leave any damaging effects after it, the work should also receive a cleansing of pure water immediately after the application of the solution. It is only necessary to clean about as much of the wall at a time as can be easily reached by the workman. The next operation to be performed is the *stopping*. *Red stopping* is composed of one part fine putty lime to three parts fine white, washed sand. This is colored with venetian red and Spanish brown and made to suit in shade as near as possible a brick stained with the subjoined *stain*. There should be sufficient amount of the stopping made up at once to complete the building on which it is to be used; say, three hods of stopping to 200 square feet of work. This stopping should be *stayed* with copperas, say 1 pound to every three hods of stopping, dissolved in hot water and incorporated when cold. The joints are then pointed up or *stopped*, in a rough manner, and no more should be done at a time than can be *immediately finished by applying the putty joint* before the stopping has become *too hard.* If this is not done, the stopping gets so dry and hard that the putty joint will not combine with it as it ought, and it will fall off in a very short time.

When a sufficient amount is stopped in, it is usual to rub it well with a piece of dry carpet or sacking, or something of that kind, and rub the stopping well into the pores of the bricks that the work may appear as uniform as possible.

When this is properly performed the wall is ready for the color, which is composed of the same minerals as the stopping: Venetian red and Spanish brown one pound of each to one and a half gallons of water, and as this color has no setting properties it is necessary to add about one pound of copperas to three gallons of the *stain,* prepared in the same manner as for the stopping. Alum is also used in the same proportions; and sometimes half a gallon of stale beer to the same quantity of color for setting. Two ounces of red analine dissolved in alcohol will brighten up a barrel of the above color if required. This is applied with a flat brush in the usual way, when the work is ready to receive the tuck-joint, which may be either white or black.

White joint, or putty, for this work is composed of the same lime and sand as used for the stopping, but marble dust should be used whenever it can be obtained instead of the sand, or both together, on account of its giving the joint a beautiful glaze. The lime is slacked and sifted through a fine sieve. Sometimes sperm oil is mixed with it to make it work better, and also to give it greater binding properties; but this must be done while the lime is hot and dry, and one pint of oil to half a bushel of lime is enough. *The black joint* or *putty* is composed of the same material as the above and colored with lamp-black, green charge or vegetable black, the last named is easy to mix with the lime and sand, and enough should be mixed at once to finish the job. And care should be taken that this color is well *worked up,* if not the joint will have a bad appearance when laid on the work. When all is **ready** the joint is laid on, and care **should** be taken that the putty joint is **laid on** the *brick joint*, and the courses kept level and of an uniform thickness, and the cross joints plumb from top to bottom of the building. The rule used to lay on the bed joints is about 4 feet 6 inches long and 5 inches wide, and about ½ inch thick, and there ought to be two or three pieces of wood a quarter of an inch thick nailed on the back to keep the rule from the work, so as to allow room for the waste putty that is cut from the joint to fall clear to the ground. The *joint* or *stuff* is laid upon this rule, and afterwards taken off it with the jointer and laid on the work that is stopped in. After this the rough edges of the joint are cut off with a knife or *Frenchman*.

The tuck joint should not be more than 3-16 of an inch thick and well pressed when laid on.

Tucked work in pressed brick whether for white, black or red joint is performed similar to the proceeding with the exception that there is no *color* or *stain* used on the brick, which are generally the best quality of *pressed*, and therefore need no *color* from their manufactured shade, but, after the stopping is laid in and well rubbed with the sacking, the work should be brushed slightly off with a solution of muriatic acid and water, say ¼ pint to a pailfull of water, this acts as a *stain*, and relieves the brick of any surplus amount of stopping that might besmear the brick. *Red joint*, putty and sand for this joint are colored with Indian red and presents a joint a shade or two darker than the stopping, not much used except for mantels, vestibules and interior work.

When coloring the mortar for the black joint, use *green charge* when it can be obtained. There are mechanics who will *stop-stain* and *joint* fifty to one hundred square feet of this work in a day, depending upon the number of angles, coves, etc., and it may be seen that the cost of the material is small.

A tuck-jointer is made of steel, **about** 4½ inches long, ⅛ to $\frac{3}{16}$ inches thick and about 1¼ inches wide; for cross-joints it is smaller.

When preparing the stopping for light colored pressed brick, care should be taken that any of the pigments used contain no iron pyrites or magnesia, as they affect the brick the same as when used in mortar for light colored stone. In preparing the stopping for tuck-pointing, as well as colored mortar for face brickwork or stone-pointing, the following instructions should be strictly adhered to and they will give satisfactory results. The lime and sand should be made up beforehand, as described in page 74; the longer the better. The pigments used to be well soaked in distilled water also, and not incorporated into the mortar until this *mortar* has some *age*. In preparing the copperas, pound it up fine, and thoroughly dissolve it in boiling water, let it stand for at least 24 hours, and then strain it from all impurities; use about a pint of this dissolved copperas to a pail of water in tempering up your mortar with the color. For red, be sure and use English Venetian or Indian red. Indian red costs more per pound, but it goes a good ways in the mixing. For black, use *bone black*, and dissolve it thoroughly in high proof alcohol for the putty joint. For stone-pointing and front mortar there is none better than Portland cement; you may obtain almost any required tint by mixing the cement and color dry to any degree first, then temper and use it; it don't require much for the front of a dwelling, and if carefully handled there is no better mortar for this purpose. When buying your Venetian red endeavor to get the genuine article, especially for that used in the *stain*.

We have in the foregoing pages endeavored to give such instruction in regard to ornamental facework which, if followed, we know from experience will produce good results. And all masons should be anxious to excel and encourage this style of work, for we believe that the greater the number there are who are capable of performing it correctly, the greater will be its demand by the public. That it requires skill and time to execute it properly none can deny, and all masons who have an opportunity to perform it should do so for a pride in the work for its own sake; that pride and love that were the parents of mechanical skill and artistic sense that old-timers in the craft used to feel when they could put their best efforts into everything they constructed; but we know that much of this work is hurried and botched in a shameful manner that is discouraging to those who have the means and capital to have it done, and consequently an injury to the workman; and no one, therefore, should be stronger than himself in the condemnation of inferior workmanship of this kind, and none should be more anxious to perform it accurately.

Fire proof buildings—A prize having been offered for the erection of a fire-proof dwelling-house of moderate cost, a model fire-proof house was erected in Chicago, and filled with representative furniture and tested with fire. The furniture and a part of the window framing was consumed, and a portion of the wall plastering fell; but beyond this, the building was not seriously injured, either by fire or water, and, in the opinion of the committee of experts, who conducted the tests, the builder was entitled to the prize. The dwellings erected on the same plan as this tested house are of the cheapest possible construction consistent with protection from fire, and as some account of this mode of construction may be of value to masons we will give a brief account of it:

The foundations are of stone, laid on concrete, and the walls are of brick 1½ brick thick at the lower story, and 1 brick thick at the second story, the floor beams and rafters for the flat roof in each case resting on a projecting shelf. These beams and rafters, though of wood, are rendered fire-proof by building them in a concrete of 50 parts sifted cinders, 25 parts mortar, and 25 parts of plaster of paris. Wired netting nailed to the underside of the beams, served for a support for the plastering. Above the plastering the concrete is poured in between the beams about 1½ inch thick, and when it sets it forms a hard fire-proof skin above the ceiling and inclosing the lower sides of the beams. Rough floor boards are laid over the beams, and on these above each beam is nailed down a beveled stick of wood about 1½ inch thick, and placed with the narrow edge uppermost. Between these strips concrete is poured in the form of a pasty mass till the floor is covered to the top of the strips. A stream of water from a hose is used to temper the concrete and smooth it down, and when it sets it gives a hard white stone like floor. Finishing floor boards are then laid over the concrete and nailed down to the strips. The roof is also covered in the same way, except that the tin roofing is laid down over the concrete. The partitions are made either of hollow brick or concrete laid up against iron wires. The plastering is spread over this and against the brick walls of the house. The stairs are of brick, laid in cement mortar, and the flues in the chimneys are lined with clay pipes. Houses built on this plan, two stories high, entirely finished without and within, provided with pipes, gas, and water pipes, bath-room, etc., and with garden in the rear, marble door steps and terra cotta window caps have been erected for $2,000, and smaller houses have been erected for $1,200. These houses more nearly represent cheap fire-proof houses than any thing erected in this country, and are valuable as illustrating some of the more recent applications of concrete in domestic construction. Old rails (second-hand from the railroad), have also been used for fire-proof floors in Chicago. They are laid about 20 inches apart, and are fastened together by rods passing through them and secured to the walls in front and rear of the building.

A table is raised just under the rails and then concrete—cinders—or powdered coke—mortar and plaster of paris, is poured in between the rails. When it sets, the tables below are removed, and the floor may be plastered below and boarded above. Though only about four inches thick, it is sufficient to resist fire and sustain the load on the floor.

Boiler setting.—The foundation for all boilers should be of the firmest character, either of stone or brick, and the best material used throughout. Less than a 12 inch wall should not be allowed even in the smallest class of horizontal boilers.

Large boilers have 12 inch, 20 inch and 24 inch additional to the fire-brick lining of furnace.

In setting a boiler, arrangement should be made to carry

on combustion with the greatest possible heat. This requires good non-conductors of heat, such as fire-brick to line the furnace box, and continued over the roof of boiler, as well as top of bridge wall should be of fire-brick, and laid as an inverted arch, for stability.

The arch over the back connection of boiler should not be turned against the boiler, but should be sprung from the side walls, and free a $\frac{1}{2}$ inch from the boiler. The lugs of a boiler should rest on iron plates, built in the wall for the lugs to *give and take* on the rollers, otherwise the expansion of the boiler will crack the wall. The arch over a boiler should spring from the side walls and be self-supporting, and not turned on the boiler, which should be 1 or 2 inches from the fire-brick.

Lay strips of wood lengthwise on the boiler, and turn the arch on them, when the arch is keyed remove what you can of them, the fire will remove the remainder. Many claim that an air space within a boiler wall is not of any service, and the same thickness of brick would be better, and the wall stronger.

Deep ash-pits are the best, and a second or ash-grate will help preserve the grate proper; as there is less reflection of heat from it than there would be from a hard brick bottom. The bars of a furnace should be 18 or 20 inches below the boiler or crown of the furnace. They should slope downward toward the back part, about $\frac{1}{2}$ inch to the foot.

There is one object that requires very particular attention, and which must be of a certain size to produce the best effect, and that is the flue leading from the boiler to the chimney, as well as the size and elevation of the chimney itself. (See Chimney.)

Fire-cement.—Fire clay, wet 100 parts; white lead, 3 parts; powdered asbestos, $\frac{1}{2}$ part; mix all together and use as mortar.

Fire clay mortar is generally used: One fire-clay to one or two of ground or powdered old fire-brick or refractory sand.

The brick work about boiler setting is often imperfectly

laid. It is mostly done by contract, with no one to supervise it who understands the severe use to which it is to be put. The bricklayer, who may never have worked on a job of this kind before, builds good looking inside and outside walls, but the space between is apt to be filled up with odds and ends in the most promiscuous manner. Furthermore, he puts the same joint in that he would use if he were building a house, and this is just what we do not want in boiler setting, particularly in the fire brick lining of the furnace. The joints throughout the setting should be *thin*, and the work should be done as faithfully inside as outside. Kaolin or prepared fire clay is used in laying the fire brick, and it should be mixed up so thin that it cannot well be used with a trowel. Some mill owners who have had experience in this direction will not allow a trowel to be employed at all, but require the man to use iron spoons. The fire brick should be dipped in water as they are used, so that when they are laid they will not immediately drink up the water from the cement. They should then receive a thin coating of the prepared fire-clay or kaolin paste, and be carefully placed in position with as little of the kaolin or fire-clay as possible. Every sixth course, beginning with the grates, should be a row of headers, *well bonded into the masonry behind*. The headers are of little use unless they are well secured into the walls of the *setting*, for when the lower courses of fire brick have burned away more or less, we have to rely on their headers to a considerable extent to hold the front of the wall in position. In repairing fire brick linings the lower courses, which burn out fastest, can be removed and replaced without disturbing the upper part of the wall, provided the headers are secure, while if they are not, the entire wall may have to be rebuilt, and this cannot be done without either removing the boiler or tearing down a considerable part of the setting. *The locomotive*—Those who have had considerable experience in setting and repairing boiler settings, claim that it is not best to put in the fire brick header course until the lining is carried up nine courses above the grate.

Composition for covering boilers, etc. — Road scrapings, free from stones, 2 parts; cow manure, gathered from the pasture, 1 part; mix together thoroughly, and add to each barrowful of the mixture 6 lbs. of fire-clay; ½ lb. of flax shoves or chopped hay, and 4 ozs. of teased hair. It must be well mixed and chopped; then add as much water as will bring it to the consistency of mortar—the more it is worked the tougher it is. It may either be put on with the trowel or daubed on with the hand, the first coat about 1 inch thick. When thoroughly dry, another the same thickness, and so on, three inches is quite enough, but the more the better. Let each coat be scored like plaster to prevent cracks, the last coat light and smooth, so as to receive paint, whitewash, etc. The boiler or pipes must be first washed with a thin wash of the mixture to insure a catch.

The setting of a horizontal boiler is a matter that almost any competent mason may accomplish, either for heating purposes or power by following these instructions and the examination of the *setting* of a boiler in place.

When upright boilers are inclosed in brick-work for heating purposes the outside is usually built square, to suit the door castings, and for appearances; but the inside is generally built *round*, three or four inches from the boiler; to make a flue or an air space, which will be the same distance from the boiler, at every part. If it is necessary to have a flue so constructed, with the outside still square, build two walls; a round one and a square one; but the inner one must not touch the outer or the latter will *crack;* otherwise build the square inside and outside.

Baker's ovens.—In building ovens, the work is generally done according to the situation and the owner's convenience, as well as a thorough examination of an oven that gives satisfaction, when almost any skilful mechanic will be able to perform the task. To construct a baker's oven to heat with coals; the size of the base being arranged, it should be carried up to the height of the furance door, and the ash-pit left according to the width of the door and the length of the furnace bars, allowing for the door being set

4½ inches from the face of the brick-work. Let the frame and the door be about 1 foot square, like the furnace door of a copper, and the bars about 20 inches long, and level with the bottom of the oven and of the door. Let the flues be about 16 inches square for the fire to shoot into the oven from the shoulder, where the furnace is straight across to to the opposite angle of the oven, and the fire catching the crown in its course it will spread all round. Let a register be fixed in the flue, and the copper five or six inches above the furnace, not so as to get too hot, for it is usually *warm water* only that is required in a bake shop. A register should be fixed within a little of where the flue enters the oven, and rise slanting; which, being stopped when the oven is hot enough, leads into the chimney flue. The general rise of the crown above the flue is from 18 to 20 inches, which form is often made from sand. Sometimes the oven is constructed without the copper; and perhaps it is the best plan; for it is certain the two will act better apart than they do together; but of course the latter is a little the cheapest as regards fuel. The side walls, from which the crown of the oven springs, ought not to be less than 2½ bricks thick, and the crown springing from about 9 inches above the floor.

The angles should all intersect, and all be laid with as close joint as possible The brick lining the oven are now generally of fire brick laid in fire clay mortar. When the oven is *domed*, spread some sand on the top so that when the work gets dry the sand may fill up any cracks.

Brickwork impermeable to acids construct with bricks which have previously been dipped in very thick boiling tar, then lay in a mortar made of resin and a refractory sand applied hot, and rub the joints with iron (used around chemical works, etc.).

Brick Stack.—Much care and caution is required in putting down the foundation for a chimney of any great height, as are generally used for manufactory purposes; that it should be of the firmest nature there can be no doubt, as the weight it is supposed to bear is confined to a small base, which should be broad enough to insure against settlement. Sometimes the chimney is built of one solid wall, which surrounds the flue, in which case the brickwork is apt to split and crack from the heat expanding it; whereas, if there was an air chamber between the main flue wall and the exterior wall this would never happen. The following cut illustrates a cross section of a chimney 8 feet in diameter at base, with a flue 2 feet in diameter, 8 inch wall, an air chamber surrounding it, and exterior wall of 1 foot 4 inches.

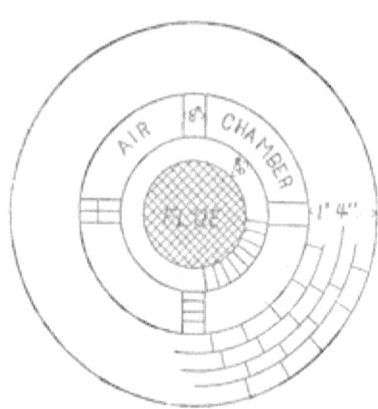

This chimney may rise to any available height according to the batter given to the exterior wall, and when the air chamber closes from that account, 4 inches at a time may be dropped from the interior of the main wall to form another one, until the required height and thickness of wall is required to top out in. It is of the utmost importance that a chimney of this kind be built perfectly plumb, that it may withstand the wind and storm. Small air flues may be built across the main wall to admit cold air into the air chamber. Of course when a chimney is built battering, we mean by being built plumb, that the battering angles are perfectly regular in that respect, so that the whole shaft shall stand plumb on its centre, and consequently secure against high winds. The stability of a chimney-stack depends on the weight of the brickwork above the joint at the base, being such that it preponderates over the wind pressure at the centre of gravity of shaft to such a degree that the resultant of the two forces shall fall within the base of stack at the joint sufficiently to prevent crushing of the material on that side, or tension on the opposite or windward edge. For the sake of stability, the line of pressure, or resultant of the weight and wind pressure, should fall within the shaft thickness at the joint level by at least $\frac{1}{4}$ of the whole width of chimney. It is easy to find the weight of the brickwork above the level of joint. Then if we know the superficial feet exposed to the wind pressure, multiplied by the wind pressure, we shall obtain the total force which acts against the side of the chimney at its centre of gravity, and this force has to be counteracted by the weight of brickwork acting through the centre of the chimney's thickness. There are thus three external forces acting upon the stack exposed to the wind; the weight of chimney acting vertically, the wind pressure acting horizontally, and the reaction of the resultant. By taking moments about the centre of gravity, and assigning definite values to each force, the actual stability of the chimney can be found.

A smoothly plastered chimney gives a better draft and keeps clean longer than any other, but for durability the joints of the flue should be struck flush with the trowel and all built in the most substantial manner. The flue must be capable of passing sufficient air for the greatest consumption of fuel likely to be used.

Less air will not do. More than is needed does no harm for it is in the power of the fireman to diminish the draft if necessary. However, before constructing a shaft, it would be well to examine one that has proved sufficient from practical results in regard to the capacity of the boiler used; for the size of the flue depends upon the grate surface of the furnace, or the amount of coal it is capable of consuming per hour, for a greater or less horse power boiler. A factory chimney suitable for a 20 horse-power boiler is commonly built 20 inches square inside, and 80 feet high, and these dimensions are correct for consumption of 15 pounds coal per horse-power per hour, a common consumption for factory engines.

Every chimney should be built several feet above all surrounding structures, so that there is no obstruction to break the air from the top of the chimney.

The small abutting brick piers which are built from the main shaft wall to sustain the flue wall in its position, should have no connection with the latter wall, and free from it at least ½ of an inch, which will allow the flue wall to expand without injury to the main shaft.

Retorts for gas houses.—Although there are masons who make a specialty of the setting of retorts and building the *benches* for them, I am satisfied that any practical bricklayer may accomplish the task by a little careful attention.

The party who manufactures and supplies the retorts, firebrick and blocks for the setting of a bench, generally sends a complete plan for their building, and if that be carefully carried out there can be no mistake made; for I have myself built benches and set the retorts, and followed the plan furnished for their execution, which have given the very best of satisfaction, and prior have never seen one built.

The fire clay should be well soaked in water, and well pounded before used; and each fire-brick and block should be well pounded to a close joint. The fire-clay is mixed with a refractory sand, two of which to one of clay. Kaolin is now generally used for this purpose.

Brick-measurement.—Mr. Trautwine, C. E., gives the following scale for brick measurement. Allowing for the usual waste for cutting brick to fit corners, jambs, etc., the average number of $8\frac{1}{4}'' \times 4'' \times 2''$ bricks required per square feet of wall is:

Thickness of Wall.			No of Brick.
$8\frac{1}{4}''$	or 1	brick	14
$12\frac{3}{4}''$	" $1\frac{1}{2}$	"	21
17	" 2	"	28
$21\frac{1}{2}$	" $2\frac{1}{2}$	"	35
$25\frac{3}{4}$	" 3	"	42

As a rude approximation, a bricklayer with a laborer to keep him supplied with materials, will in common house walls, lay on an average about 1,500 per day of 10 hours work.

In neater outer faces of brick buildings from 1,000 to 1,200; in good ordinary street fronts, 800 to 1,000, and for the very finest fronts from 150 to 300, depending upon the number of angles, arches and plumbing, etc. In plain massive engineering work he would average about 2,000. In estimating upon brick buildings, we must take into consideration that the *labor* item changes from the above according to the massiveness of the work, and the distance which the *tender* may have to carry the material, etc. But as a rule in practice one *tender* to each mason answers in many cases, whereas not so much is required sometimes, and again when the carrying is very *high*, one tender to each mason will not answer and the judgment of the contractor must be used.

In making out an estimate for brick work, the several grades of work should be figured separate and a price made for each. Arches, cornices, moulding courses, should be estimated by the foot, which varies according to the amount of cutting and size, etc. At the present time brickwork for ordinary buildings, including scaffolding, mortar, etc., averaging an entire building, is worth about $8 per 1,000 brick, to lay in good manner, but good first-class front pressed brick is worth from $15 to $20 per 1,000.

For large works a certain amount of percentage should be added, according to the time such works would take to complete them, and the amount of risk incurred, etc.

Almost any mason can learn to estimate upon the cost of brickwork from the above items, knowing the cost per thousand for bricks in his neighborhood, as well that of lime, cement and sand, and making himself familiar with the rules of mensuration, there is no reason why he should not be ready at any time to estimate on brickwork. (See proportions of brick and mortar in a wall according to joint used.)

Ordinary bricks are about 8 inches in length, and, with the mortar joint about half that in width, so that each brick on flat will give horizontal surface of about 32 square inches, or $4\frac{1}{2}$ bricks will cover 1 square foot. As ordinarily laid, there are nine courses to every 24 inches, or $4\frac{1}{2}$ to the foot; $4\frac{1}{2}$ courses, with $4\frac{1}{2}$ bricks to the course, will give $20\frac{1}{4}$ bricks to the cubic foot. Waste, cutting and closer joints will easily require an allowance of 21 bricks per cubic foot, laid 9 courses to 24 inches in the rise of the wall.

Generally, one thousand common bricks laid in a wall makes about 50 cubic feet, varying somewhat in different kinds of bricks.

Fire brick generally lay 6 brick to superficial foot of lining, and 1,000 for 170 feet of face lining, as generally laid.

The bricklayer's **tools consist of** the *trowel*, the *brick hammer* and *scutch* **for shaping his brick** into any required bevel **or shape. The** *banker* **is a** bench upon which the bricks **are cut. The** *jointer* **and the** *jointing rule* **are employed for running or marking the** centres **of the mortar joints.**

The *camber slip* is a thin piece of wood with one curved edge for the lower part of the camber arch.

The *bevel* is used for drawing the soffit line on the face of the bricks; the *templet* takes the length of the stretcher and the width of the header; and the *mould* is for forming the face and back of the brick. The *raker* is for raking out mortar for the purpose of pointing. The *compass* for drawing and spacing out his several grades of work. The *plumb rule* with a line and plummet, and the *level* for keeping his work vertical and horizontal.

The *square* is adopted for setting **out right** angles, and *templets* and *battering rules* **for** circular and battering work; **the courses are guided by lines and pins; and when brick and stone** work **are carried up together, the** *gauge-rod* marks **the** height **of the courses. Dimensions are taken by** means **of** measuring rods. **In the construction of the bricklayer's** scaffold, *standards,* **ledgers** and *putlogs* are **used for outside** scaffolding and **wooden horses** for ordinary **building. The standards, or uprights, are tapering poles,** usually **of fir, forty or fifty feet in length and six or** eight inches **in diameter at the lower ends which are let** into the ground, **or barrels filled with broken** stone **and sand.** Increased **height, when necessary, is** obtained **by lashing** additional poles above and tightening the junctions **by driving** wedges between the poles. Ledgers are horizontal poles parallel with the wall and secured by cords to the standards. The putlogs are cross-pieces, generally of birch, placed at right angles to the wall, into which they are let in *putlog holes*, and the other end rests on the ledgers. Stout scaffold boards, hooped at the ends, are laid on the putlogs.

Plain and Ornamental Plastering.—The plastering of the inside of buildings, whether done on laths, bricks or stone, generally consists of three separate coats of mortar. The first of these is called by the mason *scratch-coat*; and consists of about one part of quick-lime to 4 of sand (which latter may not be of the purest kind), and $\frac{1}{8}$ measure of bullock's hair; the last of which is to make the mortar more cohesive, and less liable to split off in spots. This coat is about $\frac{3}{8}$ to $\frac{1}{2}$ inch thick; is put on roughly; and should be pressed with the trowel with sufficient force to enter perfectly between the laths; which for facilitating, these should not be nailed nearer together than $\frac{1}{2}$ inch. In rude buildings, and for cellars, etc., this is often the only coat used. When this first coat is put on, it is roughly *scored* or *scratched* (hence its name) with pointed sticks, nearly through its thickness by lines running diagonally across each other, and about two to 4 inches apart. This gives a better hold to the second coat, which might otherwise peel off. If the first coat has become too dry, it is well to dampen it slightly as the second one is put on. The second coat or *browning* is put on about $\frac{1}{4}$ inch to $\frac{3}{8}$ inch thick, of the same hair mortar, with an additional amount of sand, as this coat should be *poorer*, and will not be so liable to crack. The rough surfaces of walls are more or less warped, or out of line; and it is not possible for the plasterer to rectify this perfectly by the eye, as may be seen in almost every house; even in those called *first-class* houses, a quick eye can generally detect unsightly undulations of the plastered surfaces. To prevent this the process of *screeding* must be resorted to. *Screeds* are a kind of guage or guide formed by applying to the first coat, or *scratch coat*, when partly dried, horizontal strips of plastering mortar, about 8 inches wide and from 2 to 4 feet apart all around the room. These are made to project out from the first coat to the intended face of the second coat; and while soft are carefully made perfectly straight and out of wind with each other, by means of the *plumb line, straight edge*, etc. When this is done the second coat is put on, filling up the broad horizontal spaces between them; and is readily brought to a perfectly flat surface, corresponding to that of the *screeds*, by means of long *straight-edges* extending over two or more of the *screeds*. The third coat, $\frac{1}{8}$ inch thick contains no hair; and for giving it a still whiter and neater appearance more lime is used, say 1 of lime to 2 of sand; and the purest or white sand free from salt, and marble dust is used. This mortar is by plasterers called *stucco*, which name is sometimes given to mortar when used for plastering outside of buildings. Or, instead of *stucco*, the third coat may be and usually is of *hard finish* or *guage-stuff*; which consists of one measure of ground plaster of Paris to about two of quick-lime *putty*, without sand. *Hard finish* works easier, but is not as good as *stucco* for walls intended to be painted in oil. The plaster of Paris is for hastening the hardening. Either of these third coats is smoothed or polished to a greater or less extent, according as it is to show or to be papered, painted, etc , and stucco should be well worked with the float in a circular direction, if not it will crack. The polishing tools are merely the trowel, the hand-float (a kind of wooden trowel) and the water brush (a short-handled flat brush for wetting the surface part at a time with water in order to polish more freely). For finer polishing, a float made of cork is used.

The smooth piece of **board about** 10 to 12 inches square with a handle beneath, **on which** the plasterer holds his mortar until **he puts it on the wall** with his trowel, is called a hawk.

The more thoroughly **hard-finish** is gone **over with the water-brush** and trowel, the firmer and stronger will it be. Frequently only two coats of plastering are put on in **infer-**

ior rooms; or when great neatness of appearance is not needed.

The first is of hair mortar; this is *scratched* with a broom and then covered with the finishing coat of finer mortar (*stucco*). If this last is nearly all lime, or with but very little sand, to make it work easier, it is called a *slipped coat* or *skimmed coated*.

A very good effect may be produced in school houses, churches, etc., by only two coats of plaster in which fine clean screened gravel is used instead of sand.

When lined into regular courses, it resembles a buff-colored sandstone, very agreeable to the eye. In purchasing *hair* for plastering, care must be taken that it has not been taken from salted hides; inasmuch as the salt will make the walls damp. For the same cause sea-shore sand should not be used.

It is almost impossible to wash it from salt. In brick walls intended to be plastered, the mortar joints should be left very rough, to let the plaster adhere. If it is put on smooth walls (for outside *mastic* or *stucco*), without first raking out the joints, it is very apt to fall off, as can be seen any day in any of our cities. The walls should also be washed clean from all dust; and should be slightly dampened as the plaster is put on.

To imitate *granite* on wall: After the second or smooth coat of plaster is dry, it receives a coat of lime wash, slightly tinted by a little umber, or ocher, etc. After this is dry, in case it appears too dark, or too light, another may be applied with more or less of the coloring matter in it. Finally, a wash of lime and mineral black is *sprinkled* on from a flat brush, to imitate the black specks in granite.

By this simple means a skilful workman can produce excellant imitations.

The horizontal and vertical joints of the imitation masonry, may be ruled in by a small bush, using the black-wash, and a long straight edge.

A day's work at plastering.—This varies greatly according to the quality of the work and material used, but the following items will greatly aid the mechanic in his calculations. A plasterer, aided by one or two laborers, to mix his mortar, and to keep his *hawk* supplied, can average from 100 to 200 square yards a day, of first coat, or *scratch coat*, about 50 to 75 yards a day of second coat or *browning*, and the same amount, or average of *hard finish, sand finish* or *stucco*, and of *slipped* coated, or *skimmed* about from 200 to 300 square yards per day. These amounts depends upon the number of angles, size of rooms, whether on walls or ceilings, or if the work be properly screeded, *darbied* or *floated*, and if the finishing coat be thoroughly *troweled*, etc.

The cost of plastering.—We can only give the quantities, the prices must be arrived at according to local circumstances, which varies in almost every locality. *Plastering* laths are usually of split white or yellow pine, or hemlock, and come in lengths of about 3 to 4 feet, and are about $1\frac{1}{2}$ inches wide, and $\frac{1}{4}$ inch thick.

They are nailed up horizontally about $\frac{1}{2}$ inch apart. The upright studs of partitions are spaced at such distances apart that the ends of the laths may be nailed to them. Laths are sold by the 1,000 of 50 and 100 bunches. A square foot of surface requires $1\frac{1}{2}$ four feet laths, or 1,000 such laths will cover 666 square feet, but in estimating on plastering we should allow about 1,400 laths and 5 lbs. of nails to 100 yards of plastering. A lather will nail up from 10 to 20 (100 bunches) bunches in a day. It requires about six bushels of lime, $\frac{1}{8}$ of a load of sand (or about 18 bushels), and one bushel of bullock's hair to *scratch coat* and brown 100 yards of plastering. It will require about 2 bushels of *putty* lime and about $\frac{1}{4}$ of a barrel of plaster of paris to do 100 yards of *hard finish;* if for *stucco* or white *sand finish*, about one bushel of putty lime to 2 bushels of the sand.

Plasterer's work is usually charged by the superficial yard. At the present rate of wages, mason at $4 per day and laborer at $2 at the current rate for material, plastering is taken from 30 to 45 cents per square yard, depending upon the style of finish, etc. Take friezes, soffits, etc., according to description, by the foot, measure raised panels extra by the foot superficial. Take the mouldings on the panel by the foot running. *Cornices* are generally taken by the foot. **If the** girth **of the** moulding from the ceiling to the wall **line is** under **6 inches**, take it **by** the running foot, **and if over 6 inches take** it at the superficial foot. If there are coves to the cornices, take them by the superficial foot. Number all angles and mitres above four, **stopped ends, etc., stating the girth whether** the mitres are **internal or external.** The *cost of cornices* and mouldings **varies according to size of mould, and whether** plain or ornamental, **it is** generally **taken by** the **running** foot, and at **the present rates** of **wages, masons at $4 and laborers at $2 per day, from 20 (small panelling) to 50 cents per foot running.** Plaster arches are taken by the piece, **and the mechanic must place a price** upon them **from** former experience; **but for ordinary** buildings they **run** from $3 up to $20, **and even more for** very stylish **and** ornamental arches. **Trusses,** center-pieces, etc., **are** bought by the piece, **and at the** present time from $1 up **to $15.** From the rules under *mensuration* almost any mason can determine the number **of yards in any** building to be plastered.

First find **the number of yards of** lathing **and how much** per yard it will **cost to put it on.** Then **the** number **of** yards of *scratch coat* **and cost per** yard; as well that for *browning*, then the **number of** yards of *finishing*, and whether it be *hard finish*, **stucco,** or *skimmed coated*.

Ornamental Decoration.—*Cornices (Plaster)*—Cornices are either plain or ornamental. In order **to** execute a cornice according **to a given** design, it is necessary to prepare **a** mould of the **several** members, which mould is **usually** made of sheet **brass,** iron **or steel,** indented so as **to represent** exactly **the forms and** projections of the **said** members, and fixed **into a wooden frame with** a handle. **If the** cornice **is of unusual size, such as are used for** large halls and dining-rooms, **it is** necessary to **frame them.** This is done **by** nailing brackets to the **wall about** 16 feet apart, to which laths are nailed; the whole **is** then covered with rough mortar, allowing about an inch to receive the putty which forms the cornice. To run cornice two masons are necessary to do it properly. Before using the mould they gauge a *screed* on the wall and ceiling, formed of putty and plaster, and wide enough to receive the top and bottom of the cornice to be formed.

Then fit the cornice mould squarely in the angle at one end of the room and mark the outer edge of the mould on the ceiling screed, repeat the same at the other end of the angle, from the two marks obtained strike a dark line with a cord. On the screed formed on the wall nail a pine straight edge about ½ inch thick and 3 inches wide, have the underside of the mould to set squarely upon this, and at the same time the upper outside edge of the mould to line with the dark line upon the ceiling; this forms a guide to *run* the cornice. When all is so far ready, the *putty* is to be mixed with about one-third of plaster of Paris, and rendered of a semi-fluid consistence by the addition of clean water. One of the workmen then takes two or three trowels full of the prepared putty on his hawk and spreads it along upon the parts where the cornice is to be worked, the other occasionally applying the mould to see where more or less of the material is required. When a sufficient quantity has been put on to fill up all the parts of the mould, the mould is worked backwards and forwards, being at the same time held firmly to the ceiling and wall, by which means the superfluous material is removed and the contour of the cornice completed to the form required. Sometimes it is necessary to repeat this operation several times in order to fill up such parts as are deficient in the former application. Sometimes when the cornice is large it is necessary to use three or four moulds, which are used in succession. The mitres at the angles are finished by hand, and requires skill and taste by the workman. Ornamental cornices and other enrichments are formed, in the first place, in the manner already described, excepting that additional sinkings are left in parts of the plain mouldings to receive the several enrichments, which are cast in plaster of Paris by means of moulds prepared for the purpose. All the ornaments, which are cast in plaster of Paris, are previously modelled in clay, or some other tractable substance, from designs made for the purpose. It requires both skill, taste and judgment to make a model for a plaster cast; but a certain measure of success is within the reach of any plasterer possessing an ordinary amount of perseverance. When the model is finished it must be left until it hardens, when it is oiled all over with sweet oil and placed in a wooden box prepared purposely for it; the several parts are examined and touched up wherever required and oiled again. The next operation is to pour melted wax and rosin into the box until the model is covered, when it is left to cool and fix itself. When cold and hard it is turned upside down and the wax mould easily separates from the clay model and becomes the matrix or mould for future castings. The wax moulds are so made that they will not cast more than a foot in length of ornament at a time, greater lengths being difficult to handle. The casts are made with the purest and finest of plaster of Paris, saturated with water; and the wax moulds must be well oiled before the plaster is poured in.

When the intoglios or casts are first taken out of the mould, they must be handled with care, as they are not very firm; they must then be placed in the open air, or in a hot oven, where they will dry and become very hard. When hard enough to bear handling, they must be scraped and cleaned preparatory to being used. Enriched friezes and *bas relief* are formed in a similar manner to the ornaments just described, excepting that the wax mould is so formed as to allow of a ground of plaster being left behind the ornament of about an inch in thickness; this is cast to the ornaments or figures and strengthens and defends their proportions, as well as promotes their general effect, when fixed in the situation for which they are intended. The capitals of columns are produced by a similar process, but they require several moulds to complete them; still, there is no difficulty in producing them, but such as the ingenuity of the operator will readily overcome. In forming the Corinthian capital, it is necessary first to prepare the bell or vase, which must be so shaped as to promote a graceful effect in the foliage and volutes, for each of which, as well as the other details, separate and distinct cameos will be required. These are all cast separately, and afterwards attached to the bell or vase by means of liquid plaster of Paris.

To make plaster ornaments known as gelatine, and which are greatly used to make the above ornamental casts. Good glue soaked and swelled; pour off excess of water; mix glycerine six times the weight of the dry glue used. Heat and evaporate water sufficient to make the mixture the proper consistence for use.

To make modeling clay, knead dry clay with glycerine instead of water, and a mass is obtained which continues moist and plastic for a length of time, thus removing one of the greatest inconveniences experienced by the modeler.

Cornices under usual circumstances, in ordinary rooms should be light, extending rather along the ceiling than down the walls, as giving the effect of increased height. If columns or pilasters are introduced attached to the walls the received proportion according to the order should be adhered to; and if an entablature is adopted without columns or pilasters, its height will be in good proportion, if from one-seventh to one-ninth that of the room. Plain, large cornices may be from one-fourteenth to one-twenty-fourth.

In coved ceilings the cove may be from one-fourth to one-sixth of the height. For running plaster arches and rib work, the plasterer should understand the rules for drawing the arches shown in this work, and he may apply them in setting his rods for the execution of this work.

Interior Decoration.—Much attention has been given of late in many localities to the interior decoration of walls, ceilings and cornices; and kalsomine, painting and frescoing seem likely to partially supercede paper for the interior walls of our private and public buildings. While this is a gain to the workman, it has one disadvantage in the finishing of dwellings. The paint, if applied too soon, cuts off the air from the plaster or stucco and retards its hardening, so that experts now recommend a delay of one year before coloring the walls or ceiling of new buildings. This has led to the suggestion of employing colored plaster and mortars, and it is thought that in time some modifications may be made in decorative plastering by this means. The design is to replace the sand commonly employed in making mortars with colored sands, or powders made from durable colored substances, like marbles, slate, glass, pottery and stones. Any material would answer that is free from metalic substances which might oxidize on exposure to air. Mica and bone ash are reported as giving good shades of gray, and many of our natural sands would give fine tints of reds, browns and yellows. Cement bricks colored in this way have already been extensively used in the neighborhood of Boston, both for the interior and exterior decorations with good results, and, by use of properly colored plasters, mortars and stucco judiciously combined, this field of the mason trade might be extended.

When it is desirable to finish the interior of buildings in tints or colors, it can be done also by mixing with the putty coat such coloring material as are not affected by lime. Blue tints may be obtained by using ultramarine blue, blue vitriol or indigo. Blacks by using lamp black, powdered charcoal, or ivory black. Red and its tints by using vermilion, venetian red, or Indian red. Browns, by using Spanish brown and the umbers. Yellows and all its tints, by using chrome yellow, or clay pulverized. Orange by using a mixture of red and yellow. Green, by using blue and yellow. And any color that can be produced by combining any of the above colors.

That many are preferring hard wood for cornicing, panelling, etc., instead of plaster for interior decoration of rooms is apparent. And the public prefer ornamental wood work rather than have their rooms defaced by unsightly cracks, in work designed for a better purpose. That the mechanic is often to blame for much of this inferior workmanship and the improper manner in which the material is prepared for interior decoration there is no question, and consequently he is the loser in an artistic sense; but by far greater blame should be attached to those who employ the mechanic, not giving him sufficient time to gauge his material properly and to execute his workmanship in a thorough manner, and, not having the mortars properly prepared for him. It must be remarked, also, that the substantiality of ornamental plaster work depends too upon the general character in which the structure in which it is being used was erected—if the foundations were poorly put down, no damp-proof courses, and the walls constructed of inferior brick, poor mortar and large joints, and the timber used of a green and unseasoned quality, surely the plasterer and workmanship should not be censured for the failure of the interior decorative plaster work of a building of this kind; and those who are paying for such work either through their ignorance of constructive principles or their penuriousness in not employing competent mechanics to perform their work are in many cases to blame; for this work will endure to the best satisfaction of its employment for decorative purposes as many examples in the past testify to its endurance, when, the building in which it has been employed, was constructed from its foundation to its finish in a thorough and workman like manner consistent with the true principles of scientific construction and the employment of the best materials for its stability and endurance; and when the plaster has had sufficient time to exclude the humidity occasioned by its use, impervious washes have been applied to protect it against its absorbent nature, and a protection for its future enrichments of tints and colors. That decorative papering has attained to a high state of perfection is evident, but will never satisfy those who are genuine lovers of art in decoration, for at its best it is simply imitations and not the real panelled arrangements and broken surfaces they pretend to be. And for sanitary purposes they rather increase than otherwise the objection to dampness, as paper is absorbent; and the size used in its manufacture, the glue, and the paste particularly, are all more or less objectionable. "The old wainscotted rooms and relieved decorations in composition of the last century were far more satisfactory, as expressing genuineness at least; and there appears no good reason why a return to the same principle as respects wall decoration in plaster should not be indulged in; at all events to an extent applicable to modern wants and received notions in style. Walls enriched in plaster-work might be made very effective and pleasing; and the medium affords opportunity for extensive and elaborate enrichment, where such might be desired. Witness the character of the enrichments of this kind in Moorish architecture, and the somewhat similar compositions applied to stone-work and wood-work in mediæval times as relieved ornament to plain surfaces."

Metal Lath and Mastic Construction.—The use of plastic material for exterior finish in modern building construction is not, strictly speaking, a novelty, although its employment in this country is by no means general. Examples of work of this kind, which are to be found in various parts of the land, having been erected many years ago, are in many cases unsatisfactory in evidences of durability, and for this reason architects and builders have been loth to repeat the experiment. It should be explained, however, that such buildings have been for the most part inadequately constructed, and to a certain extent the lack of durability of the exterior finish has been due to weakness in the building itself and the material composing the covering. The idea of using cement is, in some respects, quite recent, but the best cement has not been used generally on account of its excessive cost. German Portland cement, in the proportion of one of cement to two of *sharp, clean sand*, has been used to good results. Great care must be taken in the execution of the work that the consecutive coats follow each other as rapidly as possible. Even brackets on gables, the overhangs and lower course moldings, as well as those about the arches of the porches, are *run*, while the fascia work at the eaves, dentil and capital moldings are applied. Window sills **and heads are** also *run* in place with this material, which may be colored and tinted to suit the taste. Frame buildings covered with metal lath for the exterior with this cement forms a construction which adds in a very large degree to the fire-proof qualities of wooden buildings. The cement also lends itself readily to moldings and to other architectural features, and if intelligently applied goes to ornament the house as well as to make it serviceable and durable. Heavy water-proof paper prevents waste on the back of the lathing, while also checking too rapid drying and setting of the cement. It is a well-known fact that this Portland cement becomes hard and durable like artificial stone, and when employed in the manner indicated above, it is practically impossible to tear it from the strong steel netting to which it is applied without the use of tools.

A new style of wall and ceiling plastering has been introduced which claims to offer some advantages in ease and speed in covering the walls and in securing the plastering against falling, and fire. In place of spreading the plaster on laths fixed to the wall, it is prepared in solid blocks or slabs, and these are nailed to the rafters or joists. The slabs are made of any convenient shape or size by a simple process that may be carried on in buildings, or at the plasterer's shop. A smooth, hard surface is prepared, and a sloping edge is set up to give the slabs a beveled edge, and on this is spread a layer of plaster of Paris. Upon this, and securely bedded in it, is spread a sheet of canvas or other heavy fabric, or a layer of some loose fibres; laths are then laid along two opposite sides of the slabs, and over it all is spread a thick layer of common plastering mortar; before this sets it is brushed over with a coarse broom to give it a rough surface to make a key for the finishing coat of mortar. When the mortar has set, and the slab is hard and dry, it is raised to its place and fastened there by nails driven through the laths. The finishing coat is then applied in the usual way, covering the division between the slabs so that the surface is uniform. Such a system of plastering has the advantage of quick and cleanly work, but we should judge of no saving to cost, and making a wall covering that will not fall in masses when wet, nor take fire, as the laths are bedded in the plaster.

Stucco or *mastic panels* might be formed on the exterior of rural cottages by spreading on a background of reeds, or on *wattles*, which should *have the bark on* so that the moisture from the plaster will not expand the wood. This panelling is best in coves and other positions not much exposed. Intaglio decorations may be scraped in the plaster and afterwards colored. Very pretty effects can be had by sticking necks and bottoms of bottles, fancy shells, etc., into the damp mortar so as to form patterns, or to represent flowers and plants cut into the plaster and then colored afterwards. The play of light on many colored glass so exposed is often very beautiful.

Scagliola is used in the formation of columns, walls and ornamental works in imitation of marble, which is performed with astonishing effect. In forming columns, a frame or cradle is made of slips of wood, about two inches and a half in diameter less than it is intended to be when finished. This cradle is then lathed round, and covered with a rough coat of lime and hair mortar. When this is quite dry, the plasterer lays on the composition, which is made to imitate the most beautiful and costly marbles, and which when dry receives a high polish, and proves so complete a deception, that nothing but a fracture of its substance can discover the difference. The plaster used in making the scagliola must be of the best plaster of Paris. It is composed of plaster, with alum and some color mixed into a paste, and afterwards beaten on a prepared surface with fragments of marble and as many different shades of color must be mixed up separately as there are in the kind of marble to be imitated; the colors are put upon the work as it forms, by which means it becomes incorporated with its substance; forming the veining appearance so much admired. The workman, when the composition is properly hardened, smooths the work with a pumice stone with one hand, while with the other he washes it with a sponge and water; he then polishes it with tripoli, charcoal and a piece of fine linen; then he polishes it with a piece of felt, dipped in a mixture of oil and tripoli, finishing his operations with the application of pure oil laid on with cotton wool.

The bases and capitals of these columns are generally of real marble.

Scraffto is a modification of plaster filling where layers of different colors are put on, and the scratching made deep enough to reach the different colors as desired, just as cameos are engraved. Specimens of this, centuries old and still in good condition, are to be seen in Italy. The two foregoing methods are almost untried in this country, but they are successfully used in England, and there is no reason why skillful mechanics should not introduce the work in this country. *Rough-cast* plastering, with gravel or pebbles thrown on it, is not an unknown here, but it is generally used to cover the walls of inferior buildings. Tastefully introduced in panel work it could be advantageously used in good houses. It should not come near the ground, as it would soak up moisture. Many believe the less hard-finish on walls the better, and especially for surface decoration the walls should be sand finished, which gives texture to the work, just as rough paper does to a water color.

It is well known that the above external rough-casting of old timber houses was stamped or wrought in small devices, known by the name of *pargetting*. Why not further extend the art of decorative plastering by impressing the common stucco with geometrical or other forms, and applied according to taste, either under string courses, cornices, around arches, in spandrils, sapphites, or in large masses of diapering; and texts may be imprinted on the plaster instead of being simply painted on the walls. If color be desired, it can be effected by mixing the desired color with the coat forming the groundwork, then by laying the stencilled pattern against it, and filling in the solid portions of the device with the ordinary stucco or plaster. These patterns can be made so that they may be used repeatedly. The process does not pretend to do more than enliven wall surfaces, but for this purpose it can be made very effective.

Preparing Ground for Fresco Painting.—The wall to be treated must contain no damp or decaying stones or bricks, and the latter should be hard burned. If the wall be already covered with stucco or mortar, this will serve as the first ground, provided it be in a thoroughly sound and dry condition, and it will then be sufficient to clean and level it before applying the second, or painting ground. If not, the stucco must be cleaned off, the bricks laid bare, and the mortar between the bricks picked out to a depth of about ¾ inches. This more thorough preparation is always preferrable in a work of greater importance, or where special pains are advisable to secure durability, as, for instance, when undertaking the exterior decoration of a building. Upon this surface a thin squirting is cast, composed of the following mortar: Course quartz sand, infusorial earth, and powdered marble, mixed in certain proportions. Of this mixture four parts are taken to one of quicklime, slaked with distilled water. Upon this squirting-cast, the object of which is to secure adhesion to the surface of the wall, follows mortar of the ordinary consistency, composed of the same ingredients, to fill up all inequalities and produce a smooth surface, and upon this again the second, or painting ground, is applied. The painting ground is composed of the finest white quartz sand, marble sand artificially prepared and free from dust, marble meal and calcined fossil meal (infurocial earth). The sand composed of these materials, carefully mixed in the proper proportions, is mixed with quicklime slaked with distilled water, in the proportion of 8 parts sand to 1 of slaked lime. This mortar is applied to the wall as thin as possible, not exceeding ⅛ to ¼ inches in depth. When coated with a stucco of this composition the wall presents so hard a surface as to admit of sparks being struck from it with a steel. It is absolutely essential that throughout the work only distilled or filtered rain water be employed, otherwise the painting would be impaired. When used on the exterior of buildings as a *mastic*, pumice stone, in addition to the other ingredients of the mortar, is employed.

When the **mortar is perfectly dry**, down to the stone or

brick of the wall, it is treated to a solution of hydro-fluosilicic acid, to remove the thin crust of crystallic lime carbonate which has formed on the surface, and thus to open the pores. It is then soaked with 2 applications of potash water — glues (potassium silicate) dilated with distilled water, and when dry, the ground will be found hard, but perfectly absorbent, and ready for painting. The ground may be prepared in any tint or color that may be desired, and, therefore, as a preparation in imitation of stone it cannot be surpassed.

Carton-pierre. —This is a material used for the making of raised ornaments for wall and roof decorations. It is composed of the pulp of paper mixed with whiting and glue, this being forced into plaster moulds backed with paper, then removed to a drying-room to harden. It is much stronger and lighter than common plaster of paris ornaments, and is not so liable to chip or break if struck with anything.

A beautiful plastic substance can be prepared by mixing callodion with phosphate of lime. The phosphate should be pure, or the color of the compound will be unsatisfactory. On setting the mass is found to be hard and susceptible of a fine polish. The material can be used extensively, applied in modes that will suggest themselves to any intelligent plasterer, to high class decoration.

Putty-lime.—This is made by slacking *fat-lime* in a barrel or box with a small portion of water, and then sufficient water is added to *run* the whole through a fine seive into a box, where it is allowed to settle some time, the longer the better, when it is kept covered with water that all the particles may be thoroughly slakened and prevent future *popping* in the walk and insure sound work.

Plaster of paris.—A new process in the manufacture of plaster of paris has been announced, that is said to give excellent casts that set slowly, and are of a pure white color, instead of the usual grayish white. The unburnt gypsum is first immersed for fifteen minutes in water containing ten per cent of sulphuric acid, and then calcined.

Sugar in plastering mortar.—A correspondent of the *Sci-*

entific American has used beet sugar, costing four cents a pounds, and all lumps mashed up before putting in the mortar, where the sand was poor and loamy for plastering purposes with good results. The mortar must be dry or *stiff* when the sugar is put in, as it makes it very soft when mixed thoroughly. It is put in the hair mortar only and for the first coat, and use about forty pounds sugar for one hundred yards. It does not color the white coat any, and where good sand cannot be obtained for the purpose, as is often the case, it may be used.

Sawdust in plastering.—Two western inventors have obtained patents for the use of sawdust in place of sand in plastering mortar. One of the patents is for the use of equal parts of plaster of paris or cement and sawdust, with the ordinary amount of plastering hair and water, and the other calls for the use of about $4\frac{1}{2}$ pounds each of slaked lime and sawdust to 1 pound of plaster of paris, and a $\frac{1}{4}$ pound of glue, and $\frac{1}{18}$ of a pound of glycerine with plasterer's hair. Sifted sawdust has before been used to some extent by experienced workmen for mixing mortar for plastering external walls, exposed to the alternate action of water and frost, as a preventive of scaling. Certainly the experiment of introducing sawdust in place of sand in mortar is worth trying, for in many places sharp sand suitable for the purpose is difficult to obtain.

In plastering the ceilings of the fire-proof houses in Chicago the following method is pursued: The joists of the floor having been laid, strong iron wire is nailed to the lower sides of the timbers at distances of a few inches so as to make a course netting in place of lathing. Woven wire netting has been found in other cities to be much better. A movable platform of convenient size is brought under the joists and raised by screws to within an inch and a half of the wires. Prepared concrete is then poured down from the floor above till the space between the beams and the top of the table is filled. As soon as the concrete is set, the platform is lowered and rolled away, and when dry the plastering is sufficiently strong to support the weight of a man upon it. The underside of the plastering is then ready for the usual hard finish. The concrete is composed of 50 parts cinders, crushed slag, or pounded bricks, 25 parts good common hair mortar, and 25 parts strong plaster of Paris.

A fire-proof plaster composed of one part talc and three of plaster of Paris is also used for fire-proofing the interior of buildings.

Portland cement stucco is a mixture of Portland cement and chalk. It is of good color and close texture; weaker than Portland cement, but not so liable to crack.

It may be used for the best class of internal plastering, and, as they set very quickly, they can be painted within a few hours, which is a great advantage. They are capable of receiving a very high polish, to obtain which the surface is rubbed down with grit-stones of various degrees of courseness; afterwards *stopped* or laid over with semi-liquid neat cement which fills up the pores; rubbed again with snake-stone, and finished with putty powder. These plasters should not be used in situations much exposed to the weather, on account of their solubility.

Cement or mastic for outside walls.—Indeed, there is no subject hitherto so little understood by the majority of our practical masons as that of cements suitable for resisting the attacks of the weather on exterior walls. However, there are a number of cements that will resist the weather for a long time, if they be properly incorporated and laid on. Mr. Downing says the frequent failures in exterior cements arise, 1st. From the use of sand composed of rounded worn particles, mixed with earthy matter; 2d. From the employment of hydraulic cements of inferior or unsuitable quality; 3d. From the use of poor lime; and 4th. From the imperfect mixture and application of the materials. In making the cement choose a hydraulic lime that has been thoroughly tested, and is known to be well adapted to resist the weather *in the air*, as well as under water, and let it be perfectly fresh, as it will be nearly *worthless* if it has been long prepared.

The *very best* and purest lime should also be selected, of the greatest tenacity in mortar, and such as will slacken thoroughly throughout. Especial pains should also be taken to procure sharp *angular sand*, which, if not perfectly *clean*, must be freed from any admixture of earthy particles, by repeated washing. Let the lime be thoroughly slaked, and a good mortar made of sufficient *quantity* for the whole of the work, of the lime and sand. When the masons are ready for plastering, open one of the casks of cement, and mix the latter in equal proportions with the mortar, making a hod of the mixture at a time, as it would otherwise partially set before it could be used. Only one coat of cement should be put on, as it will then form one homogenous mass with the wall. In finishing the surface, *float it off as smoothly* as possible, and mark it off in courses to resemble stone, coloring it while the cement is yet only partially dry, so that the coloring matter may set with the cement. In mixing the coloring material, choose some of the ochres, or earthy colors, for a base, rendering it liquid by the use of *milk*, and vary the tint by adding other colors until the desired tint be obtained. In order to protect the cement against moisture it is the practice of the most successful plasterers to incorporate with the coloring wash, or paint, a quantity of thick boiled grease or fatty matter, in proportion of six or eight quarts to a half barrel of the paint. The cement should be applied in fine weather, free from frost, and it is better in all cases that buildings to be covered with it should be finished in time to allow them to become thoroughly dry before winter.

The common hydraulic cements of New York are unfit for plastering the exterior of houses, and many persons who have personally seen these employed (mixed perhaps with dirty, instead of sharp, clean sand) suppose that all cements are equally liable to crumble by exposure to damp and frost. The cement (or hydraulic limes) of Connecticut and Pennsylvania are greatly superior for stucco, or external plastering, becoming, when well applied, nearly as firm and durable as stone.—[Downing.]

Portland cement of the *best quality*, thoroughly mixed with an equal quantity of *clean*, sharp sand, and perhaps, one-fourth as much saw-dust. Brush and wash the wall off thoroughly, roughen it by hacking, unless it already presents a good key for the plastering. If well done, the mortar will last as long as the brick and will never come off. Do not paint it until the whole is well dried out, which will take two or three months, as the paint will blister if put on over the damp work.

The *best* quality of Rosendale cement may be used in place of Portland at half cost, but is not half as good for the purpose. (See Mortars.)

Whitewash, Kalsomine and Coloring. — Whitewash is made from pure white lime mixed with water. It is used for common walls and ceilings, especially where for sanitary reasons, a frequent fresh application is considered preferable to any coating that would last better. It readily comes off when rubbed, will not stand rain, nor adhere well to very smooth or non-porous surfaces. It is cheap, and when used for sanitary purposes should be made up of hot lime and applied at once, under which conditions it adhers better. It is improved by adding 1 pound pure tallow (free from salt), or one pint linseed oil to every bushel of lime. The process is generally described as *lime whiting.*

Common coloring is prepared by adding earthy pigments to the mixtures used for lime whiting. The following proportions may be used per bushel of lime; more or less according to the tint required: Cream color, 4 to 6 pounds ochre; fawn color, 6 to 8 pounds umber, 2 pounds Indian red, 2 pounds lamp-black; buff or stone color, 6 to 8 pounds umber, and 3 to 4 pounds lamp-black, dissolved in alcohol, the pigments should be soaked well at least 24 hours before being added to the lime wash.

Kalsomine is the name for all coloring mixed with water and size.

While kalsomine is a mixture of whiting and size, the best way of mixing is as follows: Take 6 lbs. best whiting and soak it in soft water sufficient to cover it for several hours. Pour off the water and stir the whiting into a smooth paste, strain the material, and add 1 qt. size in state of weak jelly; mix carefully, not breaking the lumps of jelly, then strain through muslin before using;

leave in a cold place, and the material will become a jelly, which is diluted with water when required for use. Sometimes add about ½ tablespoonful of blue **black** before the **size** is added. It is sometimes directed that **the size** should **be used** hot, **but in that case it does not work so smoothly as used in** the **condition of cold jelly, but on the contrary drags and becomes crumpled, thus causing a rough surface.** When **the white is required to be very bright and clean, potato starch is used instead of the size.**

Colored kalsomine **is tinted with the same pigments as are used for colored paints,** whiting **being used as a basis instead of white lead or zinc** white. **In** mixing **the tints, whiting is first** prepared, **then** the coloring pigments, **the latter being** introduced sparingly; **size** is added, and the **mixture is** strained. **The** colors are **classed as** *common*, *superior* **and** *delicate*. **If the** ceiling **is new,** nothing **further is required than a coat of** good **Paris white** (whiting **of a superior kind) with** just sufficient glue-size added **to bind it,** provided **the** finishing plastering was **of** good workmanship; **but if inferior and very** porous, it will **require a** preparation **of strong size,** soft-soap and **a handful of** plaster of Paris. **For old ceilings,** all **the previous** whiting, **etc., must be thoroughly washed off with an old white-wash brush or sponge and hot water, and allowed to dry before re-whiting. When this is** done, **if the ceiling is** *hot*, *i. e.*, **porous, and soaks in the** moisture **very quickly, it must be prepared with a mixture of one handful of lime, the same of whiting, ½ lb. glue, ¼ lb. soft-soap, and if smoky or damp, about 2 oz. alum, to make a pail ¾ full When this is dry, it is ready for the finish. Use the preparation thin.**

Before putting on the whiting or kalsomine shut all doors and windows to exclude **the draught,** take **a sweep right across the room,** and **continue till finished. If two** are **engaged in it so** much **the better, as it** requires to be done **quickly; be** careful to **cover well or you** will not make **a nice job.** When finished, **the doors** and windows can be opened, **as the** sooner **it dries after** it is **once** on the more **even and solid it will** look. **For** whiting and coloring walls, great care is required in preparing them if old; all the old stuff is to be cleaned off, well rubbed down with dry lump pumice, all holes well and evenly stopped with plaster of Paris, and a preparation of strong size, whiting and alum thickly laid on of the color you are going to finish, but a little darker in shade. When this is well dry, rub it well down to a good level and smooth face with lump pumice, or course sand paper. The finishing coat may be made in the same way for the ceilings; but if exposed to the liability of being touched or rubbed against, a little more or stronger size is to be used; and if in any way to damp, a little alum. To get any of the colors required, it is necessary to get the dry powders and rub up with the whiting prior to mixing with size, adding by degrees till the required depth of tone is arrived at. For the different shades of drab or stone color, yellow ochre, umber, black and red are used. For shades of blue, from the French grey to sky blue, ultramarine, etc. If glue is employed to give body, it is destroyed by the corrosive action of the lime, and in consequence the latter easily rubs off the walls when dry. This is the case also if the lime is employed, as is often absurdly recommended, simply slaked in water, and used without any fixing material.

The colors most commonly mixed with whiting to produce the various tints are as follows: Straw color may be made with white and masticot, or Dutch pink; fine grays, with white and refiners veroditie; and inferior grey may be compounded with blue black or bone black, and damp blue or indigo; pea-greens with French greens, Olympian green; and fawn color, with burnt sienna or burnt umber, or white, crome yellow, with yellow ochre, and so of any intermediate tint. All the colors used in distemper should be ground very fine, so as to insure the most minute divisions of their particles. When the old plastering has become discolored with stains, and it be desired to have it colored, it is advisable to give the old plaster, when properly cleaned off and prepared, one coat at least of white lead ground in oil, and used with spirits of turpentine, which will generally cover all old stains, and, when quite dry, will take the water color very nicely.

When it is required of the mason to mix tints for kalsomine, the following combination of colors may be referred to, to produce the required tint, of course whiting being the basis of them all, the amount of which to use depending upon the tint sought:

For Buff—White, yellow ochre, red.
For Chestnut—Red, black, yellow.
For Chocolate—Raw umber, red, black.
For Claret—Red, umber, black.
For Copper—Red, yellow, black.
For Dove—White, vermillion, blue, yellow.
For Drab—White, yellow ochre, red, black.
For Fawn—White, yellow, red.
For Flesh—White, yellow ochre, vermillion.
For Freestone—Red, black, yellow, white.
For French Gray—White, Prussian blue, lake.
For Gray—White, black.
For Green Bronze—Chrome green, black, yellow.
For Pea Green—White, chrome green.
For Lemon—White, chrome yellow.
For Limestone—White, yellow ochre, black, red.
For Olive—White, yellow, blue, black.
For Orange—Yellow, red.
For Peach—White, vermillion.
For Pearl—White, black, blue.
For Pink—White, vermillion, lake.
For Purple—Violet, with more red and white.
For Rose—White, madder lake.
For Sandstone—White, yellow orchre, black, red.
For Snuff—Yellow, Vandyke brown.
For Violet—Red, blue, white.

Washes.—The following washes will be found useful to the plasterers and masons generally:

Washes used on the Croton reservoir, N. Y., and proved to be impervious to water. The process consists in using two washes or solutions for covering the surface of brick walls; one composed of castile soap and water; and one of alum and water. The proportions are: ¾ pound soap to 1 gallon water; and half pound alum to 4 gallons water; both substances to be perfectly dissolved in water before being used. The wall should be perfectly clean and dry; and the temperature of the air should not be below 50 degrees Fahrenheit, when the compositions are applied. The first, or soap wash, should be laid on when at boiling heat, with a flat brush, taking care not to form a forth on the brick work.

This wash should remain 24 hours, so as to become dry and hard before the alum wash is applied; which should be done in the same manner as the first.

The temperature of this wash when applied may be 60° or 70°; and it should also remain 24 hours before the second coat of the soap wash is put on; and these coats are to be repeated alternately until the walls are made impervious to water.—Trautwine, C. E.

Painting on cement.—According to a French journal, it is known that the caustic lime that is not in a state of combination in cement saponifies the oil used in painting; consequently, painting on cement is only practical when, under the influence of the air, carbonic acid has united with the caustic lime to form carbonate of lime. When it is desired to paint cement without delay, attempts are made to neutralize the lime by acids; but the above journal recommends in preference carbonate of ammonia, the acid of which combines with the lime while the acid is liberated. The effect produced is however, only superficial. Various other expedients are referred to, but the solution of the problem would seem to consist in the use of caseine. Fresh white cheese and slaked fat lime are added to the color. This mixture hardens rapidly, assumes the consistency of stone, and insoluble in water, a formation of albuminate of lime taking place. It is according to this system that the mural paintings at the Berlin war museum were executed. To make composition, three parts of cheese and one of slaked fat lime are stirred, the quantity of color to be added being regulated by practice. Only earth colors or oxides of iron would be used for light red to dark brown shades; for blue, ultramarine or cobalt blue would be used; for white, oxide of zinc or sulphate of baryta; and for black, animal black. Inorganic colors, such as those of aniline, would not be used. Prussian blue, vermillion, blue ochre and white lead not to be employed on account of the injurious effects of the sulphur present in the cheese in combination with these substances. If the painting surface is too dry, it can easily be damped. The caseous lime should be prepared daily, and the brushes should be cleaned after the applicatian of each coat of paint. The process thus described is recommended for its economy. The caseous paint does not easily take fire, and is, therefore, considered particularly suitable for theaters, halls and churches.

Zinc Kalsomine is composed of zinc white mixed with water and glue sizing. The surface to which it is to be applied must be clean and smooth. For ceilings mix ¼ lb. glue with 15 lbs. zinc; for walls 1 lb. glue with 15 lbs. zinc. The glue, the night before its use, should be soaked in water, and in the morning liquified on the fire. Paris white is often used, but it is not the *genuine article*. The zinc kalsomine mixture may be colored to any required tint by mixing appropriate coloring matter with it.

Wash for *brickwork, masonry, mastic, rough-cast, etc.* —Slack ½ bushel lime in a tight barrel by pouring over it boiling water sufficient to cover it 4 or five inches deep, stirring it until slaked; then fill the barrel ⅔ full of water, and add a bushel of hydraulic cement. Add 3 pounds of sulphate of zinc, previously dissolved in water.

It may be colored by adding powdered ochre, Indian red, umber, etc. It is improved by adding to it a peck of white sand, stirred in before being used. Use best quality of Portland cement for all exterior washes of masonry, which is a good wash in itself.

Wash for brickwork.—Apply two coats of Ransome's Patent Liquid Glass to surface of brickwork, it is most effective in preventing damp from penetrating through the wall, and will not discolor the bricks; also to make brick or stone walls impervious to wet, wash the walls with a hot solution of ¾ pound of mottled or soft soap in a gallon of water, laid evenly with a brush. As soon as this is dry, another coat composed of ½ pound alum thoroughly dissolved in three gallons of water. Fair weather should be selected for the work.

Porous bricks have been effectively *weathered* by this process.

Coal tar wash for masonry.—Coal tar has recently come into extensive use abroad as a means of rendering masonry impervious to water, especially in positions exposed to direct contact with water. The tar is employed in a boiling state in one or more layers, or it may be made to flame up before being used.

The first is suitable for surfaces exposed to the air, while the second is appropriate to parts intended to be covered up. This method of treating foundations is of special application in all public buildings, especially those designed for the preservation of works of art. It prevents the disagreeable consequences of the exudations of water charged with lime salts from the mortar.

To whiten or color over smoked stained walls, make a wash with about ten cents worth of white vitriol, pulverized, in two quarts of water; wash the walls with this solution and let it dry over night, when you may apply your other wash.

A wash that is made of ¼ pound diluted glue and 5 pounds of plaster of Paris, kept well stirred while being applied, will cover a room 15 x 18 feet. To cover over old ceilings and walls with a wash of alum water composed of about a piece of alum as big as an egg pulverized and diluted with water, 1 pint of plaster of Paris, and ½ pint of soft soap for a pailful, well stirred while being used, generally answers; if the stains still show through the first coat of kalsomine give that another coat of the wash, thinner, and the second coat will come out all right. To walls that are damp intended to be kalsomined apply this wash first.

A water-proof compound for brickwork: Dissolve soft paraffin wax in benzoline spirit in the proportion of about one part of the former to four to five parts of the latter by weight.

Into a tin keg place one gallon of benzoline spirit, then mix 1½ pounds or two pounds of wax, and when well hot pour into the pail. Apply the solution to the walls whilst warm with a white-wash brush. To prevent the solution from chilling, it is best to place the tin in a pail of warm water, but on no account should the spirit be brought into the house or near a light or a serious accident might occur.

Fire-proofing exterior surfaces.—It is found that a most effective composition for fire-proofing exterior surfaces may be made by slacking a sufficient quantity of *freshly-burnt quick-lime* of the best grade, and when the slacking has become complete, adding such an amount of skim milk or water in its absence as will make a liquid of the consistency of cream. To every ten gallons of this liquid are added separately and in powder and with constant stirring the following ingredients in the order named: Two pounds of alum, 24 ounces subcarbonate of potassium or commercial potash and one pound of common salt. If white paint is desired no further addition is made to the liquid though the whiteness is found to be improved by a few ounces of plaster of Paris. Lamp black has the effect of giving a number of shades from slate color to black. But whatever tint is used it is incorporated at this stage, and the whole after being strained through a sieve, is run through a paint-mill. When ready to apply the paint is heated nearly to the boiling point of water and is put on in its hot condition. It is also found that the addition of a quantity of fine white sand to this composition renders it a valuable covering for roofs and crumbling brick walls.

M. Sarel, of Paris, has made an invention which is pronounced better than plaster of Paris for coating the walls and ceilings of rooms. A coat of oxide of zinc, mixed with size, made up like a wash, is first laid on, and over that a coat of chloride of zinc is applied in the same way as the first wash. The oxide and chloride effect an immediate combination, and form a kind of cement, smooth and polished as glass, and possessing the advantages of oil paint without the disadvantages of smell.

A red wash.—To remove the green that gathers on bricks, pour over the bricks boiling water in which any vegetables, not greasy, have been boiled. Do this for a few days. To color them red again melt 1 oz. glue in a gallon of water; while hot, put in a piece of alum the size of an egg, ½ lb. venetian red and 1 lb. Spanish brown. Try a little on the bricks, let it dry, and if too light add more red and brown; if too dark, put in more water.

Fire-proof white-wash.—Make ordinary white-wash and add 1 pint silicate of soda or potash to every 5 parts of the white-wash.

White-wash that will not rub off.—Mix up a half a pailful of lime and water ready to put on the wall; then take ¼ pt. of flour, mix it up with water; then pour on it boiling water, a sufficient quantity to thicken it; then pour it while hot into the white-wash, stir all well together, and it is ready for use.

To make glue sizing.—Break up the glue into small pieces, put it in a vessel with sufficient cold water to just cover it; let it soak over night, and in the morning the glue will be soft enough to melt readily with a moderate heat, or in a water bath. Never boil it, or you will, in a measure, destroy it altogether; 3 ounces of glue to one gallon of water. Be sure that the glue is all dissolved before using any of it. If a wall is to be painted or kalsomined that has never been washed, or even washed, size it with two coats of the size. Let the first coat dry before the second is put on.

Washes for blackboards.—Incorporate flour-emery with shellac varnish, adding sufficient lamp black to give the required color. If too thick, reduce its consistency with alcohol. This varnish, applied to the surface of wood with a camel's hair varnish brush, produces an excellent black writing surface; or pulverized slate or quartz rock moistened to the consistency of a thick fluid with silicate of soda (water-glass of commerce), and applied to the boards by means of a brush; or merely paints, such as asphaltum or grahamite dissolved in petroleum naptha.

Whitewash that will Stand Washing.—The following for a wash which can be applied to lime walls and afterward become water-proof so as to bear washing: Mix together the powder from three parts of silicious (quartz), three parts marble dust and sandstone, also two parts of burned porcelain clay, with two parts freshly slaked lime still warm. In this way a wash is made which forms a silicate if often wetted, and becomes after a time almost like stone. The four constituents mixed together give the ground color to which any pigment that can be used with lime is added. It is applied quite thickly to the wall or other surface, let it dry one day, and the next day frequently cover with water, which makes it water-proof. This wash can be cleaned with water without losing any of its color; on the contrary, each time it gets harder, so that it can even be brushed, while its porosity makes it look soft. The wash can be used for ordinary purposes as well as for the finest painting. A so-called fresco surface can be prepared with it in the dry way.

Wash for Whited Brick Walls.—In an interesting article published in *The Builder* on the efflorescence of brickwork, H. C. Standage suggests a very cheap and simple remedy. He says that the white discoloration that appears on the surface of brick walls is derived from soluble salt of sodium in the mortar. Mr. Standage says: "Acting on the hint conveyed by the fact that the excess of sodic hydrate in soap-making is expelled from the soap by salting it, *i. e.*, strewing the surface of the soap as it floats on the lye with common salt (soda chloride), he applied a solution of common salt to the white efflorescence on the bricks that were badly stained therewith. In every instance where such fluid was applied the white efflorescence was instantly removed; and what is more, has never reappeared. In obstinate cases three applications, or one application, well saturating the bricks with the common salt solution, has sufficed to affect the desired result."

To Clean Marble.—Brush the dust off with a piece of

chamois, then apply with a brush a good coat of gum arabic, about the consistency of thick mucilage, expose it to the sun or wind to dry. In a short time it will pull off; wash it with clean water and a clean cloth. If the first application does not have the desired effect, it should be tried again. Another method is to rub the marble with the following solution: One-quarter of a pound of soft soap, one quarter of a pound of whiting, and one ounce of soda and a piece of stone blue the size of a walnut; rub it over the marble with a piece of flannel, and leave it on for twenty-four hours; then wash it off with clean water, and polish the marble with a piece of flannel or an old piece of felt, or take two parts of common soda, one part of pumice stone, and one part of finely powdered chalk, sift it through a fine sieve, and mix it with water; then rub it well over the marble; then wash the marble over with soap and water. To take the stains out of white marble, take one ounce of ox gall, one gill of lye, one and a half tablespoonfuls of turpentine; mix and make into a paste with pipe clay; put on the paste over the stain, and let it remain for several days. To remove oil stains, apply common clay saturated with benzine. If the grease has remained in long the polish will be injured but the stain will be removed. Iron mould or ink spots may be taken out in the following manner: Take ½ ounce of butter of antimony and 1 ounce of oxalic acid and dissolve them in one pint of rain water; add enough flour to bring the mixture to a proper consistency. Set it evenly on the stained part with a brush, and after it has remained for a few days wash it off, and repeat the process if the stain be not wholly removed.

Sand in building is chiefly used as an ingredient in mortar, and is known as *argillaceous, silicious* or *calcareous* according to its ingredients. It is procured from pits, shores of rivers, sea-shores, etc.

Pit sand has an angular grain, and a porous, rough surface, which make it good for mortar, when free from impurities. River sand is not so sharp or angular in its grit, and is, therefore, well suited for plastering. Sea sand is not fit for building purposes, as it contains alkaline salts, which attract moisture, and it can hardly be washed free from them. Sand should be well screened when the strength of the mortar is taken into consideration.

Sand found to contain impurities such as clay, loam, etc., should be washed and the impurities carried off.

Sand which contain these impurities can be detected by rubbing the sand between the moist hands, and will leave no stain when it is of a pure quality. Salts can be detected by the taste.

Staining bricks red and black.—For staining bricks red, melt one ounce of glue in one gallon of water; add a piece of alum the size of an egg, then one pound of Venetian red and one pound of Spanish brown. Try the color on the bricks before using them, and change to light or dark with the red or brown, using a yellow mineral for buff. For coloring black, pint of asphaltum to a fluid state, and moderately heat true surface bricks and dip them. Tar and asphalt are also used for the same purpose. It is important that the bricks be sufficiently hot, and be held in the mixture to absorb the color to the depth of $\frac{1}{16}$ of an inch.

Sill.—The stone, iron, or wood, on which the window or door of a building rests. In setting stone sills the mason beds the ends only, the middle is pointed up after the building is inclosed, they should be set perfectly level, and have an inclination for the water to flow from the frame and have a projection from the the line of the building.

The strength of manilla ropes, like that of bar iron, is very variable; and so with hemp ones. Ropes of good Italian hemp are considered stronger than manilla; but their cost excludes them from general use. The *tarring of ropes* is said to lessen their strength, and, when exposed to weather their durability also. We believe that the use of it in standing rigging is partly to diminish contraction and expansion by alternate wet and dry weather. The common rule for findieg the strength of ropes, by multiplying the square of the diameter, or the circumference by a given coefficient are entirely erroneous. Well made ropes vary in strength, that of $\frac{3}{4}$ of an inch in circumference will break at 560 pounds, and one of 14 inches in circumference, or

$4\tfrac{45}{100}$ inches in diameter, at 37 tons or 82,880 pounds. A rope 3 inches in circumference, will break at 6,115 pounds, one 2 inches in diameter at 29,120 pounds.

Terra cotta, which although it has been long known, is really brick material, but brick of the highest quality, produced from the purest and best clay, and moulded and burnt with the greatest care. Thus produced, the material lays claim, and with justice, to a high place as a building material, and is capable even, at least in many cases, of supplanting stone, this being more especially true where ornamentation is to be carried out to any extent; the ornaments in terra cotta, well moulded, being produced at a much cheaper rate than the ornaments cut by hand with stone. Terra cotta possesses a hard and dense body, with a fine surface quite untouchable by any of the causes which bring about decay in stone, and possesses moreover a beautifully diversified, or, what may be called, a grained-colored surface, which vies with that of rich and old marble.

Terra cotta is subject to unequal shrinkage in burning, which sometimes causes the pieces to be twisted. When this is the case, great care must be taken in fixing the blocks, otherwise the long lines of a building, such as those of the string-courses or cornices, which are intended to be straight, are apt to be uneven, and the faces of blocks are often in *winding*.

Twisted and warped blocks are sometimes set right by chiselling, but this should be avoided, for if the vitrified skin on the surface be removed, the material will not be able to withstand the attacks of the atmosphere, etc. Terra cotta is made in several colors, depending chiefly upon the amount of heat it has gone through. White, pale grey, pale yellow, or straw color, indicate a want of firing. Rich yellow, pink, and bug varieties are generally well burnt.

A green hue is a sign of absorption of moisture, and of bad material. A glazed surface can be given to terra cotta if required. Inferior terra cotta is sometimes made by overlaying a coarsely prepared common body with a thin coating of a finer and more expensive clay. Unless these bodies have been most carefully tested and assimilated in their contraction and expansion, they are sure in course of time to destroy one another; that is, the inequality in their shrinkage will cause hair cracks in the fine outer skin, which will inevitably retain moisture, and cause the surface layer to fall off in scales after winter frosts. Another very reprehensible custom is that of coating over the clay, just before it goes into the kiln, with a thin wash of some ochreish paint, mixed with finely ground clay, which produces a sort of artificial bloom, very pretty looking for the first year or two after the work is executed, but sure to wear off before long.

Testing cement.—Rough testing of cement, as to enable a workman to get a crude and imperfect idea of its value, is easy, says the *Popular Scientific Monthly*. Enough of the pure cement should be taken to make a ball an inch in diameter, and mixed with just sufficient water to make it mould readily and be rolled into a ball. Then it should be exposed to the air and left for two hours. At the end of that time it should be set; then it should be put into water and left. It should grow gradually harder, and show no signs of cracking or crumbling, even when left for ten days. Any cement that does not endure this test is not of sufficiently good quality to make satisfactory structures; any cement that stands this properly will be generally satisfactory if properly used. In determining how to construct a building, a series of tests is often required that shall show tensile, breaking, twisting and crushing strength, and also adhesion of the materials used for the mortar. No one of these can be dispensed with, since material that will endure one satisfactorily will often fail utterly in another, and hence prove worthless for the use desired; but for general purposes the test of cement which is the most valuable is that which determines its *tensile strength*.

Proportions of chimney flues.—The old rule concerning chimneys was to the effect that the flue should be tapered to the top on the theory that, as the hot gases pass upward they become cooled, and in the process of cooling, become contracted. Also, that it was important to reduce the size of the flue in proportion to the reduction in volume of the gases, as otherwise cold air from the top would descend and fill the vacancy caused by the contraction of the gases and in this way the draft would be checked. Reasonable as this theory seems practice has shown that cylindrical boiler or furnace flues are, at least, as good as the tapered ones, and within a few years practice engineers and architects of experience in such matters have shown a disposition to make them slightly larger at the top than at the bottom, the increase of diameter being, perhaps, $\frac{1}{2}$ inch to 10 or 12 feet. Not long since a Swiss engineer made experiments to see whether the facts bear out the old rule or support the modern practice. To make the test he built a chimney over a furnace grate, the stack having two flues. One flue tapered upward and the other downward, and the flues opened side by side over the grate, with openings of the same size. On lighting a fire on the grate with unlimited access of air under it, the smoke was seen to issue nearly equally from the top of both the flues, but with an unmistakeable preponderance in favor of the flue which enlarged toward the top. On partially shutting off the access of air to the fire, the difference became much more marked; the current in the flue tapering upward diminished, and finally stopped altogether, the smoke finding its way entirely through the flue with the *wider top*.

Walls.—Walls of permanent structures are almost excluively composed of either stone or brick, or both; and are included in one general term *masonry*. The interior of the wall is called *filling*, and when mortar in a thinnish condition is poured into, so as to fill up the interstices of the stones, the operation is called *grouting*. The term *course* is applied to each horizontal layer of stone or brick; if all the stones in a layer are of equal thickness, it is termed regular *coursing*. Footings are the lower projecting courses, resting on the foundations, usually not less than double the width of the walls about in buildings, but for other walls, the width depends upon the nature of the foundation as well as the intended weight to be sustained. The stones for *footings* should be chosen as can be conveniently obtained and square stones are not so good as those which are rectangular in shape. It is not essential that the courses should be of the same thickness; but it is essential, in order to prevent unequal settlement, that all stones of the same course should be of the same thickness Rock foundations need no extra width of wall. *String* courses or *belting* are upper courses projecting slightly beyond the face of the wall. *Coping* is the top courses, usually got out in considerable lengths in comparison with stones in the rest of the work.

The *beds* of a stone or brick in a wall are the surfaces on which they rest; the *build* is the upper bed on which the stone above is placed; the interstices between the stones are called *joints*. *Stretchers* are stones or bricks which have their length disposed lengthwise in the wall; *headers* have their length crosswise; *quoins* are the corners of a wall; *bond* is the lapping of the stones or brick on each other in the construction so as to tie the separate pieces together. The most common bond of brick in this country is to lay a certain number of stretching courses, and then a heading course. Walls are composed of stones laid either with or without mortar. The latter is called *dry masonry*; *rough wall* is dry work with rough stones; if laid in mortar, it is called *rubble* work, but frequently this term is made to include all rough work. Cut stone is called *ashlar*; if only cut on beds and joints, it is called *rock* or quarry-faced ashlar. Before forming or filling up the embankment behind walls, it is a good precaution against future accidents to allow the mortar of the work to be firmly set, and a great point will be gained if the immediate back of the wall for some depth is filled up with loose material, such as broken bricks, stones, old mortar, sand, etc. Where there is likely to be much moisture in the soil, it will be advisable to set the work of the wall on hydraulic mortar; and the whole area of the cellar should be covered with concrete or asphalt, and if the former is used Portland cement is the best to mix with it. Great care is necessary in depositing and ramming the soil near the wall; the more completely the soil can be made to slip, or have a tendency to slip, from the wall the better.

Thickness of Walls.—Retaining walls are such as sustain

a lateral pressure from an embankment or head of water. The width of a retaining wall depends upon the height of the embankment which it may have to sustain, and the kind of earth of which it is composed (the steeper the natural slope at which the earth would stand, the less the thrust against the wall), and the comparative weight of the earth and the masonry. To find the breadth of a wall laid in mortar, multiply the whole height of the embankment above the footings by $\frac{285}{1000}$; for dry walls make the thickness one-fourth more. Most retaining walls have an inclination or *batter* to the face, sometimes also the same in the back, but *offsets* are more common. The usual batter is from 1 to 3 inches horizontal for each foot vertical. To determine the thickness of a wall having a batter, determine the width by the rule above, and make this width at one-ninth of the height above the base. In most large cities there are building acts in force to which all constructions within their limits must conform. Walls built of *rubble* should be somewhat thicker than those of brick; on an average, at least, one-quarter thicker, but depending on the character of the stone. The common form of cut-work is to make the face ashlar, and back-up with rubble or brick. When brick footings are used for walls they should be carefully constructed of whole bricks, the hardest and best burnt being selected. The bottom courses should be double, and no back joints be allowed beyond the face of upper work, except in double courses, the projections being kept very slight (2 or 4 inches), or fracture of the footings and consequent settlement of the wall will probably occur. Mortar should be sparingly used; and sometimes footings are laid dry.

Unequal settlement in walls.—From the earliest times of construction there has invariably been this difficulty to be overcome in the employment of separate and distinct materials, viz., the different manner in which they may behave under similar circumstances. It is often assumed that they will act together, or that, even if their action is not identical, it will be so insignificant in diversity of influence that there will be no necessity for taking any precaution to guard against unforeseen contingencies.

Unequal settlement generally proceeds when employing two different descriptions of material in the same structure, such as stone and brick, or by using two or more varieties of work. If a wall, a pier, the abutment of a bridge, or a house, be built entirely of brick, there can no unequal settlement take place, unless the *foundation yield*, which would cause cracks in the best structure ever erected. But if a structure be erected partly of brick and partly of stone, then, if the two materials be very *unequally distributed* and badly *bonded together*, there is considerable likelihood that there will be a settlement originating in the vicinity of their *union*, and spreading gradually over the entire building. The absolute difference of settlement between the two materials depends upon the much greater number of joints that there are in the brick work compared with the stone work, especially in the *backing up* of the latter with brick. Another fruitful source of the collapse of piers and abutments in which two classes of work are used is the want of bond between the facework and the *hearting* or filling. It is manifest that if the bond be insufficient, the facework is nothing more than a mere veneering, and the least inequality of settlement would cause the face to sheer clear off from the rest of the structure. Manifestly, too great care cannot be adopted in the *bonding in* of *rubble* or *brick work* in the backing with coursed ashlar-work in the face. If the stones in the face be all *stretchers* and no *headers*, then there is no union between the face and the interior, and the structure as a whole is *defective, unsound* and *unreliable*. To the use of *bad mortar, large joints* and *inferior workmanship,* may be *attributed* the downfall of many a *building*. The proper use of iron is to employ it and make it available where other means for effecting the desired object cannot be obtained, but not to use it to the prejudice of more substantial materials simply because there is a difficulty in getting them *put together* so as to constitute *sound* and *durable* work.

Beton.—How walls are constructed with it. Specifically the French word for concrete; a concrete the invention of M. Coignet, composed usually of sand 5, lime 1, hydraulic cement .25. The materials are mixed with a shovel, ground violently in a tampering-mill, water being added sparingly from time to time. The pug-mill has a vertical cylinder and a shaft armed with knives spirally arranged, beneath which is a cycloidal presser which drives the plastic below out of holes in the bottom of the mill. This is carefully and persistently rammed in molds, a stratum at a time till the mould is full. The top of each stratum is deeply scratched to bind its successor thereto. The molds are coffers *in situ*, or ordinary molds, according to circumstances.

The reduction by ramming is very great, about 1, 7 to 1. The resistance to crushing is 5,000 pounds to the square inch; ten times that of a common mortar made of the same materials and proportions. Sewers made on this plan may have the centering removed in 8 hours, and in 4 and 5 days may be used.

Arches with a pitch of 1 in 10, have proportions: Sand 5, lime 1, hydraulic cement 5. In Paris, arches, floors, foundations, barracks, and churches are made of this material.

A dwelling of five stories in Paris is constructed of a single mass of beton; a staircase of the same material runs in helicoidal form from the basement to the highest floor. English recipe for making Beton:

Puzzolana 12, quicklime 9, sand 6, stone spalls 9, iron scales 3, molded or mixed in a box.

M. Coignet erected a test arch at St. Denis, near Paris, whose dimentions are as follows: Span, 196 feet; rise of arch, 19 feet; cross section at the crown, 4 ft. x 3.25; cross section at the springing, 6.5 x 6.5; specific gravity of the material 2,200; weight of arch 260 tons.

The arch was constructed in six days being formed in thin concentric layers. After it had reached what was deemed a sufficient size, it was allowed to remain for 5 or 6 weeks, at the end of which time all extraneous supports were removed. This was several years ago, and it yet stands uninjured, and promises to remain an enduring monument of the skill of its constructor. The mason who often has to handle concrete may judge from the foregoing to what perfection this material may be used, in the construction of buildings, when the best materials are used in its composition.

The Kansas City Architect and Builder has recently given some good practical tests for selecting brick for substantial walls: 1st, the power of resistance under pressure; 2d, the appearance of the fracture which should present an even texture, and a fine, brilliant grain, without cavities in the interior, and neither ribbony nor stony; 3rd, the exterior, which should be smooth and regular, the angles and edges sharp and straight. When the size of the bricks is equal throughout the mass it is a proof that the brick earth has been well prepared and the bricks generally well made. A brick when struck should give forth a clear, ringing sound. Good bricks are generally of a dark reddish brown color, and sometimes they show vitrified spots on the surface; it is not well, however, to depend too much on this last fact, for it is often only an indication of the amount of heat to which the brick has been subjected, while the clay of which the bricks is made may be impure and ill prepared.

Bad bricks are generally recognized by their reddish yellow color, but still more by the dull sound which they emit when struck; their grain being soft they crumble easily and absorb water with avidity. A good brick should not absorb more than about $\frac{1}{15}$ of its own weight of water. It should appear, and in reality be, dry. All brick that does not take up any water at all is too much burned; the mortar adheres to it imperfectly, but it is a good conductor of heat. Such bricks may be used in damp soil and for pavements. When a brick left in water either scales or swells it is of bad quality and contains caustic lime. A brick which being made red hot, and then having water poured on it, does not crack, is of extraordinary and rare quality, and those which have borne the effect of moisture and dryness during two or three winters without scaling or cracking are excellent. In order to try if bricks will bear the effect of frost, let one be boiled for half an hour in a solution of sulphate of soda, saturated cold, and then suspended by a string over the vessel in which it has been boiled. In 24 hours the surface of the brick will be covered with small crystals; the brick is then to be immersed again in the solution until the crystals disappear, and again suspended, repeating this operation for five days, the crystals reforming after each immersion. If after this treatment a number of particles of brick are found at the bottom of the vessel containing the solution, the bricks are incapable of supporting the effects of frost.

The propriety of using mortar beds as thin as possible in walls has been inculated in this book. In Roman and most eastern work the joints in some instances were one, and one and one-half inch thick, and when the mortar has been good, such buildings, after centuries of wear, have been found sound and good, but we have no such faith in mortar made in modern times. Mr. Rawlinson says: "As a general rule, buildings whether of marble, limestone, sandstone, or of brick-work alone, or of brick and terra-cotta combined, which are ornamental in character, must all have *thin* joints and beds. Thick beds and joints of mortar would destroy the harmony of design by deteriorating the appearance of labor bestowed on the rich materials in such buildings."

Union of new and old brick.—In attaching any new work to a building, every allowance must be made for the sinking of the footings under pressure, and for the settlement of masonry into itself. Thus, while it is necessary that a vertical groove, or indent, be made in the old work, to receive a corresponding pier of the new, it is still more essential that a freedom for the downward motion of the latter should be secured; otherwise if it be tightly toothed and bonded into the old work, a fracture will take place.

To stay-lath walls.—In the construction of brick walls, and especially walls backed up with brick having an ashlar facing, too much caution cannot be exercised by the mechanic that they **remain perfectly plumb until the** building be properly inclosed. In **building walls of** the **above** description, a block, or piece of scantling should be laid *dry* in the pier or wall at a proper distance from the floor joist, so that a stay-lath may be fastened to it and nailed to the stay lath on the floor joists, and a sufficient number of these as the case may require. And to insure against the *drawing in* of the walls as the construction progresses, none of these stay-laths should be removed until the building is inclosed, and, it becomes necessary to do so for the carpenter to lay his floor. It must be remembered, that no matter how careful a mechanic may be in the vertical construction of a brick wall, and especially where the joints are *struck* on the face, or the wall be of ashlar facing, and the backing up be either of brick or rubble, there is a natural tendency for such work to draw inward, and the above precaution should be resorted to.

www.ingramcontent.com/pod-product-compliance
Lightning Source LLC
Chambersburg PA
CBHW021827230426
43669CB00008B/894